Laura Greaves is a multi-award winning journalist, author and proud 'crazy dog lady'. She has spent nearly twenty years writing for newspapers and magazines in Australia and around the world and is the former editor of Dogs Life magazine. A freelance writer for the past eight years, Laura has written extensively for countless dog and pet-specific print and web publications. She is the author of the collection Incredible Dog Journeys and three romance comedy novels, Be My Baby, The Ex-Factor and Two Weeks 'Til Christmas, all of which feature an extensive supporting cast of cheeky canines.

Find out more at www.lauragreaves.com
and www.facebook.com/lauragreaveswritesbooks

DOGS with JOBS

INSPIRATIONAL TALES OF THE WORLD'S HARDEST WORKING DOGS

LAURA GREAVES

Text Copyright © Laura Greaves 2017
First published by Penguin Random House Australia Pty Ltd.

The right of Laura Greaves to be identified as
the author of this work has been asserted in accordance with the
Copyright, Designs and Patents Act 1988.

This edition first published in Great Britain in 2018 by
Trapeze
an imprint of the Orion Publishing Group Ltd
Carmelite House
50 Victoria Embankment
London EC4Y 0DZ
An Hachette UK Company

1 3 5 7 9 10 8 6 4 2

Cover design by Louisa Maggio © Penguin Random House Australia Pty
Ltd Front cover photograph courtesy Department of Defence,
© Commonwealth of Australia; back cover photograph by Brian Edwards

A CIP catalogue record for this book is available
from the British Library.

ISBN: 978 1 4091 8015 9

Printed in Great Britain by CPI Group (UK) Ltd, Croydon, CR0 4YY

www.orionbooks.co.uk

Properly trained, a man can be a dog's best friend.
—Corey Ford

Here's to all the dogs willing to train us.
And all the humans willing to learn.

CONTENTS

INTRODUCTION

It's a steamy early summer's morning and I'm standing in a car park attached to a vast suburban Sydney reserve with a drop of petrol the size of a pinhead on my foot. Across the other side of the car park, in the back of a red truck emblazoned with the Fire & Rescue NSW logo, Viking the black labrador sits calmly in his travel crate.

'It might take him a little while,' says Viking's handler, Station Officer Phil Etienne. 'It's a big area and I'll start him well away from you so you can see what he does.'

Phil lets Viking out of the vehicle and in an instant the rangy young canine has his nose to the ground. He roams quickly over the surrounding bushy terrain, moving closer to me by the second. He's excited now, I can tell – thrilled to have an opportunity to use his considerable smarts and motivated by the thought of the reward that awaits should he do his job well.

I stand statue still in the middle of the empty asphalt expanse, feeling vaguely guilty about the fuel on my big toe, though there's nothing untoward about it – Phil put it there so that I can see first hand what a valuable weapon Viking is in the fight against arson. But if I feel a bit shifty when I've done nothing wrong, I can only imagine how a person who *had* started a fire might feel watching the determined dog at work.

As it turns out, Phil is incorrect. It doesn't take Viking a while to find the tiny spot of petrol. In fact, it takes virtually no time at all. In under a minute, he's sitting next to me with his wet nose pressed against my foot. Phil tries to dissuade Viking, encouraging him to look elsewhere, but the dog's not having it. He doesn't budge. *Come off it*, his expressive eyes seem to say. *I know petrol when I smell it, and I smell it right here.*

Phil rewards Viking with a chorus of effusive praise and a few minutes of rough-housing with a rolled-up towel. Meanwhile, I stand there thinking, *I am so lazy.*

I have virtually no useful skills. Sure, I can string words together in a somewhat interesting fashion, but I can't do anything that's truly beneficial in a broader sense. My abilities don't solve big problems or save lives. And I definitely don't have the all-consuming drive to work that Viking has. If given the choice between working and not working, like most human beings I would choose naps and bad TV every time. And so would you. It's cool, you can admit it.

I often say that dogs are a gift we don't deserve. That's true of *all* canines, but perhaps working dogs even more so.

What did we do, for example, to deserve a creature with a nose so powerful it can smell a sick little girl's plummeting blood sugar levels? What makes humans worthy of an animal that would literally throw himself under a bus to protect us? How did we get lucky enough to share our lives with four-legged mood boosters that can calm us when we're angry and wake us when demons plague our dreams?

And why don't we appreciate how absurdly fortunate we are to be able to get away with paying these tireless workers in little more than cuddles and treats? Would you do *your* job in exchange for a brief chew on a towel? Me either.

If dogs could talk, the phrase 'I can't be bothered' would not be in their vocabulary. Working dogs are on call 24/7. They will do their jobs in the middle of the night if we ask them to. They will show up and work whether they're tired, hungry or not in the mood. They are conscientious in the extreme. If Employee of the Month awards were open to all species, working dogs would win every single time.

Everybody knows about working dogs on farms, in law enforcement and therapy roles. But the sheer array of what dogs can do is staggering. From keeping wildlife away from warships and commercial aircraft to acting as 'eyes' not just for humans but *for other dogs*, there is truly no end to their talents. They are utterly incredible.

Yes, compared to a working dog, we are *all* lazy. So you might as well do that lazy human thing and sit back, put your feet up and read all about the wonders of working canines. Warning: you may feel slightly inadequate – but I promise you will also feel amazed and inspired.

Laura Greaves
2017

FIGO

GUIDE DOG

If there's one canine career that springs to most people's minds when they hear the words 'working dog', it is surely guide dog. These dedicated dogs help their vision-impaired handlers make their way in a world that would otherwise be frightening and almost impossible to navigate. Their job description spans everything from safely crossing busy streets to manoeuvring on and off crowded public transport. Guide dogs have even led their people through marathon races and up towering mountains – American man Randy Pierce is in the midst of a quest to climb forty-eight New Hampshire mountains higher than 1200 metres with his guide dog by his side.

A guide dog is rarely off duty, acting as their handler's eyes virtually twenty-four hours a day – all in exchange for a warm bed, a full food bowl and a steady stream of belly rubs. Although when they're not wearing their work harness they're free to play and lounge all they want, there's no doubt guide dogs are among the hardest-working dogs in the world. Without them, their handlers simply could not do many of the daily activities most sighted people take for granted.

Some guide dogs, however, take their jobs particularly seriously. Some seem to see their role not as a job, but as a calling. They go above and beyond the call of duty, literally putting their lives on the line for their two-legged companions.

Figo the golden retriever is one of those guide dogs.

Figo was born in 2007 as part of the US Guide Dog Foundation's in-house breeding program. The foundation has a breeding colony of more than 100 dogs, mostly labradors but also golden retrievers, standard poodles and lab–golden retriever crosses. The charity, which places about eighty-five guide dogs a year, breeds only enough dogs for the needs of their programs. They say foundation-bred dogs are more than twice as successful in guide and service dog roles than dogs donated as puppies by breeders or from shelters, though they have occasionally trained shelter dogs to work as service dogs for disabled veterans.

Figo lived at the foundation's headquarters in Smithtown, on Long Island in New York, until the age of eight weeks, when he moved in with a volunteer puppy raiser. For the next year, the puppy raiser worked to ensure Figo was well socialised with people and other dogs and that he was exposed to as many different environments as possible, from city streets, supermarkets and busy shopping centres to doctors' offices and even subway trains – every conceivable situation he might encounter once he began working as a fully-fledged guide dog.

At around a year old, Figo went back to the Guide Dog Foundation to begin his formal training. 'For the most part, our dogs all go through the same formal training,' says Doug Wiggin, who is the Guide Dog Foundation's field representative for the north-eastern United States. 'While we're training them, we're trying to see what type of a person will be most suitable for the dog. Is it a slow dog or a fast dog, a city dog or a country dog? Is it the type of dog that doesn't mind doing the subway or the bus or does it like more of a quiet environment where there's not as much activity?'

Becoming a guide dog is a tough process for a curious and excitable young dog. Plenty of pups don't make the cut and are instead deployed as detector dogs for law enforcement agencies, physical or occupational therapy dogs working in military medical centres, or as other specialised therapy dogs. If they're deemed unsuitable for any working or service dog role, the foundation's dogs are adopted out to loving families.

'Being a guide dog is the most challenging job for a dog to do. Everything that's natural for a dog to do, such as sniffing, chasing and playing with other dogs, we don't want it doing while it's working,' Doug says. 'We're trying to see what the dog is like under distraction. Is it so interested in another dog, for example, that it's not going to focus on its work? Does it just want to keep sniffing, sniffing, sniffing? When it's "in harness" the dog is working. When it's out of harness, it's a pet.'

Fortunately for Figo, he passed his formal training with flying colours – so much so, he graduated a month early. 'Figo showed low animal distraction and people distraction. It was funny to watch him work. He could be a little funny and slow, but was very eager to work. He's a very gentle dog and was really enjoying it,' he says.

The next phase of guide dog training is the team training – training the dog and handler to work together – which is Doug's domain. Happily, he already had a perfect match in mind for dedicated little Figo.

Audrey Stone has been legally blind, with limited vision, since birth as a result of macular degeneration, though the condition wasn't properly diagnosed until she was in her twenties. She used a cane for many years before deciding to apply for a guide dog. Now 64, she relies on four-legged help to get around her home town of Brewster, a small village in Upstate New York.

Her first guide dog, a black labrador called Buddy, didn't stay long – he developed allergies that hadn't been present during training and had to be redeployed. Her second, a golden retriever called Leilani, which is a Hawaiian word meaning 'heavenly flower', was with Audrey for nine years until she sadly passed away from lung cancer at the age of ten in June 2008.

Audrey was dogless for five months while the Guide Dog Foundation searched for her next canine companion. She didn't mind the delay – good things come to those who wait, after all. The third time, Audrey hoped, would be the charm.

At last, in November 2008, Audrey received a call from the foundation. 'They said they had a dog, a golden retriever cross labrador, a little bit older, and would I like it? I said, "Whatever you want,"' she recalls. 'Whichever dog they feel is best is given to you and that's fine by me. Beggars can't be choosers is my motto.'

On the day she was due to meet her new dog, however, she found it wasn't an older dog but a 'bouncy little thing' called Figo that came strutting in. 'He was wagging his tail and happy to be there and just wanted to work,' she laughs. 'I said, "What happened to the other dog?" and Doug, who trained me with my first two guide dogs, said, "We felt this dog was right for you so we let him out of the training program a month early." They saw the potential in him.'

Audrey fell for the exuberant little dog in an instant. 'He was slow to bond with most people, but we bonded within minutes. It was very quick. I just felt that it was meant to be; for some reason Figo was meant to be mine.'

Audrey and Figo set about working with Doug to get a feel for each other and cement their bond. 'It's like a marriage. You learn your dog's habits just like you'd learn your husband's or your wife's habits,' she says. 'If the weather is bad, for example, Figo is like, *Forget it. Not going anywhere today.*'

Doug also describes the dog-and-handler training phase as a marriage. 'They're learning the pros and cons of each other. This a new set of eyes that she's getting, and it's a totally different personality than the last set of eyes that she had,' he says. His job is to help the dog's handler learn how to hold the harness, the correct body position while walking, footwork and more. 'She's learning the pull of that dog and the feel of how that dog moves. I always tell people, "The dog is not perfect and you're not perfect either, but together you become the perfect team." It's amazing the confidence the dog can give them. It's an incredible bond that we can only imagine.'

Audrey quickly learned that Figo can be a little silly. 'He's very playful. In the yard he'll roll around and kick his feet up. He likes to dig under the leaves. He loves to give hugs and kisses,' she says. 'The puppy raiser said he loved squeaky toys so I got a lot of different ones for him. I named them all and he knows which one is which. He doesn't chew them; he just likes to have them in his mouth.'

She also discovered that Figo is 'all business' when he has his working harness on, and the pair quickly became a familiar sight out and about in Brewster. 'Figo only has eyes for Audrey. You can see that,' says Doug. 'He wants to keep working for her. Figo enjoys his work.'

During a routine vet check-up in early 2015, Figo's vet remarked, 'You know, I see a lot of animals, and owners that love their animals, but this dog really loves you with all his heart and soul.'

And Figo was about to prove it.

*

June 8, 2015, was a day much like any other for Audrey and Figo. In their six-and-a-half years together, the pair had refined their day-to-day routines to a fine art. 'I tell him we're going to go somewhere and he knows where we're going, which way to go at the bottom of the driveway, right or left,' she says.

It was a warm early summer's day, a little overcast, as Audrey and Figo set out to run errands around 8.15 a.m. They were just a block from home when they came to the intersection of North Main Street and Michael Neuner Drive, a crossing they had traversed countless times previously. When Audrey determined it was safe to cross, she gave Figo the command and he guided her into the street.

Figo, like all guide dogs, is trained to avoid oncoming traffic. If a guide dog sees an approaching vehicle, it will refuse the command to go forward. It's called 'intelligent disobedience'. Turning vehicles, however, can appear without warning when the dog team are already in the street and are much harder to dodge.

Audrey and Figo were halfway across the road when a yellow school minibus with two kindergarteners onboard suddenly turned into the street. Audrey, of course, could not see the vehicle and the driver later said he simply didn't see the blind woman and her golden dog. As the minibus bore down on them, Audrey was directly in its path. There was no way out; disaster seemed imminent.

And then Figo's protective instincts kicked in. In a split second, he broke away from Audrey, threw himself in front of the bus and bit the tyre. Audrey was also hit and knocked unconscious, but Figo took the brunt of the collision.

'That day was a nightmare. I still don't know what happened. I gave him a clear sign, a clear command to cross the road. Apparently the bus came out of nowhere,' she says. 'I don't know what happened after that.'

When she regained consciousness, Audrey was partially pinned under the school bus and with her limited vision she could see tufts of Figo's fur stuck to the front tyre. She had a broken ankle, a broken elbow and three broken ribs as well as nasty cuts to her head that required stitches. The minibus driver was subsequently issued with a summons for failing to yield to a pedestrian.

Incredibly, Figo had survived the impact. Though his broken right front leg was 'swinging like a pendulum', he was right by Audrey's side – and refused to leave her even after emergency services arrived. The Brewster Fire Department was first on the scene – Audrey lives across the road from the fire station and she and Figo are well known to the firefighters.

Audrey's memories of the accident are hazy, but she knows her first thought was Figo. 'When I came to, he was standing there with his leg dangling in the air. I knew I was hurt, but I was more worried about him,' she says. 'Figo was trying to get to me and they were trying to take him away from me and he was very upset. He was obviously fighting his own little war in his mind.'

Paul Schwartz, who was working at a petrol station at the intersection, told local media that Figo's leg was cut down to the bone, but despite his own injuries the loyal dog was determined to comfort Audrey. 'He was limping as we put him on a big blanket on the sidewalk and it started to rain. He let us wrap up his leg without any problem. The dog was being a good sport, really calm,' Paul told *The Journal News*. 'He wasn't barking or crying or yelping, but he kept pulling toward her. After she was put on a gurney and taken away he stopped doing that. He seemed a little lost after she left.'

Figo couldn't travel in the ambulance with Audrey, so she was taken to nearby Danbury Hospital without him. Firefighters then loaded Figo into their truck and took him to the nearest veterinary hospital, which happened to be his regular vet, Middlebranch Veterinary. 'He was lucky he didn't have any internal injuries. God or somebody was with us that day,' says Audrey.

When word of the accident reached Doug Wiggin, he was not surprised to learn that Figo had put his life on the line to save Audrey.

'It was a very proud moment for me to think about what this dog did for Audrey. Obviously Figo saw something that just wasn't right and his instinct was to move her out of the way and make sure she was safe,' he says. 'Any time you train a dog, that's what you hope the dog will do, but it hits your heart. It's just amazing what these dogs will do for their humans. It shows you how dedicated the dogs are.'

*

Both Audrey and Figo spent four months in hospital after the accident. After her initial treatment, Audrey moved to a rehabilitation facility and 'had to learn to walk all over again, which is pretty frightening.'

In consultation with the Guide Dog Foundation – though Audrey owns Figo, the foundation is always on hand to assist its dog teams – it was decided the best place for Figo to stay while Audrey recuperated was at Middlebranch Veterinary. Once his injuries healed, however, his stay there became more like a holiday.

'He was well taken care of by the vet. She took him home every night and brought him to work every day. I was very lucky that she was able to do that,' says Audrey.

But Figo clearly missed his job and was eager to get back to work. 'They become a pet when they're not working for a long period of time. He'd look at his harness in the vet hospital and they had to put it away because they knew he was wondering, *Why am I not using it?*'

Audrey would receive multiple phone calls every day with requests to decipher Figo's unique personality quirks. 'The vet would call me up and say, "Figo is doing this or that – what's he trying to tell us?" and I'd tell them what he meant. We are funny. We read each other's minds.'

Though Figo was being lavished with attention, it was also clear he missed Audrey desperately. As the weeks stretched into months, he started to become depressed – so his vet arranged a visit to Audrey.

'The vet said he had this look on his face like, *Where is she?* He was getting to the point where he didn't want to eat.

They brought him over to see me and after that he was fine. He perked up,' she says.

Back at the Guide Dog Foundation, Doug Wiggin was a little concerned. He was worried Figo's confidence could have been so damaged by the accident that he wouldn't be willing or able to work anymore. Figo was recalled to training HQ in Smithtown to be assessed.

Happily, Figo's focus on his job was as laser-sharp as ever.

'After everything happened and I went to go collect him, you could just see the bond they had there and how much he really does watch out for her,' Doug says. 'The fact that he was willing to work again for her is pretty special after everything he's been through.'

Audrey had no doubt Figo would bounce back from the accident. The months spent in rehabilitation had given her plenty of time to think about his incredible act of courage and she knew there was no way Figo would forfeit the amazing bond they shared.

'I knew he could do it. I just knew it. They brought him over to me in the nursing home and I told him that he had to,' she laughs. 'He proved his love by doing what he did. After the accident, it really sunk in. It occurred to me that he was willing to die for me. He didn't care if he made it; he just wanted to make sure that I made it. He went beyond the call of duty. Thank God he survived. It's a miracle.'

A few days before Figo went home to Audrey, Doug spent some time helping the dog re-familiarise himself with the neighbourhood he hadn't seen in months. 'The first time I took him back he was a little hesitant, but with some encouragement he picked it right up,' he says. 'We were getting ready to practise crossing the street where he got hit, waiting and listening for the traffic flow, and this girl popped her head out of a car and said, "Is that Figo? Yeah!" Audrey has a lot of support around there. I was amazed to see that.'

Finally, after 141 days apart, Audrey and Figo were officially reunited on 26 October 2015. 'Once he came back it was like nothing had ever happened,' she laughs.

The brave dog quickly became a local and international celebrity. He received gifts and get-well cards from all over the world. Audrey was interviewed by media outlets across the US and as far afield as the UK. She and Figo were on the front page of their local newspaper several times and also appeared on top-rating national breakfast television shows *The Today Show* and *Good Morning America*.

The local fire department gave Figo an award for courage and heroism, and in November 2015 he was named the American Society for the Prevention of Cruelty to Animals Dog of the Year.

'A lot of people recognise us in our area wherever we go. You'd think Figo was Lassie. At the grocery store deli department they always give him two slices of bologna and say, "This is for the hero dog,"' she says. 'It's a different world now. I've always been a shy person and kept to myself, but people are always congratulating us. Figo did all the work; I just held the leash! People say, "We're just so glad the two of you are back together again." There's a saying here in New York that your life can change in a New York minute. Well, mine did.'

Figo is ten now and retirement beckons. Retired guide dogs commonly live the rest of their days with their handlers as pets, or they're adopted by a family member or close friend. If that's not an option, the Guide Dog Foundation finds loving homes for retired guides – sometimes they even go back to their puppy raiser.

Doug Wiggin says finding homes for retired guide dogs is never a problem. 'We've taken dogs that are fourteen years old and adopted them out. I myself have taken some of the dogs that have an illness and only have a short time and have them come live with me,' he says.

Even when he's no longer her guide dog, Audrey is adamant Figo isn't going anywhere. 'People have said to me, "We'll take him when he retires," but I would feel awful if he had to leave me. I just don't think he would survive without me. We're really joined at the hip,' she says.

She wonders now, with the benefit of hindsight, if there was perhaps a greater force at play when it came to pairing her with Figo. After all, he wasn't the Guide Dog Foundation's first choice of dog for her, but a last-minute twist of fate saw them matched up.

'He was sent to me for a reason. What made the training school change their mind at the last minute? Maybe in some corner of the universe they knew this [accident] was going to happen and they knew he was a dog that would take charge,' she muses. 'He's very brave. He's just a wonderful dog. He's my little angel.'

Audrey herself was raised in foster care and sees in Figo a kindred spirit – a fellow creature who has known many homes and wants only to belong. 'I was a foster child until I was three years old, when I went into a permanent foster home. I said to Doug once, "I collect these dogs like foster children,"' she says. 'They're born at the training school, they go to the puppy raiser, go back to the school to get trained and then they meet me. They kick around like foster children. There's a sense of *where do they belong?* Maybe Figo senses that.'

Whatever the reason fate chose Figo to be a guide dog and brought them together, Audrey will be forever grateful it did.

MOLLY POLLY

DIABETES ALERT AND MENTAL HEALTH SUPPORT DOG

'*And though she be but little, she is fierce.*'

So wrote William Shakespeare in his beloved comedy *A Midsummer Night's Dream*. He was referring to the character of Hermia, whose diminutive size belies her high-spirited and feisty temperament. But the line could just as easily be applied to a scrappy Australian silky terrier called Molly – and indeed to ten-year-olds Hannah and Olivia Weber, the diabetic identical twin sisters whose lives little Molly has repeatedly saved.

When Hannah and Olivia were born in Canberra in January 2007, there were no signs that anything was wrong with the bouncing baby girls. Olivia arrived first, weighing in at 2.2 kilograms, just slightly under the average twin birth weight. Hannah followed two minutes later, tipping the scales at 2.62 kilos. 'Hannah was the big boofhead,' laughs the girls' mother, Adrienne Cottell.

But as they grew into toddlers, the sisters remained thin, and by their second birthday Adrienne was becoming worried. Hannah in particular seemed to be constantly thirsty, once drinking three litres of water in a single day. She was toilet training at the time and would take herself off to the potty every few seconds, even though she was so tiny she could barely sit up on it.

But it was the fact that Hannah seemed constantly distressed that concerned Adrienne the most. She screamed relentlessly and nobody could tell her why. 'We kept taking her to behaviour specialists because she was screaming all the time,' says Adrienne, who was a single parent at the time and had no option but to return to work when the girls were just seven weeks old. She was exhausted and frightened. 'One day I got really frustrated and I smacked Hannah's bum. I realised she had no fat on her bottom and I knew straight away that she was really unwell. I just felt like it was my fault.'

It was Christmas time and the girls' regular GP was on holiday. Worried she'd simply be told she was overreacting and sent home if she took her daughters to hospital, Adrienne decided to wait the few days until the family doctor returned. When she did, a diagnosis quickly followed.

Hannah has type 1 diabetes, an autoimmune disease in which the immune system destroys the cells in the pancreas that produce insulin. Without insulin the body's cells cannot turn glucose (sugar) into energy, so the body burns its own fats instead. This then releases chemical substances called ketones into the blood that can build up and become a life-threatening condition.

Researchers don't know what causes type 1 diabetes and at present there is no cure. Unlike type 2 diabetes – which can be managed with a combination of regular exercise, healthy eating and weight management – type 1 is not linked to modifiable lifestyle factors. In other words, it can't be prevented. It occurs most frequently in people aged under thirty and is one of the most common chronic childhood illnesses.

Type 1 diabetes usually develops suddenly and with obvious symptoms, including excessive thirst and urination, unexplained weight loss and mood swings. Hannah's screaming bouts, Adrienne soon learned, happened because 'when they get too much sugar their brain malfunctions and they scream. None of the behaviour specialists Hannah saw picked it up.'

People with type 1 diabetes need insulin every day of their lives, either via injections several times a day or via a subcutaneous insulin pump, to replace the insulin the body cannot produce. They must also test their blood glucose levels frequently throughout the day.

'The GP cried when she gave me the test results because she was like, "You do know what this means,"' Adrienne recalls. But for her, the diagnosis was a relief – not only would Hannah receive the treatment she needed, but Adrienne now knew how to recognise the symptoms should Olivia ever display them. 'I wasn't remotely sad. I was just like, *This is our life now*,' she says.

Hannah was admitted to Canberra Hospital to stabilise her condition – without Olivia. It was the first time in their short lives the twins had been apart and the separation was very difficult. 'Hannah didn't have to spend long in hospital, but Olivia got left at home and that was when I did cry. She thought Hannah had died,' says Adrienne.

Though she didn't have symptoms at the time, Olivia was tested for diabetes-related autoantibodies after Hannah's diagnosis and returned a positive result. Under doctors' guidance, she was put on a therapeutic program of omega-3 and vitamin D and monitored closely. Results of subsequent tests remained negative for several years.

Even after Hannah was diagnosed and the girls began their respective treatment, life was a rollercoaster. Repeated anonymous complaints against Adrienne were filed with the Australian Capital Territory's Child and Youth Protection Services by people who assumed Hannah and Olivia's thin frames were the result of abuse or neglect. 'We got reported all the time. The girls' doctors got so angry because they were like, "These people have no idea what you go through,"' she says.

Then, shortly before Hannah's third birthday, she developed a serious infection at her insulin pump site and became gravely ill. 'Hannah was unresponsive because of the ketones and had to be resuscitated. Livy willed her back to life on the resuscitation bed,' Adrienne says. 'It was 2 a.m. and this little girl was in her sister's face going, "I love you, Hannah. Open your eyes, Hanny." Hannah wouldn't open her eyes when we said it, but she did when Livy said it. Every time, she'd do it for her. If I didn't have Livy there, I probably would have lost Hannah.'

Hannah recovered from her ordeal, but Olivia had by now developed severe anxiety and post-traumatic stress disorder. She lost a large amount of weight and started sleeping only four hours a night.

There were more scary moments to come. One night, Adrienne woke with a start and, without thinking, ran into the sleeping Hannah's bedroom. A blood glucose test revealed she was dangerously hypoglycaemic. Hypoglycaemia occurs when blood glucose levels drop below 3.3 to 3.6 mmol/L; Hannah's level was just 1.1.

'I sat bolt upright in bed and raced to her. There was no rhyme or reason why I should have done that, but I knew instantly it was her,' she says. 'We often say that Hannah has an angel. That's why I think I've still got my kids.'

As the twins got older, Adrienne, who has since reunited with their father, Martin Weber, realised that Hannah is 'hypo unaware', meaning she is unable to tell when she is hypoglycaemic. Most diabetics notice the symptoms of hypoglycaemia, which include confusion, tingling in the mouth or fingers and feeling weak. Failing to recognise these symptoms can lead to convulsions, loss of consciousness and coma.

Hypo unawareness is a dangerous condition, but fortunately the twins have a symbiotic relationship: Olivia can somehow feel what her sister feels. 'Hannah will pick up maybe one in ten hypos, but Livy actually feels Hannah's [sugar] highs and lows. Even the specialist said, "When Livy is screaming, test Hannah,"' Adrienne explains.

For four years after Hannah was diagnosed, Olivia continued taking her omega-3 and vitamin D and her autoantibody test results continued to be negative. But she constantly told her mother she wished she had the disease.

'Olivia kept asking for diabetes and Hannah kept saying, "Can she have it?" Livy used to cry all the time because she wanted diabetes. She thought Hannah was getting all the attention and they felt like they weren't twins,' Adrienne says.

Then in 2014, when the girls were seven, Olivia got her wish. She abruptly began displaying symptoms of type 1 diabetes during a three-week family campervan holiday in New Zealand.

'Halfway through the trip, we realised Livy had diabetes. She suddenly began drinking and weeing excessively,' says Adrienne. 'We called Canberra Hospital to help us and they were amazing. We put Livy on Hannah's spare insulin pump, the insulin pump company sent us a "care package" and we continued with our trip.'

Olivia's diabetes is easier to manage than Hannah's because she is hypo aware and able to tell her parents when she feels unwell. But her anxiety is much worse than her sister's.

And while many parents would worry that having two diabetic daughters would mean double the stress and heartache, Adrienne was able to take Olivia's diagnosis in her stride – because by then the family had a secret weapon; someone to help with the round-the-clock job of keeping Hannah and Olivia safe.

And that someone's name is Molly Polly.

*

In 2012, Adrienne, Martin and the girls had left Canberra for a fresh start in Brisbane. With Hannah and Olivia starting school there, Adrienne looked for a way to keep them extra safe when she couldn't be with them. The girls have a designated carer in the classroom with them, but with Hannah's hypo unawareness and Olivia's extreme anxiety, she wanted another tool in the toolbox.

Adrienne had seen reports from the United States of dogs being trained to detect abnormal blood-sugar levels and alert their diabetic owners. She found an Australian organisation doing the same type of training and contacted them to ask if it could work for children. She says the response was not encouraging.

'They told me I wouldn't be able to look after a dog on top of caring for the girls, let alone train it, but I thought Hannah was going to die and I knew instinctively it would work,' says Adrienne.

The girls were having a terrible time at their new school, and Adrienne says she felt as though staff didn't appreciate the seriousness of their condition. In Brisbane, Hannah also developed severe anxiety. There were times when she wasn't able to get to the toilet and would instead wet her pants or collapse on the floor. Only five years old, she developed migraines that Adrienne believes were brought on by stress.

She contacted another charity, which was more positive but still not able to assist, and then another, which shared Adrienne's belief that a dog could be trained to detect and alert for diabetic children. Unfortunately, the organisation's waiting list was prohibitively long. They suggested Adrienne try to do it herself.

'The lady I spoke to turned around and said, "Don't let your daughter die. Go and purchase your own dog,"' she says.

So she did. Adrienne had previously owned an Australian silky terrier called Megan, who was so intelligent she knew more than 250 words. She knew it was the perfect breed for the job of being Hannah and Olivia's guardian.

'Everyone says, "Why did you choose a silky? They're not children's dogs." They can be snappy, but that's because they're usually bought by little old ladies who don't socialise them with kids,' she says. 'They're very hardy, loyal and protective and they don't moult.'

As if throwing its support behind her endeavour, the universe soon delivered a breeder literally to Adrienne's door. 'One day I saw a lady outside our apartment with her two silkies. I asked where she'd got them and she said she was a breeder. I said, "Here's my number. If you have a litter, please give me a call,"' she says.

Soon after, the woman called to say she had a litter of six puppies. Adrienne put her name down for a female. 'Girls have a bit more of a "mummy instinct". They show a bit more loyalty,' she explains.

The girls' first meeting with the puppy they'd decided to name Molly Polly could have been a disaster. Hannah had a migraine from a tough day at school and was in a state of high anxiety, but dog lover Olivia was thrilled.

'The other female pup of the litter hated to be picked up, but Molly came straight over to them. Every time we went to visit, Molly would come to them,' says Adrienne. 'People talk about dogs choosing you and that's exactly what happened with Molly.'

Molly came home at the age of eight weeks and the sisters were smitten. Though she was ostensibly Hannah's assistance dog – at that stage Olivia hadn't yet been diagnosed with diabetes – it was Livy who bonded with Molly the most. 'Molly went in the Barbie house, the car. She was dressed up. The girls made an obstacle course for her,' Adrienne says. 'Molly essentially went to bootcamp for being around kids. All the girls' friends came over all the time. She was manhandled. She thought kids were awesome because it meant she got to play and have lots of cuddles.'

The girls even started feeling better about going to school because they knew they were coming home to Molly at the end of each day. But when Adrienne asked the school whether they would consider allowing Molly – once she was fully certified as an assistance dog – to accompany the girls, she says the answer was a firm no.

The refusal, and Olivia's subsequent diabetes diagnosis, were catalysts for the family's move back to Canberra in 2014.

For the first year or so of Molly's life, Adrienne focused on socialisation: exposing her to a variety of environments and situations she might encounter when working for the girls. Then, at the age of fifteen months, it was time for

Molly to go to work – her diabetes alert training began in earnest.

'When it came to training Molly, we rang around in Australia and no one really knew what to do aside from saying, "Expose her to Hannah while she's doing her blood sugars and let her sniff the test strips, then reward her when she's high or low,"' she says. 'So we did that. It wasn't quite the right training, but we were like, *At least we're attempting it.*'

When Adrienne's Canberra neighbours, Barb Grundy and Carolyn Kidd, launched a dog-training business, Dogs on the Run, she asked them if they thought Molly could be suitable for training as an assistance dog. They were eager to take up the challenge and began obedience training with Molly twice a week.

'There was no use in me doing all this alert-dog training if she couldn't cope with the world outside. The first time, Molly wouldn't leave the house with them but they won her over. They said, "She's very food motivated, so let's go for it,"' she says.

In March 2015, with no formal diabetes alert training – Molly was still only being encouraged to sniff the girls' blood-glucose test strips – she woke Adrienne at 4 a.m. to alert her to Hannah's high level of ketones. The amount of ketones in her blood had soared to 3.8 mmol/L; the meter only goes up to four and anything over 1.5 mmol/L usually requires hospitalisation. Adrienne immediately administered insulin and called 000, but when paramedics arrived Molly was having none of it.

'Molly was with me in Hannah's room and when the paramedics arrived she stepped between them and Hannah. She didn't know they were coming to help her,' she recalls. 'She didn't bare her teeth but she was like, *You are not stepping foot in this house.*'

Molly was eventually persuaded to allow the paramedics to take Hannah to hospital and Adrienne immediately started looking for more formalised training options for the little dog, who clearly took her job very seriously indeed.

A Google search delivered the Diabetic Alert Dog University (DADU) in the US. Run by dog trainer Mary McNeight, who lost both her father and grandmother to complications of type 2 diabetes, DADU has developed a series of videos that teach people all over the world to train their own dogs to alert for sugar highs and lows.

Adrienne immediately signed up and began training Molly according to the DADU videos. 'Molly got the training really quickly and started alerting for hypos and hypers from week six of the ten-week training,' she says.

Molly's powerful nose can detect whether the girls' blood sugar is unstable with just a sniff of their saliva. She alerts by bumping the twins with her nose or swiping at their legs with her paw. If they don't respond – and they often don't – Molly will go and alert Adrienne instead. Incredibly, she doesn't even need to be in the same room as Hannah and Olivia – she can detect ketones or hypoglycaemia from up to a kilometre away, or when they're separated by closed doors. 'We've also taught her to "talk". She alerts almost every day.'

DADU's Mary McNeight says her decision to develop the training program was driven by her belief that people shouldn't have to 'mortgage their houses in an attempt to pay for diabetic alert dog training.' Indeed, when Adrienne first started investigating the possibility of having an alert dog for the girls, she was horrified by the cost – tens of thousands of dollars in some cases.

'By the time we bought Molly, trained her and had her desexed, she still cost less than $2000,' she says.

Soon after Molly began her DADU training, and not long after her first life-saving effort, Adrienne was out shopping one day and saw a woman walking a dog sporting a mindDog vest. She chased after her and learned that mindDog Australia is a not-for-profit organisation that helps people to procure, train and accredit psychiatric assistance dogs.

At once, Adrienne wondered if Molly could possibly do double duty as both a diabetes alert dog *and* an assistance dog to help with Hannah and Olivia's anxiety and Olivia's PTSD. 'I said, "Can a child have a dog like this?" and the lady said, "I don't see why not."'

The woman in the mall was correct: Molly first donned her mindDog training vest in April 2015 and was fully accredited by September. Adrienne believes Molly is the first assistance dog in Australia to not only have two distinct jobs – diabetes alert *and* mental health support – but to work for two children at once. 'Molly is the first in Australia for a lot of things,' she laughs.

In May 2015, Molly chalked up another first when she became the first ACT assistance dog to attend school.

Hannah and Olivia's school, Ainslie Primary School, welcomed Molly into the classroom so she can monitor the girls during the school day, calm their anxiety and alert when necessary. As always, she will alert Hannah and Olivia first, but if they don't respond Molly is trained to alert their carer or a teacher.

'After she completed her DADU training I rolled up to the school and said, "Molly is now a trained assistance dog, will you take her?" They had to break so much ground to get her in. There was nothing in Australia about primary school children having an assistance dog at school. No precedent, nothing,' says Adrienne. 'Molly was all over the principal like a rash. The school posted on their Facebook page, "We're getting a new member of our school on Monday and her name is Molly Polly." I didn't realise it, but we hit around the world. The post was shared hundreds and hundreds of times.'

Initially Molly only went to school in the morning and Adrienne would pick her up at lunchtime, but now she stays all day. To say she enjoys the experience would be an understatement. 'It's very unusual for a dog to be in a school situation, but Molly loves it. She just about breaks her neck trying to get there in the mornings. I think she thinks it's an awesome job. Not once has she shown any sign that she feels like her job is burdensome.'

The only aspects of school life she's not so keen on are assemblies and music lessons, because they're crowded and noisy and often involve drums and loud, squeaky instruments.

The school community loves Molly so much they bought her 'the Taj Mahal of crates' so she has her own space to retreat to when she needs a break from all the adoration. 'The girls will say, "She's working, you're not allowed to pat her" but then they all have sneaky pats. The teachers walk around holding her like a handbag,' says Adrienne.

Molly is often so exhausted when she comes home in the afternoon that she'll occasionally miss one of the girls' hypos, but with Adrienne and Martin on hand to pick up the slack, they let her off the hook. 'If Molly ever misses one of their hypos we're like, "Molly, you're a slacker!" She's not very happy about that and then she'll have me up all night alerting,' she says.

Now four, Molly hopefully has many years of faithful service ahead of her. Her training must be continually reinforced or she can lose 'the knack'. 'What some people don't realise is that you have to keep training them all the time,' says Adrienne. 'If you don't put the effort in, it doesn't work. Sometimes Molly won't alert for Martin or for the girls' school carer because she thinks, *They're doing it.*'

The nature of her work means Molly will never 'retire', though Adrienne says if she ever stopped alerting she would remain a much-loved family pet. She passed her Public Access Test in September 2015 and as a fully-fledged assistance dog she can go anywhere the girls do, from the supermarket to the cabin of an aircraft. (The only places that are off limits are zoos and animal parks due to quarantine regulations.) Adrienne says she sometimes runs into problems with people trying to prevent Molly entering certain places because she doesn't look like a typical assistance dog such as a labrador or golden retriever, but says most people are fascinated by the little dog with the big responsibility.

Molly is certainly a conscientious 'employee' where both her jobs are concerned, but her positive impact on the lives of her young charges goes far beyond soothing their anxiety and alerting when their diabetes is unstable. Molly Polly has essentially given Hannah and Olivia their childhoods back.

'I originally got Molly for Hannah, but Livy has thrived, too. Livy's anxiety was so bad she wouldn't talk in public and would stay in the corner. Now she'll tell people about her diabetes alert dog. Molly is like the winner in a popularity contest,' says Adrienne.

And for Adrienne and Martin, tiny-but-fierce Molly has provided something they worried they'd lost forever: peace of mind. 'Having Molly Polly is like having an extra, happy family member. She's made our lives complete. I actually sleep now,' she laughs.

HECTOR, MURPH, SIDNEY, BUSTER, JET & BUDDY

DOLPHIN SPOTTERS

As anyone who has ever lived with a dog can attest, they're not backward in coming forward when they suspect something is up. When the pizza delivery guy rings the doorbell or the neighbours have friends over, our four-legged sentries will make sure we know about it. They will excitedly alert us to the rumbling of thunder as though we hadn't heard it ourselves. They will register their vociferous opposition to strange dogs passing by the front fence. They will loudly share their consternation when a leaf has the temerity to fall from a tree in the dead of night. Because these, in our canine companions' humble opinion, are things we need to know. Immediately.

What's really amazing – or annoying, depending on your feelings on the matter – about dogs' need to keep their owners apprised of affairs *at all times* is that it isn't learned behaviour. We don't have to teach them to do it (and in fact many dog owners devote considerable time and effort to trying to rid their pets of this particular habit), though with training they can be taught to notify us of specific things. For a dog, barking at stuff is just a natural instinct, as primal as burying bones and antagonising cats.

Many dog owners celebrate this canine quirk. They nurture and encourage it and appreciate the sense of security that having a vigilant pooch on the premises affords. Some savvy dog lovers have even turned their dogs' innate watchfulness to their advantage – dog lovers like Hugh and Pip Waghorn from Akaroa, a picturesque French-settled harbour town on New Zealand's Banks Peninsula.

The Waghorns have generations of family history on the peninsula. Pip's ancestor, Etienne Francois Le Lievre, first arrived from Normandy in 1838 as a blacksmith aboard the whaling boat *Nil*. The same year, Le Lievre's good friend, whaler Captain Jean Francois Langlois, bought land in the area. Both men returned to France and Le Lievre helped Langlois set up the Nanto-Bordelaise Company, whose purpose was to found a French colony on the South Island of New Zealand.

Langlois advertised for settlers to come to New Zealand and sixty-three passengers, including Le Lievre, arrived aboard the *Comte de Paris* in August 1840. Pip's family has called Akaroa and the Banks Peninsula home ever since.

Hugh's family, meanwhile, emigrated from Kent, England, onboard the HMS *Randolph*, one of the First Four Ships chartered by the Canterbury Association to carry emigrants who would establish an Anglican Church settlement in the Canterbury region. Hugh's ancestors arrived at Akaroa in December 1850 and took up farming. They are now the single biggest family group living on the Banks Peninsula.

As farmers, the Waghorns have never been without dogs – both workers and pets. And as peninsula dwellers, there are few others whose connection to the region runs so deep. So it's hardly surprising that, when a career change became necessary in 2004, they set up a business that combines their love and appreciation of dogs with their pride in their rich local heritage.

Hugh and Pip retired from farming when Hugh developed knee problems after decades of chasing sheep and cattle. He had a knee replacement and the couple swapped their country property for a more manageable home 'in town' – Akaroa. Regular exercise was vital for Hugh's recovery, so he began to take daily harbourside walks with a newfound friend.

'I had always had cattle dogs and, because I've got an artificial joint, I needed exercise, so I got a little dog to take me for a walk every day,' he says. That was Hector, a purebred cairn terrier. 'He just came with me everywhere I went. He was the one that first decided there were better things to do than just sit at my feet.'

Hector is named after another long-time Banks Peninsula resident, the Hector's dolphin (which is itself named after Sir James Hector, the nineteenth-century museum curator who formally described the first specimen found). Hector's dolphins are the smallest and rarest marine dolphins in the world, with a population estimated at just 7000. Around 1000 live in Akaroa Harbour, which was designated a 475-hectare marine reserve in 2013. The dolphins delight wildlife spotters with their friendly, curious nature and unusual appearance – they have short, stocky bodies, distinctive black facial markings and a dorsal fin shaped like a Mickey Mouse ear.

Hector's dolphins also make a unique high-frequency clicking sound. At least, the experts say it sounds like a click; humans can't hear the noise without special equipment. But, as Hugh soon discovered, dogs can.

During their daily walks by the harbour, Hugh noticed that Hector would sometimes stop and begin to whimper and cry or even bark at the water. Soon after one of these episodes, a dolphin would invariably appear. It didn't take long for Hugh to put two and two together and realise that his clever little cairn could hear the marine mammals and was alerting his master to their presence.

Soon after, with retirement proving a little too leisurely for Hugh, he decided to find 'a semi-retirement type of job.' He and Pip decided to start a harbour cruise business, ferrying tourists out into Akaroa Harbour aboard a luxury catamaran to see historic sites and spot wildlife including fur seals, little blue penguins and, of course, Hector's dolphins.

From day one of Akaroa Dolphins' operations, Hector would board the boat and go along for the ride. And, just as he always had on land, he immediately began to let Captain Hugh know when there were dolphins in the vicinity by racing to whichever side of the vessel they were on.

'He barks a bit, but we try to discourage that. Hector was once so excited to have spotted a dolphin that he slipped off the end of the boat and went into the drink,' says Hugh. 'Somebody told me that terriers go straight to the bottom, so now all the dogs wear life jackets.'

That's right: *all* the dogs. The cruises soon became so popular – and Hector's dolphin-spotting antics such a draw – that Hugh and Pip expanded their fleet of both boats and canines. They now have twelve staff and service more than 15 000 customers every year, while Hector's team has grown to include Murphy the Jack Russell terrier–Bichon Frise cross, Buster and Buddy the schnauzers, Sidney the labradoodle and Jet the kelpie.

'The little dogs are such a hit – they get more Trip-advisor reviews than anyone. They go out on every boat, so every cruise has a dolphin-spotting dog,' Hugh says. 'We get so many people coming to us saying, "Is this the company that has the dogs?" They have become a perk of our trips.'

Murphy – or Murph, as he's more commonly known – was the second dog to join the business. He became the subject of a best-selling book when one of the company's guides wrote a beautiful poem about him and a family friend illustrated it. 'We sold out the first 2500 copies we had printed and we're now on our second edition. It's just something that's grown and grown.'

Next came Buster, who belongs to the partner of one of Akaroa Dolphins' administrative staff. He started work as a puppy and quickly became a star performer.

'They all react to the dolphins, but some dogs are better at it than others. Buster is an extraordinary little dog. He has become the main man,' he says. 'He's so good with people. He doesn't mind people picking him up; he'll just accept it all. He doesn't get at all grumpy. He doesn't have a vicious bone in his body.'

Sidney is more of a part-timer; he belongs to the company's marketing manager, Rebecca Cooper, and according to Hugh is a 'beautifully natured dog'. Buddy, meanwhile, is the only dog on staff that was bought specifically to become a dolphin spotter.

'Buddy's owner is one of our skippers, Captain Bainzy. He saw the value of the dogs, so he decided he would get one himself,' Hugh explains.

Most of the dogs started work as puppies, but there is one who came on board as a comparatively middle-aged five year old. Jet started with Akaroa after immigrating to New Zealand from Australia with the Waghorns' son, George. Known by his nickname, Big Dog, Jet previously worked as a cattle dog, but a hip injury forced him into early retirement. 'George had a kelpie stud when he was working on a cattle station in the Northern Territory. He's now one of our skippers, so Jet's gone from being a cattle-chasing dog to one chasing dolphins.'

But while Jet may no longer have youth on his side, he's definitely not lacking in enthusiasm for his job. 'He's as enthusiastic as the pups. All the dogs are very excitable – they run around flat out looking for the dolphins, moving around the boat,' says Hugh. 'The little dogs are very sure-footed and good at weaving in and out of people's legs, but Jet has problems because he's the big dog. He's so frantic to get to the dolphins that he knocks people over.'

Hugh says passengers are always astonished to see the dogs at work. 'People ask me, "How do you train them?" Because they go absolutely crazy on the boat,' he says. 'I tell them, "We have our own dog whisperers," which is all a complete lie. The dogs just do it naturally.'

But there is something a little bit magical about just how and why dogs are able to hear sounds that humans can't. The science is fascinating.

Pitch is the subjective perception of a sound; it's the quality that makes it possible to judge sounds as 'higher' or 'lower' than each other. Frequency, meanwhile, is the number of sound vibrations in one second, measured in Hertz or Hz. High-frequency sound waves are short, while lower sounds have longer wavelengths. The higher the frequency, the higher the pitch.

A healthy human ear can hear low-frequency sounds of about 20 Hz and high-frequency sounds of up to 20 000 Hz. (The lowest 'A' key on a piano is 27 Hz.)

Depending on its age and breed, a dog can hear frequencies from around 40 Hz up to an incredible 60 000 Hz. (Birds, by comparison, have a frequency hearing range of just 8 to 12 Hz.)

The main function of this extraordinary ability is to help determine where a sound is coming from. Using a process called binaural spectral difference cueing, or simply sound localisation, a dog's brain can instantly compare the frequency range of, say, dolphin clicks as they arrive in each ear. Because the ear furthest from the sound is partly 'shadowed' by the dog's head, some of the short, high-frequency wavelengths will be absorbed. That means the ear closest to the clicks will hear a higher frequency, guiding the dog to the dolphin's location.

Adding to the dogs' incredible hearing abilities is the fact that they have up to eighteen muscles that allow them to tilt and rotate their ears so that they can funnel sound into their inner ear more efficiently. Dogs also have much longer ear canals than humans, and they can alter the position of these to help localise a sound.

Hugh believes there's a psychological element to the dogs' dolphin detection, too. Though they can hear and locate it, the dogs don't understand the sound of the Hector's dolphin when they first hear it. That's why they're so eager to pinpoint its source – and the positive response from their employers is what drives them to do it again and again.

'Sometimes we've got a whole group of grumpy people and we come across a pod of dolphins and the dogs go crazy and the whole atmosphere on the boat changes. Everyone's excited and happy,' he says. 'I think the dogs started to associate the happy people with the clicking noise and they then started hunting for that noise because they know it makes people happy.'

Their success rate is virtually 100 per cent. 'They can hear the dolphins long before we see them. That click must be loud for the dogs to hear it over the engine noise and all the other noises on the boat, but even if they're upstairs asleep at the captain's feet, they'll wake up and come running down and looking in that direction and the captain will then change course,' says Hugh. 'Dolphin spotting is something that's self-taught and I think people enjoy seeing the dogs so happy in their work.'

While many working dogs are rewarded for discharging their duties with a food treat or a few minutes of play with a favourite toy, the Akaroa dolphin dogs seem to see locating their targets as the prize. That said, there's certainly no lack of praise for the clever canines either.

'They also get so many hugs and cuddles. They get their photo taken,' Hugh says. 'They don't get any extra food treats. That probably comes from our farming background – I can't stand dogs begging so they get severely reprimanded if they do. We give away big free chocolate chip cookies on our trips and sometimes people like to give bits of those to the dogs, but we discourage that. I think spotting the dolphins is the reward.'

Hector's dolphins are charming creatures that, along with their North Island cousin, Maui's dolphins, are only found in New Zealand. (Maui's dolphins are critically endangered, with fewer than 50 remaining.) According to the New Zealand Whale and Dolphin Trust, Hector's dolphins live in small pods of between two and eight, and have a unique social system called 'fission–fusion'. This means that, when two pods of dolphins meet, they won't necessarily part in their original groups but split into new and different groups before going their separate ways.

Educating passengers about the dolphins is a priority for Akaroa Dolphins and part of their business licence fee goes towards Department of Conservation research. Operating the daily cruises means Hugh gets to see a side of the Hector's dolphin that most people never will. He's quite sure that, far from worrying about them, the dolphins actually seek out the dogs to tease and play with them.

'I believe that the dolphins are now familiar with the dogs. We'll see them swimming alongside the boat with their eyes slightly tilted so they can see the dogs,' he says. 'They'll torment the dogs by swimming one way and then turning around and swimming the other.'

Tearing up and down the boat for a single two-hour tour would be tiring for any dog; the Akaroa Dolphins pack do three a day in peak season. It's not uncommon for a dog, once he's finished spotting dolphins, to adopt a passenger and settle down for a nap.

'When they're on they do a full day and they're pretty exhausted at the end of that day. When the dolphins have left, the dogs will often curl up at somebody's feet or in someone's lap. I always say to people, "The dog can sense trustworthy people and that's why he's chosen you,"' Hugh says. 'They get so used to dealing with a whole variety of people, different nationalities, different colours. They're not like a little town dog that would maybe only know its immediate family. That's one thing I will say about a dog: they don't discriminate against anyone.'

Now fourteen, Hector the original dolphin-spotting dog is effectively retired. He'll still join a cruise every now and then, but Hugh says he's less tolerant of being the centre of attention these days.

'Hector sometimes gets a bit grizzly, as if to say, *Please, I've had enough.* They call him the Grumpy Old Man – a bit like his owner,' he says. 'We're phasing him out. His full-time job now will be to take me for a walk every morning. Terriers are the sort of dog that need to be with you the whole time. It doesn't matter what I'm doing, he wants to be at my feet.'

When Hector does hang up his life jacket for good, Murph, Buster, Buddy, Sidney and Big Dog will happily pick up the slack. Other dogs will no doubt join the team in the future, too. That's the beauty of utilising the dogs' natural desire to locate the dolphins: any able sea dog can be recruited into service on the crystal-clear waters of Akaroa Harbour.

While the canine crew may change, one thing never will: Akaroa Dolphins will always have four-legged sentinels aboard its vessels. 'We'll have to develop a succession plan. I think we're stuck with the dogs now because they've got such a reputation,' Hugh laughs.

Six dedicated dogs living lives of fun and adventure simply by doing what comes naturally – that's a reputation most people would be more than happy to have.

TUNA

SOCIAL MEDIA SUPERSTAR/
DAY-CHANGER

All the great captains of industry came from humble beginnings. Henry Ford, the eldest of six children, spent his childhood doing farm chores and walking 6 kilometres to church every Sunday; he didn't start the Ford Motor Company until he was forty.

University dropout Steve Jobs, the son of a Syrian migrant, co-founded tech giant Apple in his adoptive parents' California garage. Sir Richard Branson ran a discount record store from a London church while still a teenager; today his Virgin Group controls more than 400 companies.

The story of social-media sensation Mr Herschel Burns – better known as Tuna – has similarly modest origins. His ascent to Instagram eminence began on a cold Sunday morning in December 2010 at a Los Angeles farmers' market.

Courtney Dasher was a recent LA transplant, having moved from Atlanta, Georgia, to pursue a career in interior design. She loved her job and had a frenetic social life and a wide circle of friends, but somehow she felt adrift in her adopted home.

'I had a friend who was fostering a pit bull. I had just moved into my own studio apartment and she suggested fostering a dog so that I would have a companion,' she recalls.

Courtney had no idea that fostering an animal was even possible. She had grown up surrounded by animals – her father lived in the country and her mother had owned three cockapoo dogs, all purchased from breeders – but wasn't aware of the concept of animal rescue.

'I grew up without any knowledge of the rescue world, so I asked my friend more about it. She informed me that there are dogs that have been rescued in need of temporary homes while they're waiting to be adopted. I thought that would be the perfect set-up for me.'

She had already thought about getting a dog of her own, half-joking to a friend, 'If I'm not married by the time I'm thirty, I'm going to get a pug.' Instead, at twenty-eight, the idea of caring for a dog for a short period while he was waiting for a forever home seemed like an ideal way to test the waters.

Courtney's thoughts immediately swung to the farmers market she liked to visit every Sunday on her way home from church, where each week a small animal rescue would showcase the pets in its care.

'There would always be dogs and cats out in cages but I really didn't know what it was about. After talking to my friend about fostering, the following Sunday I stopped by that market,' she says. 'I told the woman with the dogs and cats that I didn't think I could necessarily adopt because I'd just moved into a studio apartment and I had a full-time job and a big social life. She said, "Take any one you want for the week."'

It was two weeks before Christmas and she would have loved to take every one of the adorable dogs home, but one in particular caught her eye. 'There was one that had a very pronounced underbite that I wanted to foster but the woman said she was spoken for,' says Courtney. 'So I walked around to look at the other dogs and all of a sudden, I saw this tiny puppy who wearing an oversized sweater, shivering. He had his head down and looked extremely downcast, very insecure and very unloved. It was like the record literally stopped for me when I laid eyes on him.'

The sad little dog, just four months old and shivering in the cold despite his unwieldy jumper, also had an 'exaggerated overbite, receding jaw and a magnificent wrinkly neck'. Courtney was instantly smitten.

'I feel like God has given me a heart for the unlovable since I was a child. I walk into a room and I feel very "others aware". I feel like I'm very alert to what's going on in other people's hearts. My reaction to this dog was just like, *Oh my gosh, this puppy is so insecure and in need of love and I want to bring him home and love him with excellence*,' she says.

The puppy was a 'Chiweenie' – a Chihuahua cross dachshund, the latter breed commonly known in the United States as a wiener-dog. He had been found 200 kilometres away, dumped on the side of the road near San Diego. A rescue group had picked the abandoned dog up and taken him to a Los Angeles-based shelter, where he had been taken in by Robin Faber, the woman Courtney met at the farmers market.

'Robin is a private rescuer who takes dogs from the shelters that need more space. She's an amazing woman; it's incredible what she does,' Courtney says.

Robin had named the puppy Wormy because he was so frightened and submissive that he would drop to his belly and squirm towards her rather than walk. The name resonated with Courtney. 'I loved worms growing up, so that really connected my heart to him,' she laughs.

Courtney was eager to take Wormy home with her that Sunday morning, but there was a problem. Robin's foster care placements generally ran from Sunday to Sunday, but Courtney was due to leave LA on Wednesday on a trip to San Francisco to visit family before the holiday season kicked into high gear.

'Robin said, "That's okay, I'll bring him tonight and you can take him for the next few days and then I'll pick him up." She usually doesn't do that, because she's just a really busy individual, but she could tell that me and this dog were going to have a connection,' she says. 'I think she knew that I would end up adopting him.'

As promised, Robin delivered Wormy to Courtney's apartment that evening and for the next three days Courtney tried intently to find him a loving permanent home.

'I was trying so hard through my network of friends to get him adopted in those three days. No one responded to me except one friend, Sunny. She was interested in taking him, but she already had a dog and didn't think that would go over well. Other than that, it was radio silence.'

Well, *almost* radio silence: plenty of people were vocal in their belief that Courtney's lifestyle was simply not dog friendly.

'On the Tuesday night, me and my friends went to a holiday party. I had to return Wormy the next day and I thought then, *I'm in love with this dog and I think I want to adopt him*. But everyone discouraged me because I was a really busy person. I had a full-time job and a lot of friendships. They were just like, "You're never home. It's irresponsible of you to get a dog right now."'

In her head, Courtney conceded that her friends had a point – but in her heart she knew she couldn't bear to give Wormy up.

That night Courtney had two friends staying over, so she and Wormy slept on an air mattress. 'He fell asleep on my shoulder and when I woke up on Wednesday morning I opened my eyes and he was still in the exact same place,' she says. 'He lifted up his little head and looked at me and I thought, *You know I'm supposed to be your mum*.'

Nevertheless, Courtney duly returned Wormy to Robin that day as promised and left for her trip. But as she drove north up the Pacific coastline toward San Francisco, she couldn't stop thinking about the funny little 'shrivelneck' pup who had wormed his way into her heart.

'I stopped off in Santa Barbara to call Robin. I told her, "I've fallen in love with this puppy, but I don't think I'm ready to keep him permanently because of my circumstances." Robin said, "People make plans for when they're going to have a child, but if a woman falls pregnant unexpectedly the baby changes your life – and this dog will change your life."' Then Robin made Courtney an offer she couldn't refuse. 'She said, "Look, if he doesn't get adopted this Sunday, or if the farmers' market is cancelled due to rain, you can take him for another week to make your decision."'

Another week with Wormy would take them up to Boxing Day, December 26. In the five years she had lived away from her home town of Cleveland, Ohio, Courtney had never missed a Christmas at home. That year, however, she couldn't take the time off work and would be staying in LA. And if that wasn't enough of a sign from the universe that Wormy and Courtney belonged together, the Saturday night before the next scheduled farmers' market delivered a torrential downpour that drenched virtually the entire state of California. The market was indeed cancelled and Wormy came to stay once again.

By the time Boxing Day dawned, Courtney's mind was made up. 'I was walking home from church and I said to myself, "I'm going to keep him,"' she says. 'Over that week it had been confirmed to me that it was the right thing to do, so I called Robin to tell her that I would be keeping Wormy – he was my Christmas present to myself.'

With Wormy now a permanent family member, Courtney decided to change her sweet puppy's name. Not only had he stopped 'worming' – he quickly became so comfortable in Courtney's company he only ever did it once – but she wanted to mark the start of their new life together with a new identity for him.

'I took him to a party with around twenty-five of my friends and they all had something to say,' she laughs. 'One of them thought he looked like Benjamin Button. Another thought that, with his overbite, he looked like Mr Burns from *The Simpsons*. I agreed to that, but I wanted to give him dignity with a first name. In high school I babysat for a little boy named Herschel and I thought that would be a cute name for a wiener-dog. So I named him Mr Herschel Burns, since he is part wiener-dog.'

But as many dog owners will attest, a four-legged friend's given name is often not what he or she is called day to day. It wasn't long before Mr Herschel Burns had acquired the nickname 'Tooney' on account of his cartoonish appearance. Over time Tooney morphed into Tuna – and the moniker stuck.

By mid-2011, when Courtney first heard about a fledgling photo-sharing social-media platform called Instagram, she had hundreds of pictures of her oddball Chiweenie stored on her phone.

And that's how Tuna got his job.

A potted history of Instagram for the uninitiated: created by Stanford University alumni Kevin Systrom and Mike

Krieger, the photo- and video-sharing social-media service was launched in October 2010 as a free mobile app.

Initially the app confined users' uploaded pictures to a square shape, mimicking the vintage feel of Kodak Instamatic or Polaroid SX-70 images; since 2015, however, any aspect ratio can be uploaded. It also allows users to apply digital filters to their images and add searchable 'hashtags' that link pictures by theme, giving rise to trending topics and creating enormous interest-based online communities.

Instagram's popularity grew rapidly, and it continues to expand. It had more than 100 million active users within the first eighteen months and in April 2012 Facebook bought it for US$1 billion. Today the platform has around 600 million active users and counting.

We can thank Instagram for the rise of the 'selfie'. It has also launched the careers of countless 'influencers', who earn an often-sizable income by promoting products and services to their legions of followers.

In 2011, Courtney was not particularly social-media savvy. She didn't have a Facebook profile or a Twitter account and resisted friends' urging to get on board the social-media bandwagon. That was until she heard about Instagram.

After six months with Tuna, she'd started to get used to the emphatic reactions her beloved dog inspired. 'A lot of people thought I was mad. They were like, "What are you doing with this dog? He's so odd-looking" or, "He's so ugly." There wasn't much positive feedback,' she says. 'Family and friends weren't really on board either, but because they know my heart and my love for the underdog, they knew he was perfect for me. My dad even proclaimed that "if anybody was going to have a dog like this, it was going to be you."'

The negativity directed at Tuna's appearance baffled Courtney. 'I've always celebrated his unconventional qualities. I think he is absolutely beautiful.'

She was sure there were plenty of people out there who would appreciate Tuna the way she did. That's why she slowly came around to the idea of starting an Instagram account dedicated to him.

'Instagram was conceived around the same time that I had adopted Tuna, but I didn't hear about it until June 2011, when friends were encouraging me to start an account for myself, since I was an interior designer,' she says. 'In November 2011, my best friend joined Instagram and when she showed me the platform I thought it was so cool. Since I had almost a year's worth of funny and cute photos of Tuna, I decided to make my account about him. I decided to post a photo a day of Tuna only. At the time Instagram was totally different to what it is today. I don't think people had the intention then of becoming "Insta-famous" and back then there certainly weren't a lot of animal-specific accounts.'

Courtney uploaded her first photo of Tuna to his Instagram account, @tunameltsmyheart (then called @dasherlikethereindeer), on 22 November 2011, and almost immediately his fellow Instagram users took notice.

'Straight away people were saying, "He's so cute", "He brings me joy", "He's changed my crappy day into a good day", "He's a great distraction from my cancer treatment", "I don't have a great relationship with my dad, but Tuna bonds us,"' she says. 'It was just so cool to read all of these strangers' testimonials about my little pup. Unbeknown to me, I had developed this brand on day one and kept with it without this hopefulness of *maybe one day I'll have a thousand followers*. I just thought, *I have this really funny dog who is bringing people a ton of joy*. It was never my intention to garner a larger following. I just wanted to be a catalyst to change people's day and Tuna was doing just that.'

Tuna's Instagram profile continued to amass followers, hitting several thousand by December 2012. Later that month, Instagram featured three images of Tuna in a single post on its own account and his followers leapt from 8500 to 16 000 within thirty minutes. By the next morning, Tuna had more than 32 000 followers.

Overnight, the little dog rescued from the side of a California highway went viral. He had his own website and Facebook page by Christmas. The tech news website Mashable published an article about him and a number of other high-profile media outlets followed suit. In January 2013, Courtney and Tuna appeared on the top-rating US breakfast TV show *Today*. Then came stories in the *Daily Mail* and on *Buzzfeed*, which called him 'the most inspiring dog on the internet'.

'In the (northern) summer of 2013, articles were being written about him all over the world. South Korea, Peru, Israel, Brazil – he just had this media frenzy,' says Courtney.

'I became a believer of Jesus when I was twenty-one and in my conversations with God I would say, "I want to be used to change the world." I had this catalyst moment about six months after Tuna went viral when I paused and said out loud to God, "Oh my gosh, is this how you're using me to change the world?"'

As 2013 drew to a close, Tuna attained next-level internet fame: he became a meme. That September, a user on the social-news aggregation, web-content rating and discussion website Reddit uploaded a picture of a McDonald's receipt on which was scrawled the word 'Phteven.' The image bore the caption, *My friend told the lady at McDonalds 'It's Stephen, with a ph.'* Underneath was a picture of Tuna, overbite looking particularly resplendent, and the word *PHTEVEN.*

Within days, other photos of Tuna began to circulate online, all with funny captions written phonetically to sound like a speech impediment caused by an overbite.

Tuna's Instagram account has now swelled to 1.9 million followers; he has more than two million followers across all his social-media channels. He has been featured in *Marie Claire* and *Cosmopolitan* magazines, the *Huffington Post* and appeared on *E! News*, BBC television and Australia's *Sunrise*, to name just a few. He has toured the US greeting his adoring fans and travelled extensively both in America and the UK to promote his book, *Tuna Melts My Heart: The Underdog with the Overbite* (Penguin Random House). He now has a spin-off Instagram account, @thetravelingtuna, that has more than 50 000 followers.

As interest in her little dog reached fever pitch, Courtney recalled Robin's words to her when she adopted Tuna back in 2010: *This dog will change your life.* 'I thought she meant I would have to come home on lunch breaks and come right home after work and it'd be a big responsibility, which it was, but in hindsight I think it was a prophetic statement because Tuna has literally changed my life in so many ways,' she says.

Courtney left her job in 2015 to manage Tuna's career full-time, but while she does earn an income from her pooch, Courtney is determined to maintain the integrity of Tuna's online presence.

'I do get offers to work with brands and companies, but I turn down about 90 per cent of them. My loyalty stands more with my audience because they are invested in Tuna,' she says. 'Sometimes it's really hard to turn down a large amount of money, but it's all about faith for me. If I say no to this one thing because I don't have a sense of peace about it, there'll be a yes to something else that makes more sense, and in the long term my audience will have more respect for me. I feel like I'm accountable and I have a lot of responsibility to his audience.

'I really feel like that is how Tuna's platform has continued to grow over the years. People understand that my motivation is to bring them joy and laughter.'

Courtney is certain that Tuna understands he has a job. When he's not working – whether that's posing for his latest Instagram post, meeting his fans at events or appearing on national television – he 'likes to be under the covers and sleep for about twenty-one hours a day,' she laughs.

'I definitely think he's aware because he's a really intelligent animal. He's not just a dog; he has this incredible, almost human-like personality,' she says. 'In fact, I always say that he has two personalities: that of a ten-year-old mischievous boy who's a little wild and an adventurer, but then he can turn into this cantankerous 87-year-old man who's grumpy and wants to be left alone. Regardless of his mood, though, I feel like he actually understands that this is our platform to spread joy to people and he lends himself well to being that source of joy for his followers.'

Above all else, Courtney's chief priority is always the wellbeing of her furry best friend. That means keeping a close eye on his energy levels and his comfort in every situation; Tuna's welfare always comes first. 'I'm very aware of Tuna's temperament. I know when he's crabby and I know when he looks exhausted,' she says. 'I think a lot of "rescue parents" understand that their pet has a story that could be evoking their reactions to things. You never really know what you're getting when you adopt a pet because they have a past that could have been traumatic for them, so I think it's important to be hyperaware of their needs or their reactions.'

Meet-and-greet events can sometimes be tricky because Tuna is somewhat fussy about the company he keeps. He's not fond of men or children – Courtney believes males may have abused Tuna in his early life, and when Tuna was a puppy Courtney worked as a nanny for a little boy who would excitedly chase him around the yard.

'I think it's because he's a rescue and he must have had a bad relationship with men in the past. Almost all women he's fine with, (but) I have to be very mindful when men are in his space as well as children, but I know the reason behind that aversion,' she explains. 'Fortunately I have a whole routine with that and I know how to manage it when he is in the presence of men and kids. We go to these meet-and-greets and I will vocalise to the audience what triggers Tuna and how to avoid making him reactive. If a child's approaching, I immediately tell the parents, "Tuna's funny with kids" and they are always very understanding. We just make it work.'

On the whole, however, Tuna loves the adulation his fans heap upon him. 'If Tuna was bothered about it, we would never do these meet-and-greets. He's very cooperative when it comes to being handled. People say to me, "My dog would never hold still for a photo or let strangers hold him," but Tuna is really relaxed and docile about the whole thing.'

Now seven years old, Tuna is showing no sign of wanting to swap his career for a quieter life. After all, who would want to give up job perks like on-demand cuddles, international travel and global adoration? But Courtney has already begun to field questions about what she'll do when Tuna is no longer able to brighten the lives of his friends and fans.

'People ask me all the time, "What will you do when he dies?" I don't look at it like that. For me it's, well, how much longer will Instagram be relevant? Or how much longer can we go posting one photo a day?' says Courtney.

But whether Tuna continues his work on Instagram or elsewhere, one thing is certain: the adorable 'shrivelneck' with the outstanding overbite will keep bringing smiles one way or another.

'I heard a really wise statement a long time ago: "When the opportunity of a lifetime comes, make the most of the lifetime of the opportunity." That really spoke to my heart. This is more than an Instagram account for me. It's so much more than that. I have been told numerous times that Tuna helped someone through cancer treatment. That is incredible,' says Courtney. 'I didn't have any intention of garnering all these followers. I feel like this is a gift.'

And Tuna, the rescued Chiweenie who became an accidental internet superstar and joyful day-changer, is a gift to all of us.

HOLLY

STORY DOGS
READING COMPANION

There's no doubt about it: twenty-first century pets are pampered beyond measure. From organic meals and designer outfits to diamond-encrusted collars and doggy daycare, our four-legged friends have never been more spoiled – or had less to do.

In this day and age of coddled canines, it's actually quite unusual for a dog to have a job. They are more likely to be found snoozing on a sofa than putting in a day's work. Dogs that have *two* jobs, then, are even more remarkable. And it's nothing short of extraordinary for a tail-wagging layabout to have had three different careers.

Well, it would be extraordinary for most dogs. Not for Holly the greyhound, though – because Holly is a truly extraordinary pooch.

Holly began her life just as virtually all of the 20 000 greyhound puppies bred in Australia every year do: destined for life as a racing dog. Not much is known about how she fared in her first career on the racetrack, whether she was a ferocious competitor or always an also-ran. Was she the MVH (Most Valuable Hound) in her racing kennel – or was she the inevitable wooden spooner?

It seems unlikely that she ever set the world of greyhound racing alight, because when Holly was just two years old she was taken to a Brisbane vet by her trainer and left there. (A racing greyhound that consistently wins or places in races will generally keep competing until the age of five.) She was lucky – according to welfare organisation Animals Australia, most greyhounds that don't cut it on the track are simply killed. They estimate that up to 17000 healthy dogs are killed every year, most before their fifth birthday, although a greyhound's natural lifespan is twelve to fourteen years.

'We're not quite sure what happened. A trainer had come to the vet. We don't know why,' says Petra Westphal who, with husband Tom, adopted Holly in early March 2015. 'I'm assuming the veterinary costs were too high and he decided she wasn't worth it so he said, "You keep her and do with her as you please."'

So Holly was given a new job. For several months, the pretty fawn-coloured dog worked as a blood donor and is believed to have lived on the premises. The blood she gave was used to save the lives of her canine counterparts, but there was a limit to how often Holly could help.

'If a greyhound only gives blood once a month, they can continue to do so almost indefinitely. But at the vet they were using her whenever they needed blood, so more often than once a month, which is why she could not keep going. At the end of that time the vet rang Friends of the Hound,' says Petra.

Friends of the Hound was started in 2003 by Lisa White, who hails from the NSW North Coast. Lisa had rescued a timid blue greyhound called Zada from her local pound and was surprised to discover what a gentle and affectionate dog she was. Zada wasn't even supposed to be rehomed – she was at the pound to be euthanised and was in fact the first greyhound ever adopted from the facility – and when she learned about the 'horrendous mass wastage' of greyhounds in the racing industry, Lisa vowed to do everything in her power to show people that the breed is an ideal family pet.

Like Lisa, Petra knew little about greyhounds when she first 'met' one. She had seen horror stories about live baiting in the media, so when she came across a Friends of the Hound stall at Eumundi Markets, not far from her home at Noosaville on Queensland's Sunshine Coast, she was curious.

'Friends of the Hound have a stall there every month or so. They bring greyhounds in for a meet-and-greet and they're available for adoption. I thought, *This is a good cause*,' she says. 'Greyhounds had been in the media with the trainers doing the live baiting, but I met some of the dogs and some of the owners and learned a lot of things I didn't know about greyhounds, like the fact that they rarely bark.'

Won over by the placid – and widely misunderstood – breed, Petra went home and tried to convince Tom that they should adopt one. They had been looking for a new dog and she was certain this was the breed for them.

Tom didn't share her conviction. 'We'd lost our other dog about in early 2013, when we lived in Melbourne, and we needed to have a break. The loss was very sudden and very unfortunate – the vet found a large spinal tumour, which was inoperable, causing her pain and starting to paralyse her. After she was put to sleep, we needed some time out,' she explains. 'We had since moved to Queensland and when we thought, *We need to have another dog,* we went to the RSPCA, but the right dog for us wasn't there.'

Petra has always had rescue dogs, ever since her first canine companion when she was just six years old, but they had tended to be quite stocky, solid breeds. A thin, wiry greyhound would definitely be a departure in aesthetic terms.

'I never had a problem with the way they look, but Tom wasn't too keen. Some greyhounds are quite tall and he wasn't sure,' she says.

But she wouldn't be dissuaded. 'We um-ed and ah-ed. I kept going back to the Friends of the Hound website, where they list all the dogs for adoption, and eventually I think I convinced Tom to meet one or two.'

Holly was by that stage living with one of Friends of the Hound's network of foster carers, and when they saw her picture on the group's website and read her description, the couple immediately thought she could be right for them. More importantly, however, they thought they could be right for her.

'She was smaller than a lot of greyhounds, which appealed. It was suggested that she was very quiet and shy and needed a bit of TLC to bring her out of her shell. We thought, *We've got the time, we can do that*,' Petra says. 'I called them and said, "We think this girl sounds like she would suit us." She sounded perfect. We were good to go.'

Before they could meet Holly, however, Petra and Tom had to pass muster with Friends of the Hound. The organisation vets all prospective adopters to ensure they can provide a loving home for a retired greyhound. 'You can't adopt a greyhound until they've met you and explained what having a greyhound is all about. It's things like making sure you have secure fencing – ex-racing greyounds don't know life as pets, so they can try to escape.'

When the time came to meet Holly in the flesh, knowing her husband was still a little hesitant, Petra left the final decision up to Tom. As it turned out, she needn't have worried about whether they'd hit it off.

'We met her in a park. I can live with pretty much any dog, so Tom was going to be the decision maker,' she says. 'The first thing I got him to do was take her for a walk around the oval. Immediately, she was by his side. They were walking like they'd walked together forever.'

Decision made.

Though Petra and Tom were instantly smitten with their new canine companion, it took some time for Holly to become comfortable in her new home. Having spent her short life in a concrete racing kennel and then in a veterinary hospital, she had no idea what it meant to live in a comfortable home with people who adored her.

'To come out of whatever environment she was in, to then go to a vet and then to a foster carer to learn how to live in a home, I think she was just like, *What's happening?*' says Petra. 'She took a while to settle in because she was like, *What's a couch?* At 3 a.m. we'd be up with her because that was what she was used to: *3 a.m. is when I go racing!* Even getting her into a car for the first time was challenging, but we got there.'

Holly was shy to the point of being almost paralysed, which made Petra and Tom wonder what kind of treatment she had suffered in her earlier life. 'She was very, very timid. You could pretty much do anything to her and she'd just stand there and endure it,' says Petra. It was as though the fight had gone out of her.

Gradually, however, Holly started to relax and enjoy her new life. She became less timid and started to enjoy longer walks – quite a feat for a breed that's built for speed rather than endurance. 'Trying to take her for a walk was like, ten minutes and she's done: *I can't walk another step!* She loves her walks now. In the afternoon, about 3 p.m., she runs madly around the house doing what we call her "zoomies". It only lasts three minutes or so, but it's crazy fast and full on.'

Perhaps surprisingly given his initial trepidation, Tom and Holly became virtually inseparable. 'She's become very attached to him – they do call them velcro dogs! He's home a lot more than I am so he spends a lot of time with her,' Petra says. 'Initially, if Tom was out and I was home, she would just be crying and fretting the whole time. We've got her out of that, but she does love him.'

By March 2015, with Holly's confidence growing by the day, Petra began to wonder if her sweet, easygoing dog might be suitable for some kind of volunteer work. A life-long volunteer for various organisations, Petra hadn't done any volunteer work since relocating to Queensland and was eager to give back.

'I thought that I'd love to do something with Holly because she's so gentle and I thought she'd be perfect for all different opportunities,' she says. 'Initially I thought about taking her to visit elderly people in aged care homes, but then I thought that was maybe more about me, because I work in aged care and have for twenty years. I love it, but I thought, *Do I really want to do it in my spare time as well or try something different?*'

So Petra took to Google and searched for volunteer opportunities for dogs and their humans. It wasn't long before her fact-finding mission led her to an organisation called Story Dogs.

Holly's third career was about to begin.

Just like Petra, it was a casual internet search that changed Janine Sigley's life. In 2007, while looking for volunteering work that her teenage daughter could do, she typed 'volunteering with animals' into Google.

Thousands of websites popped up, but two caught her eye: SitStayRead and Reading Education Assistance Dogs

(READ). Both based in the United States, each organisation operates on the same principle: that reading aloud to a friendly, non-judgemental canine can improve children's literacy skills and boost their confidence and self-esteem.

'I grew up with dogs and they have been a part of my whole life. I saw these and immediately knew that this type of support for children struggling with reading would absolutely work,' says Janine, who lives at Murwillumbah on the NSW North Coast. 'I emailed the links to a friend who I knew also loved dogs, Leah Sheldon, to see if she was interested in making this happen in the Tweed area. She said yes!'

With both Janine and Leah working in other jobs, Story Dogs started small. In 2009, they trialled their fledgling program at their own children's primary school. 'At first the principal was pretty sceptical, but he knew Leah and me and knew we were people who make things happen and were pretty passionate about kids, so he said we could give it a try,' she says. 'After one term, the feedback from the students and teachers was overwhelmingly positive. The principal was pleasantly surprised and asked how many dog teams his school could have, as all of the classes wanted one.'

Ten years on, Story Dogs now has 171 dog teams working in 118 schools in six Australian states. Melbourne and the Gold Coast are the largest and fastest-growing areas. The dog teams help around 780 children every week, with each team reading one-on-one with about five kids in each weekly session. The children generally stay with the program for at least two school terms, but often stick around for an entire year.

'Our big, hairy, audacious goal is to have a Story Dogs team in every primary school in Australia, and our goal on the way to achieving this is to have a thousand dog teams by 2020,' Janine says. 'No child should be left behind in literacy. The mission of Story Dogs is to make reading fun for children so they become confident lifelong readers.'

When Petra stumbled upon the Story Dogs website in early 2015, Story Dogs was operating in Queensland but didn't have any dog teams in schools north of Brisbane. So she sent Janine an email asking whether there were any plans to expand to the Sunshine Coast.

'I wrote about me and my dog and wanting to be involved if I could be. Janine replied and said, "This is how our program works: we find people who are interested in what we do and we help them to get started in their region,"' she says. In other words, Story Dogs would absolutely expand to the Sunshine Coast – if Petra was willing to be in charge of that expansion.

She travelled down to NSW to meet with some of Story Dogs' regional coordinators, do a four-hour training session and spend time in a school with a dog team to learn how to run a reading session. She and Holly were also assessed together by a qualified independent dog trainer and undertook a ten-point accreditation test. All prospective Story Dogs are assessed on things like walking on a loose lead, being able to be handled, not being tempted by food or toys, being able to sit or lie calmly on the reading rug and not being disturbed by loud, sudden noises.

Almost any dog can become a Story Dog (except restricted breeds) as long as it has a calm temperament and is responsive to its handler's commands. They also do not impose an upper age limit, as older dogs are often calmer and particularly well suited to the job.

'It is often the only volunteering they can do as most other therapy dogs have a cut-off at ten years old,' says Janine. 'We have a lot of labradors, golden retrievers and also small poodle crosses. One of our volunteers' husbands calls us Snorey Dogs as their labrador always goes to sleep and snores in the reading sessions.'

She hadn't had much to do with greyhounds before starting Story Dogs, but says the breed's laid-back temperament makes them ideal reading partners. 'I have been amazed at how cool, friendly, soft and happy they are in a school situation,' she says. 'Nothing fazes them. They are also quite a novel dog as many children may not have been around greyhounds, so they become quite interested in them.'

Holly and Petra started work as a Story Dogs team in September 2015. Once a week during term time, they visit the local Noosa Pengari Steiner School and work with Year 2 students aged seven and eight.

'We arrive, pop our blanket down, get our books and get ourselves set up on the verandah, then we go to our first classroom and collect our first child. Each child reads for fifteen to twenty minutes and we work with four students per session,' Petra says. 'We walk back to Holly's rug and ask, *What do you want to read to Holly today?* There's a big hug for Holly and they stroke her fur. We get into the book and, more often than not, Holly will just relax into it and sleep through the whole thing.'

The reasons why some children struggle with reading are 'many and varied', according to Janine. 'Sometimes it just has not "clicked" for that child yet and they just need more time. Other reasons are self-confidence issues, behaviour problems, absenteeism, a home life that's not conducive to reading or a physiological reason such as ADHD or being on the autism spectrum,' she says.

But regardless of the cause of the difficulty, reading aloud to a dog seems to guarantee improvement. 'The dog isn't going to judge them. She's not going to laugh at them if they make a mistake. She doesn't mind how long it takes,' says Petra. 'Holly is very patient. She's like, *I'm just relaxing here, I don't mind what it sounds like or if you get stuck.* Some kids can get really flustered when they're struggling with every word. The fact that they can have a break when they get really stuck is important.'

Most of the time, she says, the students forget entirely that they're doing something they dislike or find difficult. 'They're just having a nice time with the dog, reading an interesting book that's not a school book. The learning comes by default. Story Dogs takes the pressure and urgency and performance element out of reading and turns it on its head. Reading is great for their future, but it's the whole process.'

And as Petra has got to know the children she and Holly work with, she's realised that improved reading skills aren't the only benefit of the time they spend together. Some of the students have difficult home lives, where not only is encouraging independent reading not a priority, but one-to-one time with their parents or caregivers is rare as well.

'It creates a bit of stability for some of these kids and a space where it's a bit of time that's just their own. It's just confidence building and having a bit of a special time, which, due to circumstances, doesn't happen for some of these kids at home,' Petra says. 'It all takes time. It's a long journey for some of them. One of the students we see had real issues even with finding the right sound for the letter at the start of a word. He no longer has that problem. He still hates reading, but he's a lot better at it. I don't think he's realised how far he has come.'

Holly and Petra have come a long way, too. From being the only dog team on the Sunshine Coast in 2015, Petra is now the regional coordinator and oversees sixteen other teams in eight schools. 'I started to spread the word about the program, recruit some volunteers and do some fundraising,' she says. 'The fact that the program can make such a difference to a child's life was the thing that attracted me the most.'

Now five, Holly is happily entrenched in her third career and has no plans to give up her job any time soon. Although it's not strenuous work, Petra is sure Holly understands that she is doing something important.

'I think it's fair to say Holly enjoys the experience. How much of that is around *Here's a lovely child that's going to give me cuddles and treats and that's good*, I don't know,' she laughs. 'Dogs are incredible creatures. They have so much to give and they just make you a better person.'

There is also a touch of sadness in Holly's success as a Story Dog, because it reminds Petra of the thousands of ex-racing greyhounds that never got the chance to have a second or – like Holly – third act. In addition to her work with Story Dogs, she continues to be a passionate advocate for greyhound adoption and the importance of giving dogs something useful to do.

'We get bailed up all the time. Whenever we're walking down the street people come up and ask, "Is she a rescue dog? Where did you get her?" A lot of people also say, "I didn't realise greyhounds were so lovely,"' she says. 'I think a lot of people thought that greyhounds were all adopted out at the end of their careers. I don't think people understood they get shot in their hundreds and buried in mass graves. It's heartbreaking how many of them get killed every year for no reason, instead of being sent out into the world to do the incredible work they could be doing.'

Her wish is that every greyhound – no, every *dog* – will have an opportunity to find its vocation. 'I think it's important for people to realise that, just because a dog has finished with a certain chapter of her life, doesn't mean she can't still make a difference,' says Petra. 'Even just being a companion dog, they're making someone's life a little richer just by being around.'

There's no doubt Holly enriches the lives of everyone she meets. Whether curled up with a book or dispelling myths about her breed, this extraordinary dog surely has many more exciting chapters ahead of her.

TRUMAN
(AKA THE DIRT DOXIE)
ULTRAMARATHON RUNNER

To say that Catra Corbett attracts attention any time she takes her place at the starting line of a running race would be an understatement. With her flame-red pigtails, more than fifty colourful tattoos, multiple facial piercings and trademark neon skirt and knee-high socks, Catra certainly stands out from the crowd. But it's not just her appearance that has made the California native something of a celebrity in the world of trail and ultra running. It's not even her steely determination or her impressive race results – she has run more than 250 ultramarathons and is one of only two women in the world to have completed a hundred 100-mile (160-kilometre) runs – though there's no question she is a fierce competitor. They don't call her The Dirt Diva for nothing.

What really makes eyes swivel in Catra's direction as she gets ready to race is her running buddy – because he's a dog.

An eleven-year-old, four-kilogram dachshund whose legs are just eight centimetres long, to be precise. And his name is TruMan.

'In the long-distance world, everybody knows us. When we are running by people they're like, "Oh my god, a wiener-dog just passed me" and I'm like, "That's right, you didn't get beat by just any dachshund!"' laughs Catra.

TruMan – or TruMan Trumie the Dirt Doxie, to give him his full name – has been by Catra's side during dozens of races, from 50-kilometre ultramarathons to segments of the notorious Tahoe 200 Miler (321 kilometres). Together they completed the Rocky Ridge Trail Half Marathon, which features more than 1200 metres of arduous ascents and descents, and they regularly rack up 70-kilometre training weeks on the trails around Catra's home near Fremont, about forty-five minutes south of San Francisco. A few times a year TruMan will even pull off a 90-kilometre training week like it's no big deal. (Catra's usual weekly training covers closer to 200 kilometres, but TruMan doesn't accompany her on every run.)

But TruMan hasn't always been a runner – and the story of how he became one is every bit as inspiring as his feats out on the trails today.

Catra grew up with farm animals, but was definitely not a dog person. 'We had a pig and a horse and we raised lambs. I did have a dog, Candy, when I was about nine that we adopted from a friend. She was a poodle and she was really aggressive and I got bitten,' she says. 'By the time I was about ten I really didn't care for dogs.'

In her mid twenties, Catra's then boyfriend had a family dog, an elderly dachshund called Twinkie. She was sick and blind and, unsurprisingly, not very friendly. 'She was about eighteen and would bite your ankles when you came by. I was afraid of her – and all dogs,' she recalls.

Catra was also at that time deep in the grip of alcoholism and methamphetamine addiction and, in spite of her fear of canines, empathised with the ailing old dog, the first dachshund she had ever known. 'I felt really bad because she was so sick and she was in pain. She had tumours all over her. Every weekend, my boyfriend's parents would talk about taking Twinkie to the vet to be put to sleep, but they couldn't bring themselves to do it because they loved her so much.'

Eventually, the devastated couple asked their son and Catra to take Twinkie to the vet to be humanely euthanised. Though heartbreaking, the experience was Catra's first insight into the profound bond humans and dogs can share. She began to wonder if she might someday have a dachshund of her own.

In the meantime, there was a new dog to get to know. 'After Twinkie died, the family adopted another dachshund, whose previous owner couldn't take care of her. She was working all day and the poor dog was shut in the bathroom and tearing everything up,' says Catra. She was living with her boyfriend's family at the time and became very fond of the dog.

Even after their relationship ended, Catra and her former partner shared custody of the little dog. 'For a few months I would have her on the weekends and then he said,

"I'll pay half for a dachshund for you,"' she says. 'So I had my very own. I named him Oskar Mayer (in homage to the American hot dog and deli meats company). He was a little terror, but I loved that little dog.'

By then, Catra had taken up hiking and running on nearby trails as part of her recovery from addiction; she had been arrested and spent a night in jail for selling meth and says it was the 'aha moment' she needed to spur her into getting clean. Oskar proved to be a keen hiker and she says he was instrumental in helping her replace her vices with healthy lifestyle choices. (Now fifty-two, Catra has been clean and sober for twenty-two years and eats a vegan diet.)

'He was my recovery buddy and my little adventure buddy. He had been born with something wrong with his hind legs, I think from so much inbreeding, so he wasn't much of a runner. He was slow but he liked to hike,' she says.

For seven years, Catra and Oskar hiked around 5 kilometres together every day. Then, in November 2002, Oskar had what should have been a routine operation on his legs. He came home from the vet for a day, but didn't properly regain consciousness after the anaesthesia and Catra rushed him back to the clinic. He died the next day.

Catra was inconsolable. 'There was no reason for it. He was a healthy dog. I think the anaesthesia was just too much for him. I was devastated,' she says.

Though she kept up her running and hiking, it was more than eighteen months before Catra could even begin to contemplate adopting another four-legged friend to join her out on the trails. When she finally decided the time was right, as is so often the case with rescue pets, the dog chose her.

'A friend of mine, Mike, kept sending me pictures of dachshunds that were available for adoption. Finally he sent me one from a rescue in Berkeley, about 50 kilometres away,' says Catra. 'I thought, *Oh my god, he's so cute!* He was half dachshund, half Jack Russell terrier.'

Catra and Mike went to visit the dog at the mobile home of the woman who had rescued him. It didn't take long for them to realise the rescuer was in need of rescue herself – she had eight dogs in her trailer and seemed thoroughly overwhelmed.

'This dog came flying out of this trailer and bit Mike. I went to pick him up and the woman said, "No, no, no" but the dog was great. He looked like a dachshund, but he was hyper and springy like a Jack Russell,' she recalls. The rescuer was amazed. 'She said, "He doesn't let anybody pick him up," and I thought, *I want him.*'

Unlike Oskar, little Felix, as he was then known, definitely *was* a runner. He took to running Catra's local Rocky Ridge Trail like the proverbial duck to water, soon covering up to 20 kilometres at a time. He loved their Rocky Ridge outings so much that Catra even decided to change his name.

'He was my little trail guy. One day we were out running on the Rocky Ridge Trail and I said, "Oh my god, that's what I'm going to call him!"' she says.

But in early 2012, when Rocky was around eleven years old, he suddenly didn't want to run at Rocky Ridge any-more – or anywhere else. He would slow down or stop completely, and Catra knew something was very wrong. He passed away on February 2 that year; the vet suspected an aneurysm.

Once again, Catra was bereft – as was her flatmate at the time, who had grown to love Rocky. 'He really liked Rocky and wanted to do something with dogs, so I said, "Why not start a dachshund rescue?"' she says.

Her roommate took the idea and ran with it, setting himself up as a private wiener-dog shelter. The first dachshund that came into his care, Skye, became a 'foster fail' when he adopted her. Skye was happy to accompany Catra on her runs every now and then, and for the time being that was enough.

Then fate stepped in once more. One day in July 2012, while she was running three hours away in Yosemite National Park, Catra received a call from her flatmate giving her a heads-up that he'd just taken another dog into foster care. 'He said, "When you come home, we've got this dog. He'll be hiding somewhere because he's afraid of everything,"' she says.

Sure enough, when she arrived home Catra found the terrified dachshund curled up behind the couch, shaking with fear. Not wanting to frighten him any more, she sat down and waited. 'After about fifteen or twenty minutes he finally peeked around, like he kind of wanted to come out but he wouldn't – he was just too scared.'

More time passed. Eventually, after what felt like hours, the dog mustered enough courage to inch closer to Catra. Gently, she picked him up and set him on her lap.

'I just started talking to him. He was so afraid. Any movement, any noise, was like terror to him. He was afraid we'd hit him or do something to him,' she says. Nevertheless, something told her this dog was meant for her. 'I wasn't planning on keeping him, but right away I felt, *Oh my god, this is him!*'

The dog was around six years of age and had come to her roommate's dachshund rescue from a hoarding situation. 'The woman who owned him prior to me had twenty-two dachshunds. She'd had his dental done and got him fixed; those things aren't cheap. She meant well, but she finally realised it was out of control,' Catra says.

The woman had first adopted the dog out to a staff member at her local vet clinic, but when his new owner realised the extent of his anxiety and fear issues, she was forced to admit she didn't have the time or resources to help him. After three months, she felt she had no choice but to return him to the hoarding situation.

The original owner then surrendered the dog – along with eleven others – to Catra's friend's rescue.

It took a year of Catra's patience and gentle guidance for the traumatised dog to start to come out of his shell. 'His tail was tucked for about three months, but I worked with him. We'd sit out in front of the house in rush hour traffic or I'd get up early with him when the garbage truck was around to let him know, "It's just noise, it's not going to get you or do anything to you,"' she says. 'If I got him away from the house where there was less traffic he'd walk, but otherwise I had to carry him. If I walked him with Skye he was a little better. He watched her and would see what he had to do.

'I remember the first time, about a year after I got him, that his tail first stood up and started to wag. It took that long for him to develop that confidence. Now it's like he doesn't even hear noise; he ignores it.'

The dog's name was Truman. Catra intended to change it, but the more she got to know her new canine companion – as she watched him bravely trying to put his past behind him and conquer his fears – the more she realised the moniker suited him.

'I was trying to come up with all these names for him, but nothing fit. Then I went, *You know what? He's a true man*. It was just so fitting for him,' she says, though she changed the spelling to TruMan to reflect his newfound courage. There was the added bonus of Harry S Truman having been the thirty-third President of the United States; three is Catra's lucky number and she always asks for race number 33 in running events.

With his name settled and his confidence growing by the day, Catra knew she should start to look for a forever home for the brave little boy. Though she had developed a deep bond with TruMan, she was trying to be sensible: her flat-mate was running a rescue, after all, and every dog they rehomed meant there was room for one more.

She thought a retiree might make a good new owner for TruMan. 'Once we got him well enough, to where we felt we could put him up on the website, I thought, *He'd do well with a senior, just sitting on their lap all day*,' she says. But her heart wasn't in the search – she simply didn't want to let the plucky pooch go. 'I thought, *Do I really want to give him another home? I could show him the world!*'

Just as Catra had kicked her drug addiction years before, TruMan's recovery from his troubled past gathered momentum and soon Catra decided the time was right to see how he'd handle himself out on the trails.

'I drove him to the Mission Peak trailhead, a mile from my house, thinking, *He's either going to walk or freeze.* But I knew he wasn't going to run away. I started running and he just followed me,' she says.

And that was that. For better or worse, TruMan and Catra would be a package deal. 'I love him and he loves me. I believe he knows that nothing bad is going to happen when he's with me. He's confident that whatever we do, it's going to be fun.'

With her newly minted running companion by her side, the fun was truly about to begin.

The start of a competitive running race can be chaotic. Runners might stretch, jog on the spot or perform warm-up 'strides' as they try to calm their nerves and psych themselves up for the challenge ahead. They go through their little rituals, too: double-knotting their shoelaces, checking and re-checking their compulsory gear, mentally running through the particularly tricky bits of the course they're about to tackle.

Catra's start-line preparations are a little different. Having competed in more events than she can count, she has her own race-day routine down pat. She's more likely to be found making sure TruMan is ready to run – ensuring he has his preferred snacks, fitting his goggles and shooing away other runners who might tread on his tiny paws. They are habits that have been developed and refined over dozens of races with TruMan, from 10-kilometre fun runs to 50-kilometre ultramarathons.

'A month after I started running with him there was a 10k and I thought, *Oh, he could do that!* It was all on trail because he still didn't do well running on the road,' she says. 'We did the 10k and a couple of weeks later it was going to be Thanksgiving, so I thought we'd do a nine miler (14 kilometres) just as a Thanksgiving Day run.'

By January 2013, TruMan was running up to 32 kilometres at a time with Catra. 'I slowly built him up,' she says.

In 2014 he ran more than 2000 kilometres. In 2015, he ran his first Fremont 50k, a race co-directed by Catra and fellow ultra runner Mike Palmer. The following year he broke his own record there, completing the three laps of the 16-and-a-bit kilometre course on the East Bay Regional Park Alameda Creek Trail in seven hours and thirteen minutes. He blew that time out of the water in 2017 with a blistering personal best (PB) time of six hours and fifty-nine minutes.

In 2016, Catra entered a 72-hour race, in which participants run as far as they can in the allotted time. She signed TruMan up for the 48-hour event, just so he could be out on the course to help her maintain her goal pace. He ended up running about 44 kilometres alongside his mistress over the three days; at the time it was the furthest he'd ever run.

TruMan's marathon (42.2 kilometres) PB, also achieved in the Fremont 50k, currently stands at six hours and ten minutes – and that's slow, according to Catra. 'I ran a 50k the day before he did his marathon, so he was slow because I was slow,' she says. 'I was pushing for around six hours for him, but I had to walk the last three miles.'

TruMan is well known to race directors and always gets his own race number. In the beginning, Catra wouldn't even enter herself in races – as a race volunteer she was entitled to run for free, so she'd enter TruMan alone then go along as his pacer.

When they're running together, TruMan's wellbeing is more important to Catra than her own. 'When I'm running with him, I'm observing every movement that he's making. I watch him to make sure he's okay. How is he moving? Is he limping? I'll look at his paws, but he doesn't get any paw issues,' she says. 'Every ten minutes I'll give him water. He usually won't start eating until a few hours in because he gets in his groove, but I carry baby food and dog snacks. I'm vegan, so he eats what I'm eating.'

She also makes sure never to push TruMan too hard. 'If I'm doing a long run, like if I'm training for something and I'm doing thirty miles, I'll run most of it alone but I'll save a few miles for him and come back and get him.'

There have been mishaps along the way, of course. Just as with any elite athlete – especially those who compete in extreme endurance sports – TruMan is not immune to accident and injury. He is prone to eye problems. Because he's so low to the ground his eyes are often scratched by low-lying branches and debris kicked up by other runners. In 2015 he had surgery to repair a damaged cornea and now uses eye drops and wears dog-specific goggles to protect his peepers.

'I didn't want to get the doggles because I thought, *He's not going to wear them*, but he does. As long as he's moving he keeps them on, but if I stop and start taking pictures he wants to take them off. Although they're not just a fashion statement, he does look cute in them,' Catra laughs.

In 2016, while running on a narrow trail with a steep drop on one side, a dog lunged at TruMan. Startled, he tumbled 9 metres into a ravine.

'I was terrified. I thought he was dead or that he would have broken his back, but he'd landed in the only spot where he wouldn't have been hurt,' says Catra. 'He had a few scratches but where he landed was so soft, it was all leaves. He had his little glasses on, so that saved his eyes. The vet said, "He's in such great shape, that's the reason there's no damage."'

In the early days of their mutual racing career, Catra worried that TruMan would be trampled by keyed-up runners at the start of races. TruMan, however, has never shared her concerns.

'At the Rocky Ridge Half Marathon he was the most confident I've seen him at a race, lined up with all the feet around him. He was trying to jump up and getting patted by everybody,' she says. 'He knows when he's got that number on that it's his race. He just acts different.'

He has disgraced himself in races on more than one occasion, though. 'I know now that he's going to poop right when we start going. It's like clockwork. The very first race I took him in, it was a single track and he went right in the middle. I was like, "I'm so sorry!"'

Though TruMan's safety is always her top priority, Catra is no stranger to criticism from people who say dachshunds aren't cut out for long-distance trail running. 'I'll be out in the middle of a run and people will say, "He should have boots on," but I'm like, "No, he doesn't need them, thank you very much." They don't fit him anyway because he has little legs,' she says. 'I just say, "Please Google him, he's totally fine."'

She doesn't subscribe to the idea that people – or indeed dogs – are cut out for some things and not others. Catra's core belief is that there are no limits; that we never know what we're capable of until we try. After all, she's living proof of that.

'People who don't know him are the only ones who say he shouldn't do it. The belief is that little dogs can't run and wiener-dogs *definitely* can't run because they have short legs and they get bad backs. But TruMan is healthy, he's thin – most dachshunds are fat and that's why they get injured,' she explains.

When he's not running, TruMan can invariably be found snoozing. He takes glucosamine and fish oil to help his joints and Catra never lets him take big jumps up or down;

she picks him up and carries him instead. 'I'm not going to let him get hurt. People who know me and know him, they see how I treat him and they say, "She would never harm that dog."'

TruMan is so good at his job, she believes, because he is passionate about it. 'Rescue dogs are more grateful. They're very happy they're getting a second chance. They need consistency in life. They need to know they have a job,' she says.

'He's having fun. When I get going, he's excited to be going. His little ears are flying. His tongue is hanging out. I want to come back as him.'

He may be pushing eighty in human years, but Catra thinks TruMan probably has another year or so of long-distance running left in those four intrepid paws. Next on their agenda is a 2500-kilometre self-supported run across California with her boyfriend, Phil, a fellow ultra runner, which will take several weeks. They've kitted out a jogging stroller with a special seat for TruMan.

She also hopes to take TruMan on the 265-kilometre Tahoe Rim Trail in California's Sierra Nevada ranges between California and Nevada.

But just as he calls the shots in every race they run together, it will be up to TruMan when he wants to farewell his illustrious ultra running career and put his paws up. 'The day he decides to stop and put on the brakes, we'll stop,' says Catra. 'Every dachshund I've ever had, when they don't want to do something, they'll let you know!'

Even now, two decades after running essentially gave Catra her life back, she is still inspired by her dog. She has lived the experience of being reborn through running and now she's seen it happen for TruMan, too.

'He inspires me a lot. People say, "I could never run an ultra," and I say, "Wait a minute, I've got a nine-pound dog with three-inch legs and he's done 50k!"' she says. 'I once saw a guy who wanted to drop out of a race and I said, "TruMan ran it yesterday and if he can do it, you can."'

She may be little, but Molly has a big job to do. The tireless terrier is believed to be the only assistance dog in Australia doing two distinct jobs – diabetes alert and mental health support – for two different owners. She has changed the lives of her young owners, twins Hannah and Olivia Weber. *(PAWS by Blackmores)*

Audrey Stone says her bond with her guide dog, Figo, was instantaneous – but even she didn't appreciate how devoted he was until Figo threw himself in the path of a school bus, saving Audrey's life. *(Guide Dog Foundation)*

The Akaroa Dolphins dog team didn't require any training for their role as dolphin detectors – the dogs' incredible hearing means they can easily home in on the location of the rare Hector's dolphin, and they alert instinctively. *(Akaroa Dolphins)*

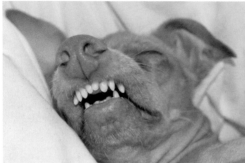

A face only a mother could love? How about a face that millions of people around the world absolutely adore! Tuna's impressive overbite and 'magnificent shrivelneck' have made him a bona fide social media superstar. *(Courtney Dasher/@tunameltsmyheart)*

Staff at Sydney's Australian National Maritime Museum had tried everything to protect its historic fleet from winged assailants, but nothing could keep the birds (or their poo) at bay – until Bailey the border collie joined the team as Assistant Director, Seagulls. *(Adrian Snelling/Australian National Maritime Museum)*

Rowdy's life story is the stuff of a Hollywood blockbuster – from a mysterious poisoning to being shot by police, it was non-stop adventure (and occasional calamity). But it was only after developing vitiligo in his twilight years that Rowdy became an international ambassador for celebrating difference. *(Lindsay Baca/Sit! Stay Pet Photography)*

From suburban pets to mascots for an award-winning country brewery, Mia, Cooper and Hoppy have plenty of reasons to flash those famous Samoyed smiles. *(Kate Henning and Simon Dunstone)*

She was a racing dog and a blood donor before being adopted into a loving home, but what's brought Holly the greyhound the most joy is her third career as a Story Dogs reading companion for kids who struggle with literacy. *(Petra Westphal)*

Dan Holt thought his life was over when he became quadriplegic after sustaining a serious spinal cord injury. Now he has a flourishing career, he's a top wheelchair rugby player and he lives independently – all with his faithful assistance dog, Charlie, by his side. *(Laura Greaves)*

What started as a bit of fun has evolved into a powerful selling tool for Brisbane real estate agent Tracey Ashley, whose adorable dog, Tiffany, now has a starring role in all of her sales campaigns – with impressive results. *(Tracey Ashley)*

BAILEY

ASSISTANT DIRECTOR OF SEAGULLS, AUSTRALIAN NATIONAL MARITIME MUSEUM

Think of a mighty warship's natural enemies and tempestuous weather likely springs to mind. Corrosive sea salt is a problem, too. And nothing challenges a military vessel like the raw, unpredictable power of the ocean itself.

Well, *almost* nothing.

As it turns out, one of the most relentless foes a naval fleet may ever face is not a stormy sea or even a hostile combatant. Those things are generally temporary and can be conquered. The thing that arguably poses the greatest risk to a ship's integrity, because of its sheer persistence both far from land and in safe harbour, is the *Chroicocephalus novaehollandiae*.

That's a silver gull, to you and me. A bog-standard, chip-stealing, squawking Aussie seagull.

For the Australian National Maritime Museum, based at Sydney's iconic Darling Harbour, these pests of the sky are a constant problem. To be more specific, their *poo* is a constant problem – because it's everywhere, all the time, and it causes significant damage to the museum's wharves and twelve heritage vessels, staining their paintwork and varnish. It's also a health risk and creates a slippery, revolting hazard for guests.

'Seagulls are a major issue in terms of the mess they leave. It creates a lot of work for our shipkeepers because they are constantly having to clean it off. The birds cause the lacquer on the boats to peel because of the acidity of their poo,' says Adrian Snelling, the museum's Head of Security.

For vessels like the 61-year-old destroyer HMAS *Vampire*, for example, repeated exterior damage can lead to corrosion and rust, not to mention requiring regular expensive repairs. The birds are a particular problem at night, when they roost on the wharves and there is no human activity to spook them.

Clearly, the museum needed a strict no-seagulls policy – and fast. Museum staff tried a number of creative anti-bird tactics, but quickly discovered seagulls are cannier and bolder than they'd given them credit for.

'We tried hanging reflective CDs to scare the birds off. We tried installing motion-activated sprinklers on all the wharves. We even tried setting up dummy eagles and other birds of prey,' says Adrian. 'They worked for a certain period of time and the birds would disappear for a short while, but they always came back.'

Frustrated, Adrian's boss, Assistant Director of Operations Peter Rout, tasked him with finding a way to keep the birds at bay permanently. His first port of call was Google, where he uncovered a novel method that had been employed successfully in America. 'I came across the dogs that work at airports in the United States, chasing birds away from runways [see Piper's story on page 278]. I said to my boss as a joke, "Let's get a dog" and he said, "Go for it,"' Adrian says.

With his boss's sole stipulation – that the dog must be his favourite breed, a border collie – ringing in his ears, Adrian began contacting local animal shelters and rescue groups. He soon found his way to Australian Working Dog Rescue (AWDR), which had recently saved a border collie cross from a pound in Newcastle, two hours north of Sydney. AWDR thought the dog, which they estimated to be nearly three years old, would be perfect for the job of dispersing seagulls because 'he was already chasing birds'.

Adrian went to meet the dog at the home of his AWDR foster carer. 'She said she had to keep him away from her backyard because he was chasing birds so much,' he laughs. 'We got a border collie because that's what my boss wanted, he just likes them, but it just happened to work out that they are probably the most appropriate breed for this job. They don't want to kill the birds; they just want to round them up.'

Still, the idea that a dog could solve a problem no human had been able to fix seemed vaguely preposterous. It was such a gamble that 'the day before we adopted Bailey, we hadn't even told Kevin Sumption, the director of the museum,' says Adrian. 'Luckily he likes dogs and was all for it.'

The new recruit's name was Bailey, but Adrian's boss wanted to change it to Haggarty after Adrian's predecessor, Peter Haggarty, who had served as the museum's security manager for twenty-four years and was quite a character. Concerned that the name change would confuse the dog, who had already been through tremendous upheaval and, at three years old, was more than familiar with his moniker, Adrian persuaded Peter Rout to bestow Haggarty as a surname instead.

First appearing in the late nineteenth century, the border collie was bred to herd and move sheep in the hilly border region between England and Scotland. Incredibly, the lineage of all modern border collies can be traced back to a single dog, Old Hemp, born in 1893. They are renowned for their boundless energy, athleticism and stamina and are often cited as the most intelligent of all domestic dog breeds. One American border collie, Chaser, has the best tested memory of any non-human creature – she can identify 1022 toys by name and retrieve them.

So Bailey Haggarty arrived at the museum in June 2016 with great expectations weighing on his handsome black and white shoulders. His foster carer was a professional dog trainer and had spent a lot of time drilling Bailey on fundamental skills like retrieval and recall. Adrian continued with basic obedience training so that the new recruit would know how to behave around the 630 000 annual visitors to the Darling Harbour site. 'The only thing we had to work on was his behaviour, because he'd had no behaviour training. He wasn't naughty – he's just a big puppy and he loves to play,' he explains.

The plan once Bailey was officially employed was to ease him into his new role gradually, with Adrian taking him for introductory walks around the complex to familiarise the eager pooch with the area he would be charged with patrolling.

Bailey, however, wasn't quite so keen on the slow-and-steady approach.

'I was "training" him as far as walking him around where he had to go, but not with chasing the birds because that was just what he wanted to do. It wasn't like training a sniffer dog, for example,' says Adrian. 'We did try to take it slowly, but because he loved chasing birds so much he just got straight into it.'

Bailey now goes out with Adrian on three bird-chasing 'runs' every day and when he hears the command 'Bailey, go!' he immediately makes a beeline for the places the gulls like to gather, such as the ends of the wharves. 'I take him down to the wharves and he knows straight away where the birds are. After the first couple of times he knew exactly where they were,' he says.

In the early days Bailey would run at the birds as fast as his legs would carry him. These days he's a little more circumspect in his approach, partly because there are fewer seagulls to vanquish and partly because the full-throttle method has had rather wet results on occasion.

'He has ended up in the harbour a few times. It's very important that he comes back when he's called, although he's not so great at that. Once he's got his eyes on a bird even food doesn't work as a lure,' says Adrian. 'Once I was calling him and said, "Let's go, you're all finished" and he just walked straight off the edge of the wharf. He just looked so surprised – he didn't know what had happened. He can't get out on his own so when he goes in we've got to get a boat to get him out. Luckily, being a maritime museum, we've got boats everywhere.' These days Bailey always wears a doggy life jacket on his bird patrols.

His reward for clearing the decks of the scourge of seagulls is a quick play with his most prized toy, a tennis ball. Nothing else will do – not even his favourite food treat, a Schmacko. 'My wife is a former Australian Border Force member and they use rolled-up towels as play rewards for their dogs. I tried a towel with Bailey, but he didn't like it. He prefers the tennis ball,' Adrian says.

In their traditional role as herders of livestock, border collies are known for their elegant corralling techniques. Not for these clever dogs is aggression or barking; they prefer stealthy tactics like crouching, stalking, intense eye contact and occasionally nipping. It's believed that Bailey has never been near a sheep – nothing is known about his background, but his rambunctious nature led his new owners to suspect he'd been a pet who was surrendered due to his high energy levels. However, Adrian was amazed to see him displaying this instinctive behaviour with birds.

'Initially he just chased them, but now he's learned that stalking behaviour is more effective and he doesn't chase them so much as stalk them,' he says.

'Effective' doesn't really do justice to how useful Bailey has been to the museum. His success at driving the seagulls away – and keeping them away – has been nothing short of phenomenal. In fact, Bailey was so impressive so quickly that at first Adrian didn't think the sudden drop in bird numbers could possibly be due to one tenacious dog.

'At first I just thought it was because Bailey started in winter and the birds had gone somewhere warmer. We were really surprised with how well he did so quickly,' he says. 'All those things we'd tried previously, the seagulls got used to. They don't get used to Bailey. Unlike a dummy eagle, they know that Bailey is real and that he's always around. Watch out, Bailey's about!'

The seagulls are not just wary of Bailey, they seem to feel genuinely affronted by his presence. 'They really do not like Bailey. It's that natural territorial behaviour. While not actually attacking him, they have started swooping at him,' Adrian laughs. 'I'd read articles that said that just knowing the dog is around is enough of a deterrent to keep them away and that seems to be the case here. They might not even be close by, but when they hear him coming the birds will come down and start swooping.'

He may have made short work of the seagulls, but Bailey still has one nemesis left to conquer. 'There's one place where we have a problem with cormorants. We just can't seem to get rid of those birds. They won't go, but fortunately they're not as much of a problem as the seagulls.'

The results where the seagulls are concerned have been remarkable. 'We were getting all our pathways high-pressure washed once or twice a week before Bailey arrived. Now it's been six months since I've had to wash them. Our fleet guys had to wash down the wharves every day so people could walk on them, otherwise it was too slippery, but they haven't had to do that since Bailey's been here. We're saving a lot of time and a lot of money.'

And that cost saving isn't just in terms of maintaining the historic fleet and museum infrastructure; Bailey himself has been quite an economical investment, it turns out. It can cost up to $70 000 for an agency or institution to buy a fully trained working dog. Bailey's adoption fee was just $350.

Word of Bailey's successes has spread across Sydney. Staff from Government Property NSW, formerly the Sydney Harbour Foreshore Authority, came to observe him at work to assess whether a dog of their own could help to manage problem ibises at heritage precincts, including The Rocks and Darling Harbour.

He has also proven just as popular a museum 'attraction' as the warships and submarines, with visitors rushing to meet the personable pooch whenever he's out and about. He has also been featured on top-rating TV shows including *Better Homes and Gardens*, 'interviewed' by a newspaper and now has his own blog on the museum's website. In 2016, Bailey even curated his own photography exhibition, *Dogs and Cats: All at Sea*, featuring images of seafaring pets from the museum's collection by early-twentieth-century commercial photographer Sam J. Hood.

He's so popular with museum staff that he has his own calendar, which his colleagues can use to book appointments with him. 'They absolutely love taking him out for walks. It's a good break from sitting behind their computers. Bailey has done wonders for morale around here,' says Adrian.

But when it comes to his seagull scattering, Adrian is careful to ensure Bailey is able to work without a crowd looking on.

'I try to do the bird runs when there's no one else around, but I do bring him out when school groups are here because the kids do love him. People always want to come up and cuddle him,' he says. 'When we're walking we do get crowds but I think it would be too much for him if he had to work while lots of people were around.'

Because of their working-dog heritage, border collies thrive when they're mentally and physically stimulated. They like to be in the thick of things; to know they have a purpose. That's why the museum decided that Bailey would live on the premises full time.

He has an outdoor kennel and a dog run, but prefers to snooze in his cosy crate in the security control room. In addition to his thrice-daily seagull quests, Bailey gets a walk every morning and at least a couple of night-time sojourns. One or two nights a week he'll go home with a museum staffer for some rest and relaxation.

'The control room is running 24/7 and we could tell he was getting really tired because his eyes were really red,' Adrian says. 'It's good for him to get away and have a rest. I'll also take him out if there's lots of people on site for events so he doesn't get overwhelmed or overstimulated. He loves coming up to my office as well. He goes to sleep under my desk.'

Though he was the one to 'hire' Bailey, Adrian didn't intend for the boisterous border collie to become 'his' dog.

But Bailey does spend the majority of his time close to Adrian.

'I took him on because nobody else really had the time. I didn't have the time either, but I made the time for him. A lot of the staff take him for walks, but for chasing the birds it's me who's his handler,' he says. 'He's just a beautiful dog and everyone thinks so. We call him The Velcro Dog because he loves to lean up against people.'

Now four, Bailey has a job at the museum as long as he wants it. 'As long as he's happy to do it, we'll keep him at it. I don't think he knows he's "working". I think it's play to him. It's his fun time,' Adrian says. 'He's adapted well to knowing when he has to work and when he can play. I wouldn't call him a working dog. He's a museum pet who gets to chase seagulls.'

In that sense, the Australian National Maritime Museum's Assistant Director of Seagulls is never off duty. *Chroicocephalus novaehollandiae,* consider yourselves warned.

ROWDY
VITILIGO AMBASSADOR

Rowdy the labrador didn't always have a job. In fact, for many of his fourteen years he *caused* rather than did hard work. It could even be argued – with tongue firmly in cheek – that the calamity-prone canine was something of a drain on his adoring family's resources.

Rowdy lived a big, adventurous life. From a mysterious poisoning to being shot by police, it was non-stop near misses, death-defying scrapes and flat-out disasters from the day the tiny ball of black fluff came home with Niki and Tim Umbenhower in June 2003.

'From when we picked this puppy up, his life story is worthy of not just a book but a movie,' Niki laughs.

Growing up in Oregon, Niki's family had always had a labrador or two. Her two brothers continued the tradition, both welcoming pet labs when they left home and started families of their own. Niki was determined to have her own labrador someday, too – and fortunately the man who would become her husband was on the same page.

'I'm married to my high-school sweetheart, Tim. We're best friends – he's the most amazing man and somehow I was lucky enough to get him,' she says. 'We always wanted a dog, but when we were in our twenties we were working and living in an apartment and it wasn't the right time.'

That didn't stop the couple from choosing the perfect name for their future four-legged friend, though. They both loved the 1976 children's novel *Summer of the Monkeys* by Wilson Rawls, which tells the story of a young boy, Jay Berry Lee, who attempts to capture a troop of monkeys that have escaped from a travelling circus. The boy's constant companion is his dog, Rowdy.

When they started thinking more seriously about adding a dog to the family after the arrival of son Josh in 1997, Niki and Tim knew immediately what his name would be.

'It's such a neat little book. The dog is the boy's best friend and does everything with him. We decided before we even had a dog that if we were to end up with a male, we'd name him Rowdy,' she says. 'Josh was about six and our daughter, Ally, was three when we decided it was time to have a family dog. We wanted our kids to have a relation-ship with their dog like the boy has in the book. Little did we know he would literally turn out to be quite rowdy!'

They began their search in earnest and met several pup-pies, but none felt like quite the right fit for the Umbenhower clan. Then they saw a litter advertised in Vancouver,

Washington, a 45-minute drive from the small town of Aurora, Oregon, where they lived at the time.

'I think there were only two puppies in the litter, a male and a female, and the female was already gone. The parents were both there. The dad was this beautiful black lab, just handsome and mellow. He came up and gave us love,' Niki recalls. 'The mum was super hyper, to the point where, when we were trying to play with Rowdy, the dogs' owner had to kennel her because she was all up in our grill.'

Her unbridled excitement was, perhaps, a portent of things to come.

The Umbenhowers fell in love with Rowdy and took him home, where, right from day one, he lived up to his name. The little lab was boisterous, rebellious and not a little naughty.

'We ended up getting an underground electronic fencing system because we had a large property and didn't have enough money to build a nice fence,' Niki recalls. 'Tim trained Rowdy very well, he'd read all the books, but there were times when Rowdy would just run right on through the invisible fence line and into the street.'

Labradors are renowned for their even temperament and easygoing nature and, for the most part, Rowdy had both. They're not known for being particularly territorial or noisy – but Rowdy must have missed that memo. 'Rowdy was always a very protective dog. If somebody came to the door he would be the first one there, barking. In all honesty, he could be scary, but he would never have attacked anybody,' says Niki. 'And we never had to lock the house.'

But for all his bluster, Rowdy was 'such a love bug' and settled easily into family life. He joined Niki, Tim and the kids on their regular camping trips to the beachside hamlet of Pacific City, where even as a puppy he would swim far out beyond the breakers and bodysurf back to the beach.

'He would swim out with the surfers. They'd go way out and he would just go with them and float around and swim, and as soon as they all caught a wave he'd come in with them. The surfers would be like, "He's the coolest dog ever."'

He also loved mountain camping trips in the Olallie Scenic Area, 160 kilometres from Aurora in the Cascade Ranges, though these annual holidays were never without mishaps.

'There's this little lake where we would take the kids swimming and there was a tree that had fallen right by the beach. Rowdy, every year, would go to this log and chew and dig at it to the point where his nails would get bloody,' Niki says. 'We'd throw an old tennis ball with a plastic ball thrower, which we call a chuck-it, and he would chase it in that lake for hours. Sometimes I would worry he was going to drown if we didn't stop throwing the ball to him.'

His beloved tennis ball once got him into strife at home when he dived headlong into a spiky barberry bush to retrieve it. Niki suspects he got a thorn stuck in his chest, because he soon had a nasty infection that developed into an angry abscess.

'It was disgusting, this hard lump that was seeping liquid non-stop. Rowdy was literally screaming in pain, but nothing showed up on the X-ray so the vet sent us home with some painkillers,' she says. 'I didn't even make it out of the parking lot before he was screaming again. I turned around and went back in and said, "I can't take him home. You have to do something."'

Rowdy was given intravenous antibiotics and the swelling soon subsided, though the cause of the drama was never identified.

Eight months later, in March 2008, Rowdy suffered another mysterious malady – and this time he was lucky to survive. The Umbenhowers were out of town and Niki's brother, Matt, was dogsitting.

'Matt had a black lab as well – Kira, who was the love of Rowdy's life – and he'd walk them down at the Pudding River. It's called that for a reason: it's kind of dark and murky,' she says. 'Nothing was out of the ordinary. The dogs were going in and out of the water, but by the time they got home Rowdy was seizing and foaming at the mouth. His eyes were rolling back in his head.'

Matt rushed Rowdy to the vet hospital, where the ailing dog had his stomach pumped. After an expensive overnight stay, he made a miraculous recovery. Once again, the vet couldn't pinpoint the culprit, but it's likely Rowdy either drank some stagnant water or decided to taste-test an animal carcass. 'We were just so glad he was alive,' says Niki.

No sooner had he recovered from his near-death experience, Rowdy was in surgery again. Since he was about five years old, he had been plagued by ear problems – he would get a minor irritation in his ear canal and shake his head so vigorously and incessantly that blood would collect under the skin within the flaps of his ears. Known as aural haematomas, these are relatively common in labradors and must be manually drained with a needle. In most cases, surgery is eventually necessary.

'We'd put a needle in and drain them and then the next day they'd be filled up again. His vet suggested surgery so he had that done on both ears in July 2008,' Niki says. 'His ears were always so soft but after the surgery they were all "crunched up". If you were to look on the inside, they were super scarred.'

If the Umbenhowers were hoping Rowdy's ear surgery would be the last of his misadventures, they would be disappointed. A year later, in July 2009, he tore the anterior cruciate ligament (ACL) in his knee while chasing the notorious tennis ball. Niki and Tim decided not to put Rowdy through surgery to repair it, because his vet warned that the success of the operation would depend largely on their ability to keep their energetic dog immobile for weeks afterward.

'They said we'd have to keep him quiet and I honestly couldn't see how we could do it,' she says. 'He'd have to have been in a coma to not be rambunctious.'

Rowdy slowly recovered from his injury naturally, but the worst was yet to come.

In May 2010, the family headed out of town for the weekend to take Josh to a baseball tournament a couple of hours away. Rowdy stayed at home with the Umbenhowers' young neighbour, Chase, on hand to feed and hang out with him.

Rowdy had always been enamoured of Chase – so much so, he would enthusiastically hump Chase's leg whenever he came to the house. When the time came to let himself in to give Rowdy his dinner, Chase decided to try and outsmart the amorous pooch.

'Chase decided that he would climb through Josh's window instead of going through the back door, because Rowdy wouldn't hump him if he was already in the house,' Niki recalls. 'Unfortunately, another neighbour, who is the sweetest lady, saw somebody climbing in the window and knew we were out of town. She called the police.'

Forty kilometres from Oregon's largest city, Portland, the town of Aurora is a picturesque little community with a population of just over 900. The police rarely see much action, says Niki, beyond doling out speeding tickets to lead-footed drivers. So the officer who responded to the neighbour's call about a burglary in progress was no doubt on high alert.

'It was a really nice summer's day and Rowdy just loves to lie out on the back deck and bask in the sun. Chase went home and was going to get his brother to help him get our cats inside,' she says. 'The police showed up and were coming onto the property. Rowdy heard them and came zooming around from the back of the house to the front, barking. The cop panicked and shot him.'

Two hours away, sitting in the bleachers at her son's baseball game, Niki received a phone call from a distraught Chase. Understandably 'freaking out', she in turn called her brother, who raced to the house, collected Rowdy and rushed him to the vet.

The police officer's bullet had pierced Rowdy's leg, passing clean through. He required emergency surgery to save the limb and was sent home with a temporary drain in it to prevent infection.

'We were on the news, because incredibly Rowdy was the second family dog to be shot by Oregon police that week. The police department paid his vet bills because they felt bad that they had shot the family dog,' says Niki.

Rowdy recovered and was a disaster-free zone for over a year – until October 2012, when he had surgery to remove an infected tooth. Unfortunately a mix up with his paperwork meant the vet extracted a healthy tooth and sent Rowdy home with the painful fang still *in situ*, requiring a second operation the following day.

By August 2014, Rowdy was eleven – and was arguably lucky to have reached such a stately age given his fondness for drama. His family hoped his 'rowdy' days were at last behind him and he would enjoy his old age quietly as a happy, healthy dog (though he did have to have a toe removed that year thanks to an infected toenail).

But if Rowdy had proved one thing to the Umbenhowers during his long life with them, it was that he had a fondness for trouble. What he needed was a distraction – a job that would keep him from following his nose straight into catastrophe.

The bad news was that there were more struggles ahead for Rowdy. The good news was they would gift him with a whole new purpose.

*

Niki knew nothing about vitiligo, a condition that causes patches of skin to lose their pigment and turn white, when she snapped a quick photo of Rowdy on 29 August 2014. Studying the picture later, she noticed his fur appeared to be greying around his eyes.

'Then in November, my daughter had her homecoming. She was in her little dress with Rowdy standing next to her and I took a photo. I noticed that the fur under one of his eyes was getting white, and on the other eye the whole top part of the fur was getting white,' she says.

Three months after that, she snapped another photo and compared it to the November image. One eye had even more white fur above it, while the other was now almost completely encircled by white.

'By then I was starting to pay attention. A little while later, it felt like we just woke up one morning and he had two perfectly symmetrical white circles around his eyes,' says Niki.

She had never seen a dog with such strangely discoloured fur before – and she was naturally concerned. Vets were baffled by what had caused Rowdy's sudden colour change and, to Niki's chagrin, didn't seem particularly interested in finding out. 'We took him to the vet and he said, "I've never seen this before." He didn't research it. He didn't call a dermatologist. I was thinking, *How do you not want to know what this is?*'

The Umbenhowers certainly *did* want to know what it was. Niki works for a large healthcare company and one day was chatting with a specialist doctor who loves dogs.

She showed him a picture of Rowdy and immediately he said, 'I think he has vitiligo.'

The diagnosis was soon clinically confirmed via a biopsy and consultation with a veterinary dermatologist.

Vitiligo is a mysterious disorder. Patches of skin turn white because the cells within them that make pigment (colour), called melanocytes, are destroyed. But exactly why those cells are destroyed is still unknown. It could be an autoimmune disease; people with certain autoimmune conditions are known to be more likely to get vitiligo. These diseases happen when a person's immune system mistakenly attacks a part of their body.

It's also possible that one or more genes might make a person more likely to get the disorder. It's believed to run in families and some researchers think a single event such as sunburn or emotional distress can cause vitiligo. But so far none of these things has been conclusively proven.

It is estimated that between 1 and 2 per cent of the population has vitiligo – potentially up to 140 million people worldwide. It affects both sexes and all races and ages, although in about 50 per cent of cases vitiligo develops between the ages of 10 and 30. There is currently no cure for the condition. The goal of treatment is to stop or slow the progression of depigmentation and possibly return some pigment to the skin.

As for vitiligo in dogs, the condition is every bit as puzzling. Certain breeds tend to be more likely to develop it, including German shepherds, rottweilers, Old English sheepdogs and dachshunds. The first signs are usually seen on the nose, muzzle and face. The fur that covers the depigmented skin will also turn white, as the Umbenhowers discovered when Rowdy developed his white 'glasses'. He also developed white fur on his belly and hind legs, and some of his toenails even turned white. New white spots continued to appear on his face 'practically overnight', too.

It's not known precisely how many dogs have vitiligo, but it's certainly not common in canines – and Niki quickly discovered just how fascinating other people found her unique black (and white) dog.

One morning in early 2015, she was sipping her coffee in front of local breakfast TV show *Good Day Oregon* when the presenters invited viewers to send in pictures of their animals for the regular Good Day Pets segment.

'I thought, *I think Oregon will get a kick out of this* so I sent in a picture of Rowdy,' says Niki. 'Within ten minutes Rowdy's picture was on *Good Day Oregon* and they were talking about him. An hour later I got a call from a news station wanting to come out and do a story on him.'

Before she knew it, Rowdy had gone viral. His story was shared on animal lovers' website The Dodo, which has more than eight million fans on social media, and viral content site Upworthy, which has around fifty million users a month. He became the subject of a Reddit 'Photoshop Battle', which saw creative users turn him into superheroes including Superman, Deadpool and Kung Fu Panda. Rowdy was soon making headlines in Mexico, the UK, Japan, Thailand and Brazil. Wildly popular Instagram dog photographer Elias Weiss Friedman, better known as The Dogist, who has

2.3 million followers, scheduled a special trip to Oregon just to meet and photograph Rowdy. He even became a Facebook meme.

'I was so excited. I started getting calls from news agencies. It just blew up. I could barely keep up with the phone calls and emails,' says Niki, who, with son Josh, set up a website, Instagram account and Facebook page for Rowdy. 'I get emails and Instagram messages from all over the world saying, "I'm officially obsessed with this dog," or, "Your dog makes me so happy." I even had a dermatologist say he diagnosed an eight-year-old with vitiligo and when he showed him Rowdy's picture it put a smile on his face.'

Best of all, however, were the messages from people with vitiligo saying Rowdy made them feel more comfortable with – and even proud of – the condition. 'I hear stories and see post after post saying, "I wish I'd had a dog like Rowdy when I was young to make me feel my vitiligo was beautiful, just like you are,"' she says.

Most people, if they've heard of it at all, are familiar with vitiligo only because the late 'King of Pop', Michael Jackson, was a sufferer. More recently, Canadian model Winnie Harlow and Sierra Leonean-American ballet dancer Michaela DePrince have raised awareness after speaking publicly about living with the condition.

But while pop stars, supermodels, ballerinas and adorable black labradors are likely to receive widespread support and find their unique beauty is celebrated, the reality for many people with vitiligo can be very different. Children in particular are often bullied, excluded and even feared because of the condition.

In his own unique way, Rowdy was able to change that. It was his (well, his family's) wish that all children and adults see vitiligo as a unique blessing that's rewarded with lots of love, attention and treats – just like he always got.

In early 2016, Niki received a message from the parent of a young child with vitiligo. 'She reached out to me and said, "My son has vitiligo and everyone thinks Rowdy is so beautiful, but these kids are being bullied at school."' Niki instantly felt that she could use Rowdy's new-found fame to raise awareness of vitiligo and help people with the condition – especially children – to feel confident and proud of their difference.

Rowdy was already an elderly gentleman by the time he became a global sensation and had mobility and other health issues that prevented him from travelling to see his adoring public (the Umbenhowers invested in hydrotherapy, acupuncture and even laser therapy in a bid to boost his wellbeing), but he was able to meet some young fans at local events and spread his positive message via YouTube videos.

Sadly, on 30 June 2017, Rowdy's incredible life came to an end. With his health declining, the Umbenhower family made the heartbreaking decision to help their beloved boy cross the Rainbow Bridge. He passed away at home in the arms of the people who had loved him so fiercely all his life.

When news of Rowdy's death reached his 90 000-plus Instagram followers, the outpouring of grief surprised even

Niki. 'We were blown away by the overwhelming support, prayers, well wishes and encouraging words,' she says. 'Our home will never be the same and I'm going to miss him every day of my life, but Rowdy touched so many people and I'm so proud to have been his mum.'

And while his loss is deeply felt by many, the Umbenhowers are adamant they will continue the important work Rowdy began.

'He had the biggest heart and we will continue on with his mission and his legacy,' says Niki. 'What an incredible dog, best friend, companion, entertainer, adventurer, protector and family pet he was.'

The Umbenhowers knew when Rowdy became the unofficial poster boy for vitiligo that he may not be in the job for long, but they're so grateful that their rambunctious labrador's 'third act' brought joy and comfort to so many people.

'There's one little boy whose life Rowdy has changed – literally. He went from being bullied to being the town hero. His mum told me he went to bed one night after watching one of Rowdy's videos and said, "Mum, aren't you sad you don't have vitiligo and aren't cool like me?"' says Niki. 'He touched thousands of people. It's really wonderful.'

It was about time Rowdy got himself a job – it's only fitting it should have been one that brought joy to so many people.

INDI

DETECTOR DOG,
AUSTRALIAN BORDER FORCE

It was only a split second, but that was all it took.

In the early morning chaos of the baggage sorting area at Sydney's international airport, Australian Border Force (ABF) detector dog handler Mick* could easily have missed the fleeting falter. With mountains of bags and suitcases ready to be collected by waiting passengers, time was against him. In his scramble to get through as much luggage as possible, he simply may not have twigged that the eager black labrador at the end of the leash was uncertain about a particular item. After all, Indi wasn't doing what he usually did when his sensitive nose caught a whiff of something illicit. Another handler might have concluded the suitcase was clean and moved his dog on to the next one.

___

* Surname withheld.

But Mick did twig. In fact, it was precisely *because* Indi wasn't doing what he usually did when he got a 'hit' that alarm bells started ringing. He felt his dog hesitate for just the briefest of moments and he got the message loud and clear: *Hey Boss, there's something funny about this one.* That was enough for Mick to act.

'A lot of indications aren't classic. Indi might start doing something differently and that's enough to signal me to investigate,' Mick says.

The suitcase was referred for further investigation by an ABF officer and opened. Socks, underwear, toothpaste – all the standard stuff a legitimate traveller might pack for an overseas holiday. But by that stage, Indi was demonstrating in no uncertain terms his conviction that this unassuming bag was hiding something sinister. And so the officer kept searching.

When the case had been completely emptied of its contents and still nothing seemed untoward, Mick wondered if he'd been wrong. Maybe he'd misread his dog's body language. Perhaps Indi was having an off day. It would be very unusual – they worked together like a well-oiled machine – but sometimes it happened.

But there was something that told Mick this wasn't a miss – something in Indi's bearing, his adamant behaviour, that seemed to say, *No Boss, I know I'm right.* Mick had always trusted his dog's nose and decided to look a little harder. This apparently innocuous bag hadn't given up all its secrets yet.

The officer lifted the lining of the suitcase to reveal what looked like a false bottom. X-rays of the bag, along with three others this group of passengers was in possession of, all showed anomalies. The officer drilled into the false bottom and Mick found himself staring at eighteen kilograms of heroin.

A dog's sense of smell is a powerful weapon – as important as eyesight and arguably more revealing than his other senses combined. It allows his brain to piece together a 'picture' of the world around him that contains as much information as a human being might glean from a high-resolution photograph.

A study by Florida State University's Sensory Research Institute found that, depending on factors such as age and breed, a dog's sniffer is between 10 000 and 100 000 times sharper than a human's. In real terms, that would mean a dog could smell a single rotten apple among two million barrels of fresh fruit. Or, in the context of sight rather than smell, it means something visible to a human at a distance of half a kilometre would be just as clearly visible to a dog from nearly 5000 kilometres away. It's a scent advantage that's almost too colossal to comprehend.

The mechanics that allow a dog's nose to be so impressive are equally astonishing. The average canine's nose contains between 125 million and 220 million olfactory cells, or scent receptors. Some breeds, such as bloodhounds, beagles and German shepherds, have up to 300 million. Humans only have around six million. Some dogs were simply built to sniff. Breeds with deep jowls and long, ground-grazing ears use those design features to sweep scent into their nasal passages and trap it. Plus, the aerodynamics of a dog's snout mean the way he breathes out simultaneously sucks new smells into his nose.

Humans recognised our own failings in the scent department and cottoned onto dogs' superior sniffing strength long ago. Dogs have been used for scent-based searching and tracking for centuries, from ancient hunting breeds right through to the highly valued detector dogs of today. We harness the power of canine noses to locate everything from land mines, termites and contraband to both living and deceased people. From prisons to ports, sniffer dogs are at work wherever people are – because where there are people, there are sure to be people who are up to no good.

The ABF is the operational arm of the Department of Immigration and Border Protection. It inherited a proud history of protecting Australia's border and serving the community that stretches back to Federation.

The department has been using detector dogs for nearly half a century, with the first two black labradors to work in a border force capacity trained and 'employed' in Sydney way back in 1968.

While those labs had moderate success, the potential for the use of dogs in customs and border protection operations was clear. When they retired in 1974, two German shepherd puppies were recruited from the Australian Army and trained with Army assistance. Those dogs had a better strike rate, contributing to a number of drugs seizures and inspiring the creation of a dedicated detector dog training unit in 1979. A purpose-built training facility followed in Canberra in 1984.

Until the early 1990s, detector dogs were only used in situations where an 'active alert' response was appropriate – think pawing, digging or jamming a wet nose right into the scent. Great for ships, aircraft, vehicles and buildings, but not appropriate where passengers are present, such as in airports and seaports. When it became apparent that dogs capable of searching people were needed, trainers taught a 'passive alert' response – usually a polite sit, drop or focused stare.

They also decided that borrowing dogs from other agencies wasn't going to work in the long term. A detector dog breeding program began in Melbourne in 1993, with the labrador retriever chosen as the breed of choice. These affable, people-loving dogs were selected not only for their drive, temperament and astounding scenting ability, but because they're, well, really cute. Some dogs look intimidating and would likely frighten a sleep-deprived traveller fresh off a 24-hour flight from the other side of the planet. Labs, however, only seem to invite cuddles and cooing, making them a perfect choice for a job that requires lots of interaction with the public.

The breeding program, which moved to a larger, state-of-the-art facility at Bulla, Victoria, in 2011, is now the only source of detector dogs for the ABF. It has produced close to 3000 puppies to date, with around 200 lovely little labs born each year, depending on operational needs. The ABF also supplies labradors to the Australian Federal Police, state and territory police, corrective services, the Department of Agriculture, the Australian Defence Force, Seeing Eye Dogs Australia, Soldier On and several international law enforcement agencies.

The demand for ABF dogs reflects the superior breeding program and natural abilities of these labradors. Those abilities still amaze Mick every day, even after seven years with the ABF. He started his career working at Sydney Airport, moving to the dog detection unit (DDU) in 2014.

'The dog unit, for me, was always where I wanted to end up because you get paid to work with a dog,' he laughs. 'Life is always a game for a working dog and not many people can say they get paid to play.'

Mick started working with Indi in mid-2014. (ABF detector dog training methods are such that any handler can work any dog, but most officers tend to work primarily with the same one or two canines.) The handsome puppy wasn't yet a year old, but his enthusiasm for detection was obvious.

'The trainers are very good at picking up the characteristics they need the dog to have and the personalities of the dog and the handler,' he says. 'Just because you work with a particular dog in your training course, doesn't mean you'll end up with that dog. The dog I had for most of my training is not the dog I've ended up with. Indi and I were paired up quite late in the course.'

ABF detection dogs like Indi are trained to sniff out a range of substances including cocaine, heroin and methamphetamine. Mick also occasionally works with a cash-detecting dog, Namba. The ABF's dogs also include tobacco and explosives sniffers.

The training isn't as simple as just drilling the dogs on the scent of various illicit substances. It has to mimic real-world situations as closely as possible.

'We might go on a plane and put some training samples down and have the dog search, but even before we do that we have to think, *Has the dog been on a plane before?*' Mick says. 'You have to go a couple of steps back, maybe start with the dog in a confined space. You have to build him up and it can be quite a challenging task.'

After completing his training at the Bulla facility in November 2014, Indi returned to Sydney with Mick to continue training on his own turf. 'We cater the training to the local environment, because an airport in Melbourne is different to an airport in Sydney,' he explains. 'The dogs never stop learning and the moment you become compla-cent is the moment they start picking up bad habits. Variety and keeping it challenging for the dog keeps them alert and focused. Even little things, like driving to the airport one way and driving back a different way, keeps away the boredom.'

For Indi and Mick, no two days on the job are the same. They might spend the morning screening arriving passen-gers and luggage at the international airport before heading to Circular Quay to search cabins on a cruise liner in the afternoon. The next day might bring a nose-led inspection of airfreight in a bonded warehouse and a quick stop to sniff parcels at Australia Post's massive gateway facility for international post before giving shipping containers a thorough going-over at the Container and Cargo Examination Facility (CEF) at Port Botany.

The jobs come in 'thick and fast', says Mick, with tasks assigned to the DDU based on intelligence gathered by the ABF and other agencies. 'Dogs are essentially mass screening tools. If there's intel to suggest there might be something on a ship, for example, the shipping operations unit will request the dog unit. They'll give us some information that will help us decide how many dogs and handlers we need,' he explains. 'If they say, "We need twenty cabins searched," then we might say, "That's a two- or three-dog job."'

The Sydney DDU works as far south as Canberra and as far north as Newcastle. Dogs and handlers are occasionally also dispatched to assist agencies in other states.

'We try not to do anything at random and with intelligence we don't need to be random,' says Mick.

Speed is essential, especially in airports. Dog teams are required to subject as many passengers and bags to 'the sniff test' as possible without disrupting the flow of foot and air traffic. 'We don't want to slow down legitimate trade or travellers. The dogs can cover a large amount of freight or a large number of passengers much more quickly than a person. We can't look at every passenger or every box and really, we don't need to, because most people aren't doing anything untoward.'

Since the detector dog program's inception, ABF dogs like Indi have been directly involved in the seizure of thousands of kilograms of illicit drugs with a street value in the millions of dollars. But even with their all-powerful noses, the fact that these conscientious canines have detected anything at all is nothing short of remarkable.

Think about it: drug smugglers are rarely helpful enough to transport their narcotics in plain sight. Instead, they're mixed with other substances and hidden inside stuffed animals or table legs or the false bottoms of suitcases. That means a detector dog must not only be able to pick up the scent of the drug it's searching for, he must somehow find it amid dozens of other strong smells.

'I think of it as being like a pot of stew: it's a combination of ingredients,' Mick explains. 'A detector dog doesn't smell "stew"; he smells all the different ingredients *in* the stew. We call it a scent picture. With drugs, it's never the same. Two shipments might be from the same country but different people made them, so the scent picture is changed slightly and it's enough to make the dog not quite sure. Our job as ABF officers is to make sure the dog can decipher what we're looking for and what we're not.'

Indi's reward for a successful 'hit' is a few minutes of play with Mick and a rolled-up towel. His drive for that reward is so strong that he doesn't want to risk getting it wrong and missing out on his playtime, so every time he alerts is a high-stakes gamble.

'The best trained dogs should be able to recognise out of the scent picture, *I know what that is and I'm not going to get rewarded for that, but this smells like something I might get rewarded for,*' says Mick. 'Some dogs are more willing to gamble and will indicate, usually by sitting down, while others aren't. He might just hesitate. Recognising that hesitation is where the handler's skills come into play.'

That was exactly what happened in 2016, when Indi made his biggest detection to date, an 18-kilogram heroin haul secreted in the false bottom of a suitcase.

'Eighteen kilos of heroin concealed in a suitcase has a very different odour to one gram that's not concealed. With that bag, Indi didn't sit. It wasn't a classic response,' he says. 'He made a very distinctive change in behaviour that was obvious not only to me but to another handler next to me. Labradors are very intelligent dogs. He was telling me, in the best possible way, that he was unsure about that bag.'

It's that symbiotic dog–handler relationship that is so critical to the success of detector dogs. Though all ABF dogs undergo the same training, every dog is different – and it's up to each handler to use his dog's unique quirks and personality traits to the team's best advantage.

'Some dogs are very independent. They'll work on their own and they don't need too much of your assistance. Our training is to try and create more of an independent dog because he's the one with the nose. We let him do his thing,' says Mick. 'Other dogs need more interaction with the handler. Labradors are very good at picking up handler cues.'

A simple 'find it' is all it takes to switch a dog like Indi into work mode. 'Even if he hasn't been given the command, we want him to be thinking, *There could be a reward around the corner*. We want the dogs to go the next level up. Any time they associate an odour with a reward they should isolate it, detect it and respond.'

As in sync as they are, though, even Mick and Indi have the occasional 'off' day. Mick says detector dog handlers often 'really step out of their comfort zone for the benefit of their dog'.

'The reality is that we have good days and bad days and so do they. Just because it's your bad day, you cannot transfer that to your dog. If he's done well and you're not rewarding him, it confuses him,' he says. 'They feed off the verbal praise. You've got to praise them for a good search even if they find nothing. You might be a timid person, but you still have to say, "This is a special moment for you as a dog." You have to constantly keep an eye not just on your dog, but also on yourself. It's those little things that are crucial to the success of a working dog.'

A day shift for Indi starts in the very early hours of the morning, well before sunrise. When he's not working, he lives at the DDU's purpose-built kennels near Sydney Airport, where each dog has a large, individual outdoor run for daytime and a climate-controlled 'bedroom' at night. On quiet days or in between jobs, Mick will take Indi to the park or a nearby beach for a run.

Indi is also a stud dog and visits Melbourne every now and then to help the ABF breeding program continue. He is the proud father of two litters to date.

Between his work duties and his other 'job' in Melbourne, Indi is one busy labrador. Mick keeps a vigilant watch for signs of fatigue and ensures his canine sidekick takes regular breaks.

'He definitely needs breaks. I can see when I'm with him that he might be a little bit tired. Sometimes it might be just too long in the same environment, and so I might change it up and take him to a different area,' he says. 'As a dog, they look up to you as their master. If you wanted to work them to death, they probably would work to death. We have to be wary of that.'

Now four, Indi will continue his work for the ABF for another five or six years. And unfortunately, there's not likely to be any shortage of work for him during that period. Drug smugglers, it seems, are only getting bolder and more technologically savvy.

'There are now websites where people can simply order illegal drugs through the mail. There's always increasing challenges in our working environment and we have to stay on par with or ahead of that,' says Mick. 'Some of these criminals have the time and resources to get quite creative.'

Not that Indi seems to mind – there's no doubt in Mick's mind that his dedicated dog would happily keep working for as long as he can still smell stuff. 'Indi recognises that, when we're in the ABF truck, we're going to work. I see his tail wagging constantly and I think, *It can't be that bad*,' he laughs. 'Work is a big game for Indi. He's the type of dog that just seems to love everything he does.'

And when Indi eventually does retire, there's a spot on the sofa awaiting him at Mick's place. Many retired ABF dogs also return to live with the foster carers who loved them as puppies. 'Indi is great with people, super friendly and lovable. Like most labradors, he just wants a pat and a cuddle. I'd love to take him home at the end of his career,' he says.

If Indi's work successes to date are any indication, he's sure to excel at loafing, too.

MIA, COOPER & HOPPY
BREWERY AMBASSADORS

Here's the thing about Samoyeds: their looks can be deceiving. You could be forgiven for taking one glance at that pristine snow-white coat and feather duster–calibre fluffy tail and thinking *prima donna*. In fact, nothing could be further from the truth. Samoyeds are among the hardiest – not to mention hardest working – dogs in history. Dapper they may be, but divas these dogs are definitely *not*.

The modern-day Samoyed is believed to descend from the Nenets herding laika, one of six sturdy laika breeds used as hunting and working dogs in Russia. Nomadic reindeer herders from Siberia bred the hirsute hounds to help with herding, as well as pulling heavy sleds when they relocated. They are made of tough stuff, able to live and toil outdoors in some of the harshest terrain and coldest temperatures on earth. In fact, their ancestors' lives literally depended on having a job to do. Winter temperatures in some parts of

Siberia frequently plunge below −50 °C; sitting still meant they risked freezing to death.

Working is in a Samoyed's DNA, as Kate Henning and her husband, Simon Dunstone, discovered in 2008. The couple were working long hours in Adelaide, South Australia – Kate as a lawyer and Simon as a software engineer – when they decided to break up the monotony of the daily grind by getting a dog. Overwhelmed by the array of breeds available, they entered their requirements into an internet questionnaire to narrow their options.

Their ideal pet, according to the website, was a Samoyed. 'I'd never even heard of Samoyeds,' Kate admits, 'but the photo and description looked really lovely. In September we went to the Royal Adelaide Show and the Samoyeds were having their display day that day. We met some and they were just absolutely beautiful dogs.'

They not only fell in love with the breed, but decided to welcome *two* dogs into their family instead of just one. The Samoyed owners they spoke to recommended they get one dog at a time, but Kate and Simon wanted their pets to be the best of friends from day one. 'Knowing we had nine-to-five, Monday-to-Friday jobs, we wanted them to be able to keep each other company,' says Kate.

They found a registered breeder in Geelong, Victoria, and were thrilled to receive news of their puppies' arrival in November. The breeder chose a male and a female for them and the couple brought the dogs home in January 2009. Kate and Simon decided to call their new canine companions Cooper and Mia – Simon was a keen amateur beer brewer whose hobby had been sparked by a Cooper's homebrew kit, while Mia was simply a name the couple loved.

'They were littermates and really good mates. The breeders picked Cooper for us because they felt he was the one in the litter who would benefit from having another dog with him from the get go,' she says. 'He didn't like being alone and would get a little bit fretty when he was by himself.'

Mia, on the other hand, was more comfortable with her own company. Her independent streak was perhaps due to her poor health – she was seriously ill as a young puppy and endured extended stays at the vet, perhaps growing used to spending time on her own.

'When Mia was desexed at five months old she didn't come out of the anaesthesia properly because her liver couldn't process the toxins. She was very, very sick and it took months to work out what was wrong,' says Kate.

The eventual diagnosis was intrahepatic portosystemic shunt (IPSS), a congenital abnormality between the portal vein and Mia's systemic circulation. In a normal dog, the toxin-filled blood that comes out of the intestines, spleen, and pancreas is drained by the portal vein into the liver for detoxification. In a dog with an IPSS, however, the blood bypasses the liver and is instead shunted directly into the systemic circulation, the part of the cardiovascular system that carries oxygenated blood away from the heart to the body. If left untreated, IPSS can lead to stunted growth, behavioural problems and liver failure. Anaesthetic intolerance is a common sign of the condition, as are vomiting, diarrhoea, seizures and even blindness.

'They say about one in ten thousand dogs has it. We were told that, if Mia didn't have surgery, her life expectancy wouldn't be more than three years. She's been back to Melbourne three times, once for a CT scan and twice for surgery,' Kate says. 'But she's doing well. She bounces around like nothing's wrong.'

With Mia's rough start in life and Cooper's separation anxiety, Kate and Simon's vision of content, self-sufficient family pets promptly went out the window – not that they minded too much. 'I'd always thought that people who got up early in the morning to walk their dogs were insane, but they quickly took over our lives. We became those people who were getting up at 5.30 a.m. to go to the dog park,' she laughs.

Early-morning exercise requirements aside, Simon and Kate were thoroughly smitten by that famous Samoyed charm – especially the wide, ready smile that's like a permanent advertisement for their happy-go-lucky approach to life. 'They're really social and really gentle and they just love to be around people,' says Kate. 'As long as they're around their people most of the time, they're happy. We absolutely love them.'

They also learned, just as their Siberian counterparts had hundreds of years ago, that a Samoyed without a job to keep her engrossed can be a challenge indeed. 'I thought we'd walk them in the evening and they'd be fine through the next day, but we would come home from work to a destroyed yard,' she says. 'They don't like being left home alone. They need to have some energy taken out. Samoyeds like to be busy and occupied.'

Little did they know, Mia and Cooper would soon find themselves very busy indeed. They were about to be put to work.

'Find a job you love and you'll never work a day in your life.' It's a lovely philosophy, but whoever uttered those words – everyone from Confucius to Mark Twain has been given the credit – was only partially right. While turning a passion into a career beats an uninspiring job hands down, making a living from a happy hobby not only requires *plenty* of hard work, it takes a team of supporters as well.

Kate and Simon were under no illusions about the hard yakka ahead when they decided in 2013 to give up their established careers and become entrepreneurs. Kate blames the same Cooper's homebrew kit that gave Cooper his name.

'It was a homebrew hobby that got a bit out of control. We discovered a bit of a passion for it and quickly went to having a full-blown set-up with fermentation and four beer taps,' she says. 'Both of us were not loving our careers or working for other people and we thought working together and doing something we loved would be a great idea.'

Kate grew up in Willunga, a suburb south of Adelaide at the gateway to the stunning Fleurieu Peninsula. The idea of returning to her former stomping ground and opening their very own brewery took hold.

In November 2012, Kate and Simon moved to the picturesque village of Myponga, forty-five minutes south of Adelaide's city centre, and leased premises just off the town's main street that offered stunning views over the Myponga Reservoir and was all but ready to roll as a microbrewery.

'It's a beautiful area, but the site also came with a very helpful bunch of licences and development approvals. We've known breweries to be stuck waiting for council approvals for years, so it was fantastic to have those already in place,' Kate says.

In other words, it was exactly what Kate and Simon were looking for. They opened as a retail outlet and bar and restaurant in November 2012, while waiting for their commercial brewing equipment to arrive. Their first onsite brewing day was August 1, 2013.

And through the whole thrilling, exhausting whirlwind of launching the business, Mia and Cooper were by Kate and Simon's side.

'The brewing and the dogs came into our lives at about the same time. We'd spend our weekends brewing and the dogs would be with us,' she says. 'When we started our commercial brewery we were working behind the bar too and the dogs would always be here with us. It's great to be able to have your dogs at work with you.'

Life got even busier with an unexpected arrival in May 2013. Word of the beer-making young couple and their flocculent, grinning dogs had spread throughout the district, so when a sad Samoyed urgently needed a new home, Kate and Simon got the call. 'Everybody knew we had

Samoyeds and there was an old Samoyed that came up on a rescue website, so somebody got in touch with us,' she says.

The dog's name was Poppet and she was believed to be about eight years old. She and her mother had been surrendered when their elderly owner went into a nursing home. But Poppet's mother had suffered a stroke and passed away and Poppet suddenly found herself in a cold, unfamiliar kennel, alone for the first time in her life.

'They wanted to rehome her with another Samoyed, or multiple Samoyeds, and we said, "Of course." Within twenty-four hours we went from having two dogs, and thinking that was it, to having three,' says Kate. 'Having lived in suburbia with a little backyard, two dogs seemed like plenty, but when Poppet came along we discovered that three dogs worked really well. I was surprised.'

Poppet wasted no time in making herself at home – and the bond with her younger canine 'siblings' was instantaneous. 'She was a very funny dog. She knew this was her chance. The minute she saw Mia and Cooper she adored them and then hated every other dog she met.'

Poppet's arrival also inspired another shift for Kate and Simon. The bar and restaurant had been operating under its existing name, Myponga Brewery, but with the commercial brewery now up and running on site, and their three adored dogs always at their heels, the couple decided the new operation needed a new name. 'We considered having a geographical name, but Smiling Samoyed was what we felt most passionate about, so that's what we went with,' says Kate.

Smiling Samoyed now produces four beers in its core range, as well as seasonal special releases. It wasn't long before the accolades started rolling in. The brewery's Dark Ale was named Most Outstanding Beer in Show at the 2015 Royal Adelaide Show, while the 12 Paws Pale Ale, the IPA and the Extra Special Bitter won gold, silver and bronze medals respectively.

As if they understood what an honour it was to be the brewery's namesakes, Mia, Cooper and Poppet took to their jobs as mascots with relish. They would greet visitors individually and patrol the al fresco dining area to ensure customers were enjoying their meals (and 'clean up' any scraps that happened to be dropped, of course). 'We get lots of feedback about the dogs that's really positive. We love the dogs, but we probably didn't expect for them to be taken in by people as much as they have been,' Kate laughs.

It was occasionally necessary to reprimand the dogs, however. 'Having grown up in suburbia, they're a bit cheeky about open gates and fences. Mia and Cooper had to be kept in an enclosure so they weren't running off all the time.'

Sadly, just two days shy of a year in the job, Poppet became gravely ill. She'd long had back problems and her veterinarian also suspected she had a tumour in her liver. It was time to free Poppet from her pain. 'One of the hardest things ever was when we had to have Poppet put to sleep. It was really sad when we lost her,' says Kate.

Even worse, with a growing business to manage, the couple couldn't take time off to grieve for their beloved pet.

'It was a Saturday and Simon and I were working in the bar. If we'd been working for someone else we would have taken the Sunday off, but we didn't have people who could cover for us,' she says. 'Having people ask, "Where's Poppet?" was really hard. It was that realisation that she wasn't just our dog.'

Poppet's ashes now sit on a shelf at the brewery. 'She's still here in spirit,' says Kate.

Cooper and Mia were bereft without their partner in crime, so when another Samoyed found herself looking for a home in September 2014, Kate and Simon once again opened their hearts.

The little dog had been taken to the vet with a broken paw at just three or four months of age. Her owners couldn't or wouldn't pay for the surgery needed to fix the puppy's damaged foot and asked the vet to euthanise her. Instead, the vet took the dog to the RSPCA.

'She had two lots of surgery on her paw, so she's got pins and things in there. The vet who did her surgery told us she was probably driven over by a car,' Kate says. 'She was in a cast for three months and lived with a foster carer during that time. They were tossing up whether to leave her in foster care until she was twelve months old and her growth had stopped, but as luck would have it, the head vet at the RSPCA had come across us when we'd been at the specialist vet with Mia.'

The vet wanted to make sure the puppy, then six months old, went to a forever home that was aware she would potentially have future medical issues and was prepared to accommodate them. After their experiences with Poppet and Mia, Simon and Kate had no qualms about taking on another Samoyed with special needs.

'I think she's a pretty lucky dog. Her life could have ended quite prematurely if she wasn't lucky enough to land in the right vet's office,' Kate says. 'We missed Poppet and when this little dog came up, it seemed destined to be.'

Just as they had with Poppet, Mia and Cooper happily welcomed their new roommate into the furry fold. 'She sometimes tries to herd them up and tell them what to do. They mostly don't pay her any attention, which is about right for a little sister.'

The new addition had a pronounced limp, so the couple decided to call her Hoppy – both in recognition of her disability *and* her job as the brewery's newest brand ambassador. Now three, with her broken paw completely healed, she doesn't 'hop' much at all. 'When you've got a dog called Hoppy, people think your dog limps and you're not doing anything about it,' says Kate. 'Now she *doesn't* hop and we get light-hearted complaints about that!'

Of the three dogs, Hoppy quickly proved herself the most dedicated to her job. 'She takes her brand ambassador role very seriously. She greets everyone and goes with the staff whenever there's a pizza that needs delivering to a table,' she says. 'Hoppy is absolutely amazing with customers. People will come and visit her specifically – they're not necessarily coming for the brewery. If she's not around because she's at home or at the groomers, people will ask where she is. They just love her.'

In fact, Hoppy can be so persuasive with customers that it now says 'Please don't feed the dog' on the Smiling Samoyed menu – though their employee clearly finds ways around that little stipulation. 'She knows she's not allowed to bark to get food – she just uses her big brown eyes to do that. She sucks everyone in. We were at a beer and barbeque festival recently and had a girl come up and say, "When we were at Smiling Samoyed, Hoppy was given nearly a whole pizza!"'

Smiling Samoyed is a family-friendly destination and the dogs are particularly fond of young visitors. The breed is renowned for its affinity with children, which was a relief for Kate and Simon when they welcomed their baby son, Alvin, in August 2016.

'Everything I'd ever heard about Samoyeds and kids was positive. There are lots of kids visiting the brewery. I have a photo of Mia and Cooper in their enclosure and somebody's child had climbed in and was sleeping on Cooper, who was also fast asleep,' says Kate. 'They've been amazing with Alvin. They're really gentle and come up and give him little licks. They're totally trustworthy dogs.'

Tragically, in January 2017, the Smiling Samoyed fur family lost another member. Cooper suddenly started coughing one Monday evening and Kate took him to the vet first thing on Tuesday. He was diagnosed with kennel cough, given antibiotics and sent home.

On Wednesday morning, 'I phoned the vet again and arranged for him to be seen again that afternoon as he didn't seem to be getting better,' says Kate. 'Before the appointment, though, he really started to deteriorate so we rushed him to the vet. They weren't able to stabilise him and he passed away that afternoon.'

Beautiful Cooper, one of the smiling Samoyeds that started it all, was just eight years old. His vet wasn't able to conclusively determine the cause of his death, but suspected an embolism. Like Poppet, Cooper now rests at the brewery, where he can keep an eye on things in spirit.

Mia, now nine, has hip dysplasia and doesn't frequent the brewery as often these days, preferring to spend her time snoozing at home. That leaves Hoppy to hold down the fort and she seems to have redoubled her efforts to make 'her' customers smile. While the appeal of brewery life for Mia and Cooper was always that it afforded constant proximity to their favourite people, Kate is convinced that Hoppy actually knows she has a job to do.

'The other two just did their own thing, but Hoppy definitely knows she's working. Having grown up at the brewery, she knows when it's a work day,' she says. 'The venue manager will come to collect her from home and Hoppy will be waiting at the door for her. If the manager wants to talk to me about anything, Hoppy will have things to say about that, like, *Come on, we're late!*'

Unlike Mia and Cooper, who would always sneak out of an open gate if given the opportunity, Hoppy almost never strays from the premises. 'Hoppy is very good at knowing that, when she's here, this is where she stays.'

Smiling Samoyed continues to expand and Kate and Simon's lives have changed considerably since they went into business in 2013. With their penchant for taking in Samoyeds in need, it may not be long before Hoppy has another canine colleague to help her out at work.

'We'll play it by ear, which is what we've done so far, seeing how it's fitting in with our life as well,' Kate says. 'But with the brewery being called Smiling Samoyed and a big dog's face on the sign as you come in, most people hope there's going to be a dog here!'

With a smile as wide as a Samoyed's greeting customers, it's no surprise people keep coming back. They're fluffy and they're cute, but more importantly they return the love they receive tenfold.

And that's the thing about Samoyeds.

CHARLIE

SPINAL CORD INJURY
ASSISTANCE DOG

It was a Friday night and Dan Holt was in a jubilant mood. After six years living and working various jobs in Canada's winter playground, the Whistler Blackcomb ski resort, the 26-year-old Australian expatriate had just been offered a full-time job in lift maintenance. But in the midst of celebrating the achievement with his friends and girlfriend, Dan fell. He tumbled down a flight of stairs and broke his neck.

He remembers the accident, on 26 September 2008, like it was yesterday. 'It went from everything going fantastic to everything being literally turned on its head,' he says.

In an instant, the life Dan had built in Whistler came to a halt. He was rushed from the picturesque mountain town to Vancouver General Hospital (VGH), 125 kilometres away. There, doctors determined he had an incomplete injury to his spinal cord at the C5-C6 vertebrae. The good news was his spinal cord remained intact. The devastating news was that Dan was now quadriplegic and would almost certainly never walk again. He would have limited sensation from the chest down, but no movement.

The native Sydneysider spent a month at VGH, followed by seven months in the hospital's G.F. Strong Rehabilitation Centre. 'It was nightmarish – everything you come across and are forced to realise. It took me years to wrap my head around it,' says Dan. 'It's not just hard on you, it's hard on the family. I had my family flying back and forth from Sydney. My then-partner had to pick up and move from Whistler to Vancouver. It wasn't pleasant.'

Eight months after the accident, Dan moved from the rehabilitation centre to live independently in Vancouver. But getting used to his new, very different way of life was tough to say the least. It was several more months before he started to think positively about his future. 'I was entirely focused on what I couldn't do. I didn't start to think about the things I *can* do for at least twelve months,' he says. 'But I have a fantastic support network of family and friends who were all telling me I could do it.'

After eighteen months in Vancouver, Dan returned to Sydney on 1 July 2010. But in his first week back on home soil, he suffered a disastrous setback.

'I got burned in the shower and spent six weeks in the burns unit at Royal North Shore Hospital. I didn't feel the pain, but I started spasming. I looked down and saw a piece of skin fall off,' he says. 'I had to have two skin grafts. It flogged me again. It was like, *What else do I have to deal with?*'

Fortunately, Dan's family was able to help him battle through those dark days. 'My family pulled me out of that pretty quick. Mum grew up in the country and has the attitude that there's always someone worse off. Sixty per cent of living with these sorts of conditions is your support network.'

Once recovered, Dan joined an intensive activity-based rehab program called Walk On (since renamed Neuro-Moves). The program involves repetitive, task-specific activities and dynamic, weight-bearing exercises performed out of the wheelchair one-on-one with a qualified physiotherapist or exercise physiologist. Run by Spinal Cord Injuries Australia (SCIA), it helps people with spinal cord injuries to maximise their functional ability and lead a more independent life.

'The aim of that wasn't to walk out of there. Of course you never give up hope, but I'm never going to walk again. It was about gaining more independence in my life, things like sitting up properly in a wheelchair and not falling over all the time,' Dan says.

Dan was a Walk On participant for three years. In 2013 he joined SCIA, where he still works as a peer support officer. He had been part of a similar mentor-style program in Canada and found he enjoyed sharing his 'cheat sheet on life' with people newly embarked on the spinal cord injury journey.

'I was talking to other clients about my experiences in Canada, travel, different equipment that I used, what it's like going home from rehab, what it's like having carers,' he says. 'It's easier hearing it from someone who's lived the injury instead of all the doom and gloom. We can break it down and show that it's not as bad as they make it out to be.'

He credits his work with SCIA with playing a key role in maintaining his positive attitude. 'I can't not work. I've always worked my entire life, ever since I was old enough to get a job. I couldn't be one of those people who just sits at home,' he says.

Dan also joined NSW Wheelchair Rugby – the fast-paced, often brutal sport commonly known as 'Murderball' – and was selected for the Australian training squad. But even as his independence skyrocketed, he still had his tough days. His work with SCIA meant he was meeting people at all stages of recovery from spinal cord injury and, though incredibly rewarding, it could at times also be confronting.

'SCIA covers all spinal units in Sydney hospitals and we follow the clients right through rehabilitation and into the community. We can even see them at week one, not that long out of surgery, no idea what's going on,' he says. 'At that point you're not so much dealing with the client, but more with Mum, Dad and family, letting them know that life goes on. Sometimes you do come across the ones that really hit home and remind you of every horrible thing that they're about to go through, because you've been there.'

In the early years, Dan also found the anniversary of his injury particularly hard to take. 'The anniversaries used to be brutal – I'd sit there and feel sorry for myself,' he says. 'But the longer I go, and with the skill set I've learned to deal with it, I realise I've come bloody far. Now I'm able to pull myself out of those darker moments. It's good for me to see how I've developed.'

That development got an added boost in 2013 when Dan met a special someone by the name of Charlie.

Dan has always loved dogs, but having a canine companion of his own remained tantalisingly out of reach when he was growing up. 'I was never able to have a dog because Mum and my two sisters are all asthmatic and my dad is allergic to things as well,' he says. So he made do. 'I'd look after the neighbours' dogs and walk the dogs that lived in my street.'

He assumed he would have a four-legged friend someday – but never could have imagined just how a dog would come into his life. While he was a Walk On client in 2012, Dan noticed that a fellow participant had an assistance dog, Barnaby.

'I just fell in love with this dog. The guy who owns him, Daniel, said, "You should apply for one,"' says Dan. He hadn't previously considered how – or even *if* – a dog could potentially help him, but got in touch with the organisation that had trained Barnaby, Australian Support Dogs (ASDOG).

Established in 1997, ASDOG is a registered charity that procures and trains assistance dogs for people with physical disabilities. 'I spoke to them about applying for a dog and they said, "For sure, but you're going to have to wait eighteen months,"' he says. 'Charlie was definitely worth the wait.'

Charlie the black labrador spent the first year of his life with a puppy raiser whose job was to socialise the young pooch with people and other dogs and expose him to as many of the environments and situations he might encounter in his 'career' as an assistance dog as possible.

Soon after his first birthday, Charlie went to live with an experienced ASDOG trainer, who drilled him in intensive obedience, skilled tasks and public access training. He learned more than fifty cues and was taught to carry out tasks including retrieving items from tables, cupboards and drawers; picking up dropped items; loading and unloading the washing machine; removing clothing such as socks; and adjusting blankets and bedding. Like all assistance dogs, Charlie is also trained to seek help for his handler should he need it.

Dan worked closely with Charlie's trainer during the year-long training phase. 'You work with them according to what your specific requirements are and they go away and sort out what he needs to do with the commands,' he says.

In the final few weeks of Charlie's training, Dan went through a training program of his own – learning how to bond, live and work with an assistance dog can be a challenging prospect for even the most enthusiastic dog lover. Dan was schooled in all aspects of general dog care and health management, tasks and reward-based training in both public and private settings, behaviour troubleshooting, and access to public venues and transport. Only when he and Charlie were *both* deemed fully trained did Charlie take his Public Access Test, earn his snappy orange ASDOG jacket and take up residence at Dan's place.

Charlie was two when he moved in with Dan in February 2013. It was pretty much love at first sight. 'I knew that having a dog was an extension of my independence, not my full independence. I was realistic about that and realistic about what tasks I was going to get him to do,' he says. 'But I didn't think the bond would develop as quickly as it did.'

Even with their respective rigorous training, however, Dan and Charlie's fledgling relationship wasn't without teething problems. It was three or four weeks before the pair was truly in sync.

'At the start I thought I'd broken him. He wasn't doing what he was meant to do and I couldn't control him,' Dan laughs. 'It was a bit of Charlie being an adolescent and a bit of me not knowing what to do. I was like, *I've got mates that have dogs and they can sit on command and do all this.* But then I realised: they just sit in the backyard all day. They're not taking me out in public. There were just so many things I was unaware of.'

There were occasional mishaps, too. 'I've run over a paw with my wheelchair a few times when he's not concentrating and turns the wrong way,' Dan admits. 'He screams so loud and it's always in a really public place, like in the shopping centre.'

Fortunately, the ASDOG training team was never far away. 'They were fantastic. One phone call and the next day they'd be there. We worked together with a lot of stuff. He's a rascal sometimes. When he sees another dog, he'll go off and say hello to it. We had to be pretty regimented just to keep Charlie in line!'

Even now, a little extra help is occasionally still required. 'If I'm struggling with something, even though I've had him for years, I can still ring up and say, "What can I do?"'

Once they'd conquered those initial complications, Dan and Charlie became a tight-knit team. Charlie's main job is retrieving: though Dan can move his arms, he has no dexterity in his hands, so Charlie truly is his right – and left – hand man.

'I can get stuff off the ground, but it takes forever, whereas I'll give Charlie a simple command and he'll do it. He can open and shut doors, turn lights on and off. People are surprised by the things he can do. They're blown away,' he says. 'If I ask him to, he'll pick up stuff that other people have dropped, but he really only works for me. It's the same with my family – they know he's not a working dog for them.'

Dan quickly discovered that, like most labradors, his sidekick is extremely food motivated. 'The more food I've got, the better the tool he is. I always have treats in my bag or on my lap,' he says. 'I'd love to be able to train him to get me a beer out of the fridge, but I also don't want him being able to get into the fridge! I actually had to sign a contract with ASDOG saying that I'll keep his weight down.'

These days, Dan is rarely without his faithful dog by his side. As a registered assistance dog, Charlie is legally allowed to accompany Dan almost anywhere. Dan does draw the line at taking Charlie to the pub, though. 'If I go somewhere and leave him at home, he looks out the window and you can tell he's choked up. Then when I get home his tail wags so hard it's like he's dislocated it at the hip, he's so excited.'

Charlie even watches from the sidelines when Dan plays rugby and is something of a local celebrity in Dan's inner-Sydney suburb. 'The whole neighbourhood knows him. Everyone pats him and plays with him. He seems a pretty good judge of character.'

Charlie also goes to work with Dan every day in Sydney's spinal cord injury hospital units. Spending months in a hospital or rehabilitation facility after a spinal cord injury is always tough, but can be even harder for dedicated pet owners who are desperately missing their animals. 'Having Charlie with me is almost like pet therapy for the clients, because they don't get to see their own pets for so long. He's a good-looking dog. It's the eyes – they just melt people,' Dan says.

Often people have resigned themselves to a life without the companionship of an animal, but meeting Charlie offers a glimmer of hope. 'That's one of the reasons I love my job: taking that "deer in the headlights" look out of people's eyes and showing them all the experiences they can still have.'

It's a pretty sweet deal for Charlie, too – he's just as hungry for attention as he is for treats. 'Charlie just loves the attention. He loves the pats and the people. Even if someone doesn't pat him, he'll snuggle into them,' Dan says.

But when push comes to shove, Charlie really only has eyes for Dan. 'Whenever Dan leaves Charlie with me for a few minutes, he's okay for a bit and then he'll be looking around like, *Where is he? You're not my person,*' says Dan's fellow SCIA peer support officer, Heidi Haydon.

While Dan has no doubt that Charlie knows he's a working dog and understands he's doing a vitally important job, he says Charlie is definitely *not* a workaholic. Some assistance dogs don't quite know what to do with themselves when their work 'uniform' comes off, but Dan says his laid-back lab is perfectly happy to shirk his duties.

'You take the ASDOG bibs off and he's different – he just wants a cuddle and a pat. Each day I take him for a run without the bibs, just to let him blow all the steam off,' he says. 'Sometimes if he's a bit stressed, like in a meeting room, he'll tap me and let me know he needs to go outside for a break.'

Though ASDOG officially owns Charlie, he is Dan's for life. Dan is responsible for Charlie's day-to-day expenses, including food, veterinary care and grooming. Now six, Charlie will continue to work for Dan for another three or four years, but even when he retires he won't be going far.

'He'll go to family or stay with me and I can get another assistance dog. They don't live with someone they don't know,' he says. 'He'd love retirement. He would sleep for twenty-three-and-a-half hours a day if he could, as long as he was around me.'

Nine years after his accident, Dan has recently regained his driver's licence and paid $130000 to have his car specially adapted. Charlie, of course, has prime position directly behind Dan, ready for their next adventure. When a hard-working guy meets a hard-working (if there's treats) dog, anything could happen.

Suffering a life-changing spinal cord injury may not be the way anyone would choose to meet their best mate, but Dan wouldn't ever want to be without Charlie. 'He's changed my life for sure. He's made it a lot more fun. He senses when I'm having a down day and he knows how to cheer me up,' he says. 'I can't imagine my life without Charlie.'

TIFFANY
REAL ESTATE MODEL

All Tracey Ashley wanted was a pet-friendly rental property. When her marriage ended in 2013, Tracey, her teenage sons, Lachlan and Harry, and their much-loved little dog, Tiffany, found themselves looking for a new place to live. As an experienced real estate agent specialising in Brisbane's south-eastern suburbs, she figured it wouldn't be that difficult to find a suitable townhouse or apartment for her family.

She was wrong.

Having previously owned her own home, Tracey hadn't experienced how tough it can be for renters to find properties that will allow pets. Around 5 million of Australia's 7.6 million households have a pet and more than 35 per cent of those pets are dogs. That's about 1.75 million four-legged tail waggers playing in backyards and loafing on sofas across the country. Meanwhile, some 4.5 million people – or 1.8 million households – live in private rental accommodation, twice as many as thirty years ago, and they have 800 000 pet dogs. But a recent Real Estate Institute of Australia survey of landlords found that nearly 40 per cent said they wouldn't lease their properties to tenants with pets, while another 28.4 per cent were undecided.

That's potentially more than half a million dogs with nowhere to call home. The odds were not in Tracey's favour, no matter how adamantly she insisted Tiffany would be an exemplary tenant.

'It was really hard to rent with a dog. As a puppy we'd taken Tiffany to training and then advanced puppy school. She's very laid-back and very social, but so many places just wouldn't allow pets,' she says.

Finally, after an increasingly exasperating search, Tracey – and Tiffany – found a place to call home. But just three months after the family moved in the vendors put the property on the market and it was back to square one. 'I was just like, *What am I going to do?*' she recalls.

This time around, Tracey decided to buy a property – but that proved just as difficult as negotiating tenancy agreements. 'When I started looking to buy something I sent emails to agents saying, 'Is this property pet friendly?' Hardly anyone even answered me,' she says. 'I thought, *This is really frustrating for me and I'm in the industry.*'

When she eventually bought a townhouse in 2014, Tracey was determined to make it easier for others – whether they were renting or buying – to find a pet-friendly home.

And she knew just the dog to help her do it.

Tracey has always had dogs with unique personalities. Her parents had a corgi when she was born, then she had a dachshund and later an ebullient 'bitser' called Buffy, who passed away six weeks after Tracey's wedding.

Her next dog chose her just two weeks later. Tina was found at a school and taken to the local vet as a stray. The vet happened to be Tracey's brother-in-law and he decided that, rather than take her to the pound, the little dog should live with Tracey and her then husband.

'We think she was a whippet cross fox terrier cross staffy. She had a whippet body, a staffy's brindle colour and a foxy face,' she says. 'We thought at the time that she'd been dumped at the school but we later realised she probably wasn't dumped there because Tina was a little Houdini – she would get out of anywhere she could get out of!'

When Tina died in July 2009, at the grand old age of sixteen, Tracey was devastated. It was more than a year before she could think about getting another dog. When at last she felt ready to welcome another canine companion into her life, Tracey knew she wanted her next dog to be the epitome of 'girlie': small, white, fluffy and female. She had already chosen a suitably feminine name, too: Tiffany.

'I wanted a Maltese or a poodle or a West Highland white terrier like in the My Dog dog food commercials. And I wanted a girl because I've got two sons,' she laughs.

In September 2010, a friend referred Tracey to a Brisbane breeder who had a litter of Shih tzu Cavalier King Charles Spaniel cross puppies. 'She said, "They're really cute," so I thought, *Okay, we'll go and have a look*,' she recalls. 'I walked in with my boys and the breeder took this little puppy out of the pen and put her down to play. I called, "Tiffany!" and she came straight to me. I said to the kids, "Ring Dad and ask him if we can get this puppy," because I knew he wouldn't say no to them!'

If it was love at first sight for Tracey, the feeling appeared to be mutual. She and Tiffany quickly built a firm bond – and it only deepened when Tracey found herself single again in late 2013.

'Tiffany is very friendly and outgoing. She loves going to the dog park, coming to my office, just going places and being with me. When she was doing her puppy training the instructors would say, "She just wants to socialise." Maybe she's taken on a bit of my personality!' she laughs. 'Over the last few years we've bonded even more than I think we would have had I still been married.'

Earlier in 2013, on a whim, Tracey had used Tiffany as a 'model' in a photo of a pet-friendly townhouse she was selling. 'It had a really nice backyard and I thought, *Wouldn't it look cute to have Tiffany sitting out there to show people it's pet friendly?*' she says.

That property sold quickly, and when Tracey faced her own pet-friendly property dilemma later that year she wondered if using Tiffany in photos more frequently might make it easier for buyers to spot properties that allowed pets.

'At that time most apartments and townhouses weren't pet friendly, and if they were, they often only allowed pets that weighed under ten kilograms – like Tiffany. I thought, *Tiffany is the type of dog that a lot of people have*,' she says.

She ran her idea past a few colleagues, none of whom shared her enthusiasm for the concept. 'At first people were really sceptical. They were like, "How is a dog going to sell a house?"'

Tracey's real estate business, The Pink Team – named after her favourite colour – is part of RE/MAX, a global real estate firm that operates on a conjunctional basis, similar to a franchise. Each of the agents she shares her pet-friendly Carina office with is self-employed and pays a fee to operate under the RE/MAX banner. The arrangement affords Tracey plenty of creativity in the way she markets her properties.

She decided to go for it. After negotiating a generous salary of treats and cuddles, Tiffany was officially 'hired' as Tracey's property model.

To the uninitiated, marketing a property for sale may not appear to be a particularly complex task. Take a few happy snaps, write a few lines – job done, right? The reality is that playing up a home's good points, minimising its not-so-good points and encapsulating the potential lifestyle opportunities a property offers is not an easy thing to do in just a dozen or so photographs. It's even tougher to make those photographs grab buyers' attention when literally thousands of other listings are trying to do the same thing.

That's why, according to property-industry experts, a growing number of realtors now include people and pets in property photographs – it helps to make their listings stand out in a highly competitive market. Gone are the days of using an uninspiring shot of the front of the property as the listing's main image; online listings rack up more views when they're a little bit different.

Twenty-first century real estate marketing is all about promoting a home's lifestyle features – the theory is that selling the lifestyle will sell the home. Vendors want buyers to not only see the best features of their home, but to be able to picture themselves living in it – and imagery that clearly illustrates what the new owners will be able to do and experience in the home is an effective way to spark the imagination.

It was this desire to see *how* to live in a property that Tracey knew Tiffany could help to illustrate. And for added 'wow factor', she would use the signature colour of her business: pink. At first she only used her camera-loving pooch in exterior shots – playing with a pink ball in the garden, sitting by the front fence in her best pink dress, even reclining on a pink inflatable lounger in the swimming pool – but when a vendor suggested having Tiffany pose indoors as well, Tracey leapt at the chance.

'The photographer was taking photos and Tiffany would jump in at random places,' she says. The unplanned 'photobombs' inspired a *Where's Wally*-style game. 'We did a 'Where's Tiffany?' campaign, where people would try and spot her in the photos. People would even come to the open houses and say, "Where's Tiffany?"'

The Where's Tiffany? campaign aside, Tracey is careful to ensure that Tiffany's appearances in photos are always in context. Prospective purchasers might find her napping on a bed in her pink hoodie, curled up with a magazine and a pink mug of tea on the couch, drying off with her pink towel in the bathroom or about to tuck into a hamburger at the dining table – on a pink plate, of course. If a property is ripe for renovation, expect to see Tiffany's pink hammer, paint brush and tool belt.

'I'm always trying to be creative with her. I don't do the same things. We had a photo shoot last year in a townhouse in my own complex and I wanted to show the laundry downstairs because it had a toilet in it,' she says. 'I thought, *Where are we going to put her in here?* So we sat her on the toilet. She was a princess on a throne!'

Tiffany the Pink Property Pooch, as she's now known, often also attends open houses, meeting prospective buyers at the front entrance. 'She sits herself down next to the For Sale sign and stands up and wags her tail to greet the buyer. Then she'll sit again and look up and down the street as if to say, *Who's next?*'

As Tracey quickly discovered, placing a photogenic pup in a photo is a great icebreaker and helps to build a rapport with prospective purchasers. 'I get people emailing me from realestate.com.au saying, "I'm not buying but I'm doing a project on marketing and I love your concept." Other people will email and say, "You've made my day even though this property isn't suitable for me,"' she says. 'Other agents from my office have met people at open houses and said, "There's a lady in our office who puts her dog in photos," and they say, "Yeah, that's Tiffany."

People that I don't even know seem to know her. That's really nice to hear.'

People often ask Tracey how she manages to get Tiffany to pose so beautifully in the various scenarios she stars in. The answer is simple: good training . . . and a little bit of bribery.

'People don't realise how difficult it is to do. None of my photos are Photoshopped,' she says. 'I've spent money training Tiffany, I know what she's able to do and I know how to get her attention.'

There's no doubt Tiffany is great at her job, and she certainly isn't a diva, but her modelling career hasn't been without mishaps. During one photo shoot, she briefly disappeared as Tracey discussed shots with the photographer. By the time she'd tracked her dog down, Tiffany was up on the kitchen counter sniffing eagerly at a mouth-watering stew the vendor's mother had left simmering in a slow cooker.

Another unfortunate incident threatened to curtail Tiffany's career all together. Tracey usually uses Tiffany's favourite chicken-flavoured dog treats as an incentive to work, but on one occasion only had the fish-flavoured variety to hand. 'Tiffany is very food oriented – she'd jump off a building for a treat,' she says. 'We were trying to get her to do particular things so I gave her a heap of treats but didn't realise how concentrated they were. I didn't realise I'd given her so many until she had really bad diarrhoea at a client's house – luckily it was outside!'

It didn't take long for Tiffany to start repaying Tracey's investment in treats. The realtor says she soon saw a spike in enquiries about properties whose listing photos featured the pretty pooch.

'I thought I'd see why it was happening so I looked it up and we get 50 per cent more internet viewings on properties starring Tiffany than without her. She keeps a property front of mind, because when you're house hunting they tend to all blur into each other,' says Tracey. 'Someone recently said to me, "It's such a great idea because you naturally remember the house."'

And it wasn't just internet traffic that Tiffany was driving – she was soon helping Tracey to nail sales, too. 'Tiffany has sold every property that she's starred in. There's been two sellers that didn't want her in their photos and they're the only two properties in the last three years that haven't sold.' Tracey was also a finalist in the property marketing category at the annual RE/MAX awards in 2015 and 2016, and was named the top marketer for her office in 2017.

Tracey gives all her vendors the choice of whether to have Tiffany in their property's marketing photos or not. For the most part, they're not only keen on the idea, but they give the pint-sized poser carte blanche.

'I ask people, "Can she sit on the bed? Can she be at the dining table?" I had one family with two dogs and when I asked if I could put Tiffany on the bed they laughed and said, "We don't even let our own dogs in the house." But they let me do it,' she says. 'Tiffany doesn't drop fur. She doesn't smell like a dog. People have allowed me to do stuff with Tiffany in their homes that they wouldn't even do in their own lives.'

It's such a deceptively simple idea – as most ingenious business ideas are – and Tracey was prepared for a barrage of copy cats, but she says she's yet to see any of her competitors attempt to cash in on Tiffany's success – and she thinks she knows why.

'No one has copied me. I've seen the occasional random shot where there's a dog or a cat sitting on a bed, but it's not a matter of just grabbing any dog off the street and putting her in the photos,' she says. 'You need a certain type of dog, and one that's been trained. Tiffany has such big eyes and she really interacts.'

She learned this the hard way when her parents were selling their house and gave Tracey free rein with the marketing. She wondered if she could double the 'Tiffany effect' by bringing a second dog, but soon found out it's not so easy to find a canine with bona fide star quality.

'I took a friend's dog, a Bichon Frise, along with Tiffany and it showed me how difficult it is because he just wasn't as good at it. It was a lot harder to get him to do things. Tiffany just seems born to do it,' says Tracey. 'She seems to know that Mum stands back, she looks at us, we take the photo and she gets a treat.'

Tiffany's fame has begun to spread beyond the world of real estate. She now has her own Facebook and Instagram accounts, both with a steadily growing fan base. She has been featured in the local newspaper and in 2016 was invited to appear on the Channel Nine morning show *Today Extra*.

'She sat on the news desk for half an hour with her pink beads and her pink bandana on. I've got photos of her sitting there, watching herself on TV. We've had some crazy moments,' Tracey laughs.

She's quite sure Tiffany understands that when she accompanies Tracey to a client's home, it's because she has a job to do. 'I absolutely think Tiffany knows she's working. When I go to work, if I'm not taking her she'll go and lie on my bed and happily stay there for eight hours, but if I've said to her the night before, "We've got work tomorrow," she'll sit by the garage door ready to get in the car,' Tracey says. 'After a photo shoot she'll come back to the office and just lay under my desk. She grew up here.'

She may be seven – that's close to fifty in human years – but Tiffany's loveliness is far from fading. Tracey hopes her sweet little dog will continue to star in her property listings for many years to come. She's constantly thinking of innovative new ways to get Tiffany even more involved in her campaigns; one project currently on the drawing board could see Tiffany leading online tours via a camera attached to her collar.

'I can't see her retiring. People enjoy seeing Tiffany in the photos and it's just amazing how much vendors love seeing their houses presented with a beautiful little dog in them,' she says.

Tiffany seems to enjoy her career far too much to hang up her pink sunglasses or tutu just yet. After all, sharing an office with your best friend is pretty hard to beat.

FRANKIE

CHILDREN'S HOSPICE
ASSISTANCE DOG

In the modern working world, 'KPI anxiety' is ubiquitous. For those who are lucky enough to be unfamiliar with management jargon, that's the fear of failing to satisfy 'key performance indicators'; in other words, worrying you'll be sacked if you don't achieve targets set by higher-ups.

There are some employees, however, who will never – *can* never – fully discharge their duties. Frankie the yellow labrador is one of those employees. Sometimes, no matter how hard she works, no matter how well trained or diligent she is, regardless of how many hours she puts in, Frankie just isn't able do what she's assigned to do. And that's okay.

Working in a children's hospice, her job is to comfort sick kids and make them smile, and there are heartbreaking days when it's simply not possible. But Frankie will never, ever stop trying. As dedicated employees go, they don't get more conscientious than Frankie.

Frankie was born on 31 July 2008, and spent the early part of her life at the Frank Baxter Juvenile Justice Centre at Kariong on the New South Wales Central Coast. A youth prison is arguably not an environment that's synonymous with industry and determination, but Frankie proved her mettle early on in Assistance Dogs Australia's Justice Pups assistance dog training program. The program is designed to equip young offenders with new skills, improve their self-esteem and confidence and give them the opportunity to meet and interact with new role models – all while training a dog that will eventually help someone with a physical disability.

Frankie and her sister, Baxter, left the detention centre in 2009, the very first Justice Pups graduates (the program is still running today). Next came more than twelve months of intensive training at the Assistance Dogs Australia National Training School in the Sydney suburb of Engadine. Then it was time to put the newly minted assistance dogs to work.

While the more reserved Baxter was paired with a family in Melbourne, exuberant Frankie's job would be a little different. She was dispatched to Bear Cottage at Manly on Sydney's Northern Beaches. The only children's hospice in NSW, Bear Cottage provides palliative care for children with life-limiting illnesses, as well as temporary respite and bereavement support for families. The facility aims to be as far removed from a typical hospital environment as possible – and what better way to do that than with a happy, cuddly, always-pleased-to-see-you labrador?

When Frankie arrived at Bear Cottage in April 2011 as an energetic two year old, she had big paws to fill. She took over from Scooter, who had retired on his birthday in February 2011 after close to ten years of faithful service. Scooter was a stoic, placid dog and his livewire replacement took some getting used to for nurse Annie Denison, who was Scooter's in-house carer for most of his Bear Cottage career.

'Our assistance dogs always have a dedicated carer and, with Scooter, his person went on maternity leave so I took over from her,' Annie says. 'Scooter was this gorgeous, jet-black lab that was big and strong. He had this lovely, musky doggy smell. I loved Scooter so much. Scooter weighed thirty-seven kilograms and Frankie only weighs twenty-six. When I saw her I thought, *She's got short, stumpy legs and a really long body, so when she walks she sways like an elephant.* She's not handsome like Scooter was. I was a bit judgemental!'

Bear Cottage is situated at the end of a quiet cul-de-sac and surrounded by a swath of open parkland and natural bush where wild rabbits are a common sight. Scooter, who came to the hospice after failing to pass muster as a guide dog, was trained not to react to other animals and 'would look at them and just ignore them'. Frankie was another story.

'Frankie wants to chase rabbits and cats. She once ran right through a screen door trying to get to a dog she saw outside. Spending fifteen months in jail with only her sister, she wasn't social with other dogs. That's the downside to being happy and extroverted,' says Annie. 'She's not big, but she's very strong. She'd just run and pull me over. I was always face down in the dirt. After a few times I was thinking, *Why is she like this?* She still doesn't really know what to do with other dogs.'

It didn't take long, however, for Annie to warm to her new charge – especially when she saw how much the lovable lab adores her job.

'Frankie is the sort of dog that grows on you. It was a bit of an adjustment to get used to a dog that was so excitable, but I could see Assistance Dogs Australia were right in sending her to us,' she says. 'The trouble with Scooter was that he was very introverted and would hide in the office. We needed a dog that loved meeting people and loves making friends. They looked at her and thought she'd be perfect for Bear Cottage. She's always happy to see people and loves interacting with people.'

Frankie's role at Bear Cottage is essentially to just be there for the kids and their families. That might mean playing ball with children in the hospice's long hallway, supervising activities in the playrooms or simply curling up on a patient's bed to watch a movie or take a nap. She can also retrieve dropped items for children in wheelchairs and even take washing out of the clothes dryer. Sometimes children will help Annie run Frankie through her training 'homework' or prepare her dinner at five o'clock every evening.

'We always ask the kids if they want to brush Frankie. We get them involved in her care and it gives them something to do to make them feel that they're valued,' she says.

Frankie has also assumed the role of 'wandering door bell', vociferously letting staff know whenever somebody comes to the main door. 'She sleeps on the sofa at the front door so she can see people coming and going,' Annie says. 'I think she feels responsible for everybody in the building. She's letting us and everybody else know that this is her house.'

Frankie makes sure she spreads her love around, ensuring she visits everyone every day. 'Every day she does her rounds of the rooms. She visits every room to see who's there and what they're doing. She's very inquisitive. She just wants to be there. She wants the children to know that she understands.'

Annie says Frankie is particularly adept at connecting with autistic children, probably as a result of her exposure to challenging behaviour in the prison environment. 'I think when she was in jail she learned to read people – to know whether she should stay away or get close,' she says. 'We have a photo of her with a boy with autism who wouldn't talk or do anything, but when Frankie was next to him he would respond. She understood what he needed and he understood that she was friendly. She sees things that we don't see.'

Entire families come to stay at Bear Cottage and some have been returning for ten years or more. Many of these families live in rented accommodation and make ends meet on a single income, so having a pet dog at home simply isn't possible. Frankie is often their only opportunity to spend time with a canine companion. She is especially attuned to the needs of well siblings, who can often feel adrift when their parents are focused on the needs of a sick child.

'Sometimes when we have a child dying and the parents are very involved, the siblings can seem lost. If they can help with Frankie and have a relationship with her it gives them a chance to get some love back,' says Annie.

She always tucks Frankie into her bed in the office at 9 p.m. because she thinks it's important that some things in Frankie's life are consistent. It's generally recommended that assistance dogs live off-site and come to work with a handler each day. That's not an option for a dog like Frankie, so scheduled time out is even more important. 'She needs to know that some things don't change, because most things do change here.'

For all her training and her tireless dedication to her job, however, Frankie is still a dog – and sometimes a dog just wants what a dog wants.

'She's not allowed in the dining room, so usually she just sits at the door and looks in, but I have walked past and seen her in there, licking the floor,' Annie laughs. 'She likes the two year olds because they walk along with their food. She'll walk up next to them and look at them and the next minute they're giving her food. They know when they're beaten.

'Sometimes we'll go into the office and the bin's been emptied and everything is all over the floor. I'll say, "Frankie!" and she'll look at me like, *Why is it always my fault?*'

She has other little quirks, too. In the prison she was taught to weave around people's legs and will do so unbidden, just to prove she can. She's also terrified of balloons and gets very frightened when they pop, which unfortunately happens often in a children's hospice.

Of course, Frankie's role at Bear Cottage is anything but simple. What she is really doing as she goes about her work at the hospice is making a potentially frightening or overwhelming place feel warm and welcoming. 'Frankie makes this building a home. She cares about everybody, whether you're staff, volunteer or family. The more you love her, the more she gives back. She's a friend to the children and their families. They think it's going to be like a hospital and she makes it not like a hospital. To me, Bear Cottage would feel very empty without a dog in it.'

It's not just the staff and patients of Bear Cottage that can attest to 'the Frankie factor': a plethora of scientific research shows why dogs like her are so good at what they do. According to several studies, spending just a few minutes with a dog can reduce blood pressure, ease anxiety and boost levels of serotonin and dopamine, neurochemicals that are essential for feelings of happiness and wellbeing. Research has also shown that performing stressful tasks seems easier when a dog is present and that dogs help to dispel workplace tension. Dog owners are less likely to develop depression, too.

Frankie has a particular knack for winning over people who aren't fond of dogs. Annie says she seems to view changing their minds as a personal challenge. 'If you're not a dog person she'll try a bit harder to engage you,' she says. 'She'll spend time making you like her and she always succeeds. It might take a week, but by the time you walk out of here you'll be saying, "Oh, we love Frankie."'

There are days at Bear Cottage, however, when Frankie simply can't make people smile. When a child passes away, Frankie feels the loss as keenly as everyone else. Not being able to ease a family's anguish can make Frankie quite distressed.

'She knows when a child dies and she gets really sad and anxious. She stresses that she can't make people feel better. She will spend more time with that family because she thinks they need to know that she cares. When a family is grieving, she knows what to do. She often just sits next to them,' says Annie. 'Recently we had two deaths in one week and she became really depressed. She wanted to sit with the families but they were really traumatised.'

Frankie's state of mind is always a priority for Annie. Although the big-hearted dog has been at Bear Cottage for more than six years, the loss of a child is still confusing for her. 'She doesn't understand why these children die. Some families come for ten years and then when their child dies they just don't come back,' she says.

She is ever watchful for signs that Frankie is feeling heartsick. 'She retreats eventually. She'll hide in the office or spend more time on the sofa by the front door. It's like she doesn't have the energy.'

When that happens, Annie takes Frankie home with her to leafy Wollstonecraft, on Sydney's lower North Shore. For a few nights each month, Frankie enjoys peace, quiet and regular visits to the nearby Chew Chew Pet Restaurant for a 'puppacino'.

'She just needs some time to have a bit of space and she sleeps a lot. Once I took her to the café and ordered sardines and couscous for her and when it was time to go she wouldn't leave,' says Annie.

But she's always raring to get back to work. 'After two or three days she'll look at me and I can tell she's bored. She's used to nurses and families, chefs, therapists. She's looking around thinking, *Where is everybody?*' she says. 'When she comes back she's so excited. She goes around to all the offices and rooms as if to say, *I'm back – did you miss me?* When I take her home and bring her back everyone says, "Thank goodness she's back." Having Frankie here just makes Bear Cottage more homely.'

In addition to her nursing duties, Annie's job as Frankie's right-hand woman is to feed her; manage her flea, tick and worm treatments; take her to the vet when necessary; and take her to the groomer for her monthly bath and summer haircut. 'I think Frankie thinks I'm her servant,' she laughs.

Frankie has arthritis, which responds well to acupuncture treatments paid for by a generous donor, though she can get stiff if she has too much exercise. Otherwise, all her veterinary work is provided free by a local clinic. Her grooming is donated, too.

She also has her own team of volunteers who take her for daily walks and for excursions into nearby Manly for a bit of time out. 'Sometimes she sits by the front door all morning waiting for them to come. I think she knows which day of the week it is because she knows which walker is coming. They adore her,' Annie says. 'They'll take her swimming, take her down to Manly for coffee. They take her to one of the beaches where the fishermen are and they throw her bits of raw fish. She's got a busy schedule.'

Frankie is nine now and plans are underway for her retirement (although some long-term families who remember Scooter still refer to Frankie as 'the new dog'). Most assistance dogs give up work around the age of ten. Scooter was retired from his post quite abruptly – he enjoyed a huge retirement party and spent three love-filled years with one of his volunteers, before passing away on Boxing Day 2014, six weeks shy of his fifteenth birthday.

'Scooter started spending more time in the office because the children were too rough with him. He had arthritis and the only way he could cope with it was to hide,' Annie says. 'He was our first assistance dog and we didn't know the best way to handle it, so we retired him quite suddenly. He got what he needed, which was a loving family. I couldn't take him at the time and I was sad about that, which is why I'm doing things differently with Frankie.'

Annie, a lifelong dog lover who grew up with corgis, cocker spaniels and beagles, is determined that Frankie's exit will be a more gradual process. She has started taking her home more frequently in an effort to help her get used to a slower pace of life.

'To Frankie, Bear Cottage is the centre of the universe. She's used to lots of people, activity and stimulation and when she retires she won't get that. I want her to get used to having fewer people around,' she says. 'I think the more breaks she has, the better she will be at her job. The time away keeps her excited about her work. There's nothing like coming to work and seeing her wag her tail because she's pleased to see you. If she had to stay at Bear Cottage all the time I think she'd lose that joy.'

Because that's the thing about Frankie: the extroverted, excitable labrador is the heart of Bear Cottage. She gives so much of herself to people whose hearts are breaking, because just being there for them is her life's great joy.

'I think Frankie knows that she is an important dog. Everybody that comes to the door is there to see Frankie, as far as she's concerned. She's a listener. She goes through sad times but she always bounces back because that's her personality,' Annie says. 'People often say to me, "I didn't like dogs, but Frankie is different" or, "I've never wanted a dog, but after spending time with Frankie I think it would be nice." I have to tell them they don't want a dog – they want a dog like Frankie. She loves people. She wants to make everybody smile. Her mission in life is to make friends with everybody that comes in.'

Well Frankie, mission accomplished.

COOP

FACILITY DOG

It is a truth universally acknowledged that five minutes in the company of a dog can change a person's day for the better. There's just something about a soft coat, a pair of liquid brown eyes and that sense of quiet, judgement-free comfort that makes all seem right with the world.

The human–animal bond is so powerful, in fact, that the simple presence of a dog can lower blood pressure and regulate the heart rate in stressful situations. In a 2002 study, American researchers set participants a timed maths task and compared the changes in blood pressure and heart rate of those who owned a dog with those who didn't. The dog owners not only had lower resting heart rates and blood pressure to begin with, they were less likely to have spikes while solving the maths problem, and their heart rates and blood pressure returned to normal more quickly than those without pets. When their dog was in the room, participants even made fewer errors in their arithmetic, which led the boffins to conclude that dogs reduce stress.

Similar research, also from the United States, found that the presence of a pet dog is actually a more effective way of lowering blood pressure in stressful situations than taking ACE inhibitors, a widely used type of blood pressure medication. Another study, published in the *Journal of the American Board of Family Medicine* in 2015, found that stroking a dog can help to lower both blood pressure and cholesterol.

The calming effect of dogs on children is even more remarkable. The US Centers for Disease Control and Prevention asked the parents of 643 kids aged between four and ten to track their body mass index (BMI), physical activity, screen time and mental health over the course of eighteen months. Fifty-eight per cent of the children surveyed had pet dogs, and while there was no difference in BMI, exercise or screen time among those with dogs and those without, the kids with four-legged friends experienced less anxiety than their dogless peers. More than 20 per cent of the children who did not have a dog had stress and anxiety, according to the standardised Screen for Child Anxiety Related Disorders (SCARED) test, compared to just 12 per cent of the kids with dogs.

And that's not all. In another study, which measured blood pressure, heart rate, and behavioural distress in healthy children aged three to six during two separate doctor visits, all the kids had lower blood pressure, lower heart rates, and less behavioural distress when a dog – not even their own dog – was in the room. Research has also revealed that seven- and eight-year-old children say pets are better providers of comfort and self-esteem than humans.

But just *why* does the presence of a humble hound have such a profoundly calming effect? One theory is that social interaction between dogs and humans increases levels of oxytocin – often called the 'cuddle hormone' or the 'love hormone' – in both the person and the pooch. At the same time, hanging out with a dog reduces levels of the 'stress hormone', cortisol. (Elevated cortisol levels impact learning and memory, lower immune function and bone density, and increase weight gain, blood pressure, cholesterol and heart disease. In other words, less is definitely best.)

Three-year-old Coop isn't up to date with all the latest data. She hasn't read the myriad scientific studies that prove our four-legged friends provide solace and support. She can't actually read, to be fair. She's a black labrador. And anyway, Coop knows that expensive research can't quantify the value of a wagging tail or a slobbery kiss. She understands that the true power of a dog's companionship is something that's felt deep within the soul.

It's a feeling that Coop's owner, Tessa Stow, knows well. As a veterinary nurse and dog trainer for more than twenty-five years, Tessa saw first hand how dogs soothed and consoled their people simply by being there. They were trusted counsellors without ever uttering a word. Vet nursing often meant Tessa assumed the role of counsellor herself, and in 2015 she formalised that experience by completing a diploma in counselling.

It was while talking with counselling staff at the Centre Against Violence (CAV) in Wangaratta, north-east Victoria, that she saw how her seemingly disparate skill sets could work together to help people, particularly children. CAV assists men, women, young people and children who are victims of sexual assault, violent crime and family violence.

'I was talking to one of the lead counsellors there about how I could possibly be a mentor for domestic violence cases and the subject got onto dogs, because we both love them,' Tessa recalls. 'We started to talk about how we could use dogs to help men, women and kids cope with their experiences and recover.'

She took to Google to research the idea and was thrilled to discover courthouse facility dogs. These professionally trained and accredited dogs work across the US in prosecutors' offices, family courts and child advocacy centres just like CAV. Their job is to be a legally neutral, calming presence and provide emotional support to vulnerable people – mainly children – during stressful court proceedings.

There are currently around 120 'comfort dogs' at work in courtrooms across America, as well as in Canada and Chile. The theory – backed up by all that research into the human–canine bond – is that dogs have a calming effect and that calm people are better able to tell their stories. Another advantage is they don't disrupt proceedings in the way that a human advocate might. According to attorney Ellen O'Neill-Stephens, who founded America's first courthouse dogs program in 2003, the presence of a dog also helps court officials by creating 'a more humane and efficient system that enables judges, lawyers, and staff to accomplish their work in a more positive and constructive manner'.

Convinced such a program would be a boon for Victoria's court system, Tessa began talking to everyone she could think of in a bid to get the idea off the ground. But just talking wasn't enough for Tessa – she was determined to start *doing* as well. She established her own program, K9 Support, and recruited her first 'employee', Coop.

Her plan was to get a dog working with an agency like CAV as soon as possible – almost like a demonstrator model to illustrate how effective comfort dogs would be in a court setting.

'Coop was chosen for me by someone who was an international dog trainer. I told him what I was going to do. He was already working with a labrador breeder and he'd got some good service dogs from this breeder,' she says. 'I wanted a golden lab but he said, "No, you're getting the black one," because he thought she was the one for me.'

In late 2014, Coop – who is named after Jodi Cooper, one of CAV's counsellors – moved in with Tessa at her home near Benalla and training began in earnest. But even for a labrador, a breed known for its exuberance and love of people, young Coop was a bit of a handful at first.

'She's amazing but she's a bit of a flirt. She just adores everybody – she's a typical lab in that sense,' Tessa laughs. 'She's just so excited to work that she can sometimes be a bit over the top. She's almost over-affectionate for the job that she's going to do. I don't want to curb that affection – it works – but the initial greeting can be a little bit overwhelming.'

It took sixteen months to train Coop to a standard that Tessa felt was appropriate for the job she had in mind. 'I trained her up to the standards of a guide dog and she had to pass the Public Access Test (PAT) to prove that she's safe in the job,' she explains.

Coop passed the PAT in 2016 and, with that ticked off the to-do list, was ready to start work. She now spends every Tuesday lending a paw at CAV and every Friday at the Goulburn Valley Centre Against Sexual Assault (GVCASA) in Shepparton. For confidentiality reasons, Tessa doesn't accompany Coop into her sessions. Instead, she leaves her in the care of a designated counsellor advocate at each centre, who take her into their therapy rooms to work with their clients.

'I only allow her to work with two counsellors. That's the limit: two people plus me. She could do a lot more than that but at the moment we're taking it slow,' she says.

Coop's job is to lessen the trauma that a victim of sexual assault or family violence may experience when telling their story. She might do that by curling up on the sofa next to that person or resting her head in their lap so they can pat and stroke her while they speak. Sometimes she'll simply lie down on her mat on the floor, doing nothing more than being there.

In some cases, the child won't touch Coop at all, but simply hold onto her leash. 'That in itself, knowing they're connected to that dog, and that sense of safety and trust, just does wonders.'

Coop is also trained to do 'tricks' that may appear to be for the amusement of kids, but are in fact part of a broader strategy designed to empower clients. 'A lot of children who are sexually abused or in domestic violence situations lose their sense of control, so we can empower them by getting them to "train" Coop,' Tessa explains. 'One of the things I teach is "search". There might be a particular toy that the child likes. The counsellor will hide the toy and Coop will go and find it, but take it back to the child.'

What Coop is really doing, she says, is creating a feeling of safety. 'When a dog is lying by your feet, sleeping comfortably, it gives the children especially the sense that there's nothing menacing in the environment: *The dog's sleeping, so I'm safe.*'

But that's the thing: even when a comfort dog may appear to be snoozing, it still has its young charge's wellbeing in mind. 'I had a counsellor say to me that she thought Coop was asleep in one session, but the little girl she was working with got up and Coop opened her eyes and checked that everything was okay,' says Tessa. 'It's unconditional love. It allows them to take a breath and feel comfortable because they have a loving creature beside them that isn't going to ask hard questions.'

Clients who feel safe are more likely to share details of their experiences that may be crucial to legal proceedings, but which they may not otherwise have felt comfortable sharing. Tessa says CAV and GVCASA counsellors have reported that Coop's involvement in sessions lowers anxiety by as much as 45 per cent.

One young child at GVCASA readily opened up to her counsellor when Coop was present in a session, despite having stuck close to Mum and barely uttered a word in six previous sessions.

'For a young child, coming in to talk about sexual abuse or domestic violence is very, very traumatic. If we can lessen their anxiety then the true story can come out,' Tessa says. 'It's something only a companion animal can give. When that labrador looks up at you with those big, brown eyes, they take that level of trauma away and bring a level of trust, comfort and non-judgement.'

And it's not just the agencies' clients that Coop is helping: the boisterous, people-loving lab has also boosted staff morale. People often don't consider how counsellors and support staff are affected by the horrific stories they hear all day, every day, but Tessa has no doubt that dogs like Coop will benefit those at the coalface, too.

'The things they have to listen to, I don't think people take into account the trauma of that. If you've got a police officer that has to look at sexual assault tapes, or a child protection caseworker always going to court because kids are not being looked after, the dogs are also helping them,' she says. 'That can help with the massive turnover of staff that we have in these really, really hard jobs. It's a huge hidden cost.'

It's another reason why Tessa is so determined to expand Coop's job from agencies like CAV into the broader justice system. Many people who have experienced sexual assault and family violence already display symptoms of post-traumatic stress disorder (PTSD) and she believes the intimidating nature of court procedures only adds to that.

'When we put people through the court system we re-traumatise them. We're adding to their stress because the court system in Australia is based on stress – apparently it makes people tell the truth,' she says.

She wants comfort dogs like Coop to work with people right through their legal proceedings, from the day they first tell their story until the day their case is resolved in court.

While Tessa has received positive feedback from politicians, lawyers and judges, the wheels of justice turn slowly and Coop has yet to receive the go-ahead to accompany anyone into court. There has been concern from some quarters about dogs barking or wandering about in courtrooms, interrupting proceedings. But Tessa says the dogs' intensive two-year training process means this simply won't be an issue.

'The dogs are trained to just lie there and not move. In training we'll yell, get angry, cry – anything they might do in the courtroom, so they just do not react. They do not disrupt anything,' she says. 'No one else can be employed to do what these dogs do. They can help in so many ways.'

Funding is another major roadblock. Tessa estimates it costs up to $40 000 to fully train and accredit a court comfort dog. They are, after all, trained to the standard of a guide dog, but while a guide dog works with just one handler, dogs like Coop can work with anyone. Court dogs will also provide around eight years of faithful service, starting work at age two and retiring around ten.

And when viewed in context of comforting a traumatised child – not to mention compared to the cost of recruiting and training new staff to replace those leaving the field in droves – $40 000 seems a small price to pay. 'I want the dogs to be where they can have the most impact,' she says. 'The way I see it, one dog that is properly cared for can help hundreds of victims, for want of a better term. And not only the victims, but the staff that they're working with.'

Coop has now retired from GVCASA and Tessa has trained a second dog, a golden labrador called Connie, to take her place there. Connie is owned by a sandplay counsellor who had worked with Coop and saw the incredible effect the gentle dog had on her clients. CAV will also soon have its own dog, a male golden lab called Amaria, who will work alongside Coop once he completes his training.

K9 Support is also a therapy-dog school, working with counsellors, psychologists, teachers and volunteers to train their own dogs to do what Coop does. She says the seasoned Coop is like a mentor for the younger dogs.

'She's like a sister to the new pups and also a trainer. Connie was frightened of a neighbour that dropped in during her early training, so I just let Coop out and Connie immediately went, *Oh, you're not an axe murderer*,' she says.

She is vigilant about ensuring that Coop and Connie, whom she still sees regularly, continue to enjoy their work, and teaches her clients at the therapy-dog school how to spot signs of burnout. Just like the counsellors and child advocates who hear these unbearable stories, Tessa says comfort dogs carry a heavy burden.

'I'm very tough on people who will take my dogs, in that they can't work them eight hours a day, five days a week, because the dogs take on much of this trauma. We don't give them enough credit for what they understand. I've seen them get off the couch and shake and shake, like they're literally shaking that session off,' she explains. 'It takes a lot to train them and you can ruin them in an instant if you work them too hard. We need to be advocates for them as much as they are for us. We need to really, really take care of them and make sure they don't overwork.'

Bureaucracy being what it is, Tessa knows that Coop may never be a court dog herself, but she is confident that dogs will one day be as ubiquitous in Australian courtrooms as stenographers and sketch artists. 'I haven't come across anyone who's not supportive. It's just a matter of finding the people who can actually make change.'

And even if she doesn't make it to the bar, Coop will continue to volunteer her time at CAV and anywhere else Tessa thinks the quiet presence of a loving dog can help. Tessa has no doubt that Coop loves her job, even if she doesn't necessarily grasp what an enormous difference she's making in the lives of truly vulnerable people.

'I don't know if Coop understands exactly how important her job is, but I do think she loves it. She understands happiness and gratitude and she knows that we're very, very pleased with her,' she laughs. 'She's so happy when I put that [facility dog] coat on. She just jumps in the car and wants to go everywhere with me. I'm just her chauffeur. I drive her to work and she's in the back of the car going,

Where are we going today? She loves to work. She gets so disappointed if I leave her behind.'

That's because Coop knows what all dog people know: dogs are pure love. And nothing is a greater balm to the soul than that.

LEXIE & FLY
STOCK GUARDIANS

The idea of leaving a beloved pet to fend for themselves is anathema to most dog lovers. We're used to spoiling our four-legged friends with daily gourmet meals, a warm bed at night and plenty of cuddles and belly rubs. But for some working dogs, indulging in the creature comforts most canine companions enjoy would be disastrous. Though they're just as treasured by their families as any other pet, success for these dogs depends on a decidedly hands-off relationship with their humans. Pampering such pooches would make it virtually impossible for them to do their jobs.

The maremma – or the Maremma-Abruzzese Sheepdog, to use the breed's full name – is that kind of dog. Bred as livestock guardians in central Italy, particularly Abruzzo and the coastal Maremma region of Tuscany and Lazio, these hardy, independent dogs have been used by shepherds to protect sheep from wolves for thousands of years.

Descriptions of white sheep-defending dogs have even been found in early Roman texts, along with statues, sculptures and paintings depicting the noble white dogs at work.

Unlike many ancient working breeds, whose twenty-first century descendants are generally more familiar with sofas than sheep, maremmas are still widely used for their original purpose, especially in Abruzzo, where the health of the rural economy continues to rest squarely on the sheep's back.

They're also hard at work in Australia. In 2015, a maremma called Oddball shot to international fame when a film based on her career was a surprise box office hit.

Oddball became a local legend in Warrnambool, a small city on Victoria's south-west coast, after she became guardian of a colony of endangered little penguins. The penguins lived on Middle Island, about 150 metres offshore, but foxes had decimated the population. By the time Oddball was stationed on the island to protect them in 2005, fewer than ten birds remained. The idea was suggested by her owner, Alan 'Swampy' Marsh, who had trained her and other maremmas to guard free-range chooks on his poultry farm.

What *Oddball* the movie didn't show was that the real Oddball quit her post after three weeks and swam back to the mainland. The people-loving dog was lonely and missed human company, but she'd been so successful at scaring off foxes in that short period that Warrnambool City Council established the Middle Island Maremma Project in 2006. Today, sister maremmas Eudy and Tula spend five days per week on the island during little penguin breeding season. They have been incredibly successful in their jobs: there has been no evidence of fox attacks since the project began and by 2013 the colony had swelled to 180 birds (it's now stable at around 130).

Oddball died in February 2017 at the impressive age of fifteen. She had spent her final years guarding chickens on Swampy's property at Dennington, just outside of Warrnambool.

Jen Dalitz doesn't need to watch a movie to know what faithful, diligent dogs maremmas are. All she has to do is look out the window of her farmhouse at Joadja, in the Southern Highlands of New South Wales, to see these tenacious canines at work.

Jen and her husband, Ric, are the owners of Eagle Rock Farm, a 1250-acre property two hours south of Sydney. As well as running a herd of about 150 Angus and belted Galloway cattle, Jen also breeds Australian and English-Irish donkeys and Waler horses, which were used by the famous Light Horse Brigade in World War I.

But while animals flourish on the farm today, that hasn't always been the case. In fact, a veritable massacre of livestock in 2010 sent Jen on a desperate quest to find some way to keep her menagerie safe.

'We've had Eagle Rock Farm since 2011 and before that we had another property not far away. At our old property we bred Dorper sheep. Dorpers are huge because they're meat sheep. The rams would have weighed a hundred kilos, and one day one of them was just gone,' she says.

When that first ram vanished, Jen was initially perplexed. 'I was like, *That's so weird*. I thought he must have been stolen and wondered who could have lifted him as he was so enormous. Then we found the blood trail in the grass.'

She knew there were foxes on the property – they're an ever-present menace in the country and, as the daughter of a professional fox hunter, Jen was more than familiar with their modus operandi. She had also spotted wild dogs in the area – both dingoes and pets that had escaped and turned feral – but hadn't counted on them being such a serious threat.

'The animal losses started as a trickle and became a tsunami. We lost seventy sheep over a week and a half. All of our lambs got taken by foxes and wild dogs, as well as two of the rams and some of the ewes,' she says. 'It was heartbreaking.'

Jen and Ric did extensive research and tried everything they could think of to keep their herd safe from the ruthless predators. They were only at the property part-time, spending most of the week in Sydney, and needed something that would keep the foxes and feral dogs out when they couldn't be there. They already had donkeys, which are known to be excellent guardians of condensed herds. Unfortunately, they're not so good at protecting sheep scattered over a wide area and are more likely to flee than fight against multiple attackers.

The couple also installed electric fencing and even brought in alpacas, which are increasingly used as livestock guardians in Australia. But nothing worked and sheep continued to meet a grisly fate.

'We thought the electric fencing would be all right, and it was originally, but it didn't take the foxes long to figure out that we'd bred the sheep back up,' says Jen. 'The frustrating thing about foxes is they don't just take one lamb to feed their family, they keep killing for fun. I used to go fox hunting with my dad as a kid and I would walk into paddocks and see dozens of sheep just ripped apart. It's just terrifying for the ewes.'

She was at a loss as to what else she could do. With the couple about to upgrade from their part-time property to Eagle Rock Farm, where Jen planned to live permanently, 'we just tried to keep the herd as intact as we could.'

'We were reading in the farming magazines about what we could do to protect the stock and thinking, *We're already doing all of these things – what more can we do?*' she says.

There was one thing they hadn't yet tried. Jen had heard about an Italian sheepdog breed that was supposedly unbeatable when it came to guarding farm animals from wild dogs and foxes. But she was wary – after all, the same had been said about alpacas and donkeys and they'd proved to be no match for the marauding killers. Plus, Jen and Ric had a young child to think about – son Ethan was two when they made the move to Eagle Rock Farm – and she'd heard these dogs were *super* protective. She wasn't sure that a big, single-minded dog was necessarily the best match for a home with a boisterous little boy.

But with their other options exhausted and their sheep still being attacked, the couple eventually decided to take the plunge. 'It was Ric's idea to get maremmas in the first place, but then he hesitated. I didn't want a repeat of the lamb situation, so I just thought we'd try it and I went off and got them,' says Jen.

In fact, Jen decided to go all in: not just one, but *two* maremmas were soon on their way to Eagle Rock Farm.

Lexie and Fly may be sisters, but they couldn't be more different. As a young dog, Lexie was sensible and serious and definitely called the shots. Fly, meanwhile, was free-spirited and adventurous and rarely stayed near the house.

But things change. Now six, the dogs' relationship has turned 180 degrees. 'They're from the same litter but they have completely different personalities. The hierarchy changes and has changed over time. Lexie was the dominant one when they were younger, but I think it's Fly now,' says Jen. 'Lexie would stay around the house more, but she's the first to go off now, while Fly is almost always within earshot of the house.'

One thing that hasn't changed over the years, however, is Lexie and Fly's passion for their job. They are essentially wandering security guards, roaming the Dalitzes' property day and night and ridding it of any predator that crosses their paths. And they're incredibly good at it. So good, in fact, that Eagle Rock Farm hasn't lost a single animal to a fox or wild dog since the maremmas moved in.

'They chase anything that runs. When we got them we also had a young beagle who liked chasing animals, so she showed the maremmas how to chase,' Jen says. 'They will run at forty kilometres an hour. If a fox comes in, the maremmas will chase it and go under fences and go after it. They're not constrained by the paddock boundaries. They have initiative.'

They never chased the sheep – though the farm doesn't currently have sheep as Jen and Ric are focusing on cattle – and don't chase the cows, because the livestock has learned not to run when the dogs are around. 'When we first got them we put them in the house yard with the sheep, so they learned to be friends. They became so used to living together the sheep weren't scared of them, so they didn't run.'

While they do hunt animals that venture onto the property, it's not as necessary these days as it was at the beginning of their custodianship. Fewer wild animals actually dare to step foot onto Eagle Rock Farm now that the maremmas are in residence.

'The foxes are on the lookout for an opportunity every day, but the presence of the maremmas stops other dogs from coming onto the property because they know it is occupied totally,' Jen explains. 'Other dogs that wander up to the property know they're here. Because Lexie and Fly are out and about all the time, they're constantly marking their territory.'

The maremmas are largely left to their own devices. Jen only feeds them two or three times a week and the rest of the time they find their own food. Wild rabbits are their staple diet, though they consider eggs an extra special treat.

'They look after the chickens but they'll eat the eggs if they can get to them,' Jen laughs. 'The geese only lay once a year. One time the dogs were out in the paddocks and I came home and there was a pile of goose eggs by the door. They were going out and collecting them.'

They sleep outside, sometimes close to the farmhouse but more often napping in the paddocks in between their regular patrols of the perimeter. Neither dog had even been inside the house until Fly had puppies in 2014. It was the middle of winter and Fly gave birth outdoors, where the temperature was close to zero – it took Jen and Ric some time to find the litter and sadly three of her offspring didn't make it. The surviving pups were promptly brought indoors, along with Fly, and ferried back and forth between the farm and the Dalitzes' Sydney home.

'Puppies have to have an ambient temperature around thirty degrees Celsius, so we had them inside for weeks and weeks. Fly had never been in the house before, ever, but not once did she have a toilet mistake in the house,' says Jen. 'Maremmas are very smart dogs.'

Motherhood seemed to mellow Fly and make her even more focused on her job. 'Lexie was fine as a puppy but Fly was crazy when she was young. When she had her pups she became much more mature,' she says.

Special circumstances aside, the dogs are happy to spend their nights in the great outdoors all year round. Maremmas have a long, dense double coat that protects them from the elements. Cold doesn't trouble them in the slightest: 'They swim in the dam in the middle of winter,' says Jen.

Night-time temperatures may drop below zero in the Southern Highlands in winter, but Lexie and Fly are dressed for the winter in mountainous Abruzzo, where daytime temperatures struggle to crack double figures and there's thick snow on the ground for half the year.

'Sometimes they come back up to the house and stay here for the night. Otherwise they go out all night hunting for rabbits or chasing foxes, which happens a lot as the foxes come up looking for a stray chicken to pluck off,' she says. 'Their job is to keep the animals safe, so they mostly go outside and do that.'

Some people can find it hard to reconcile the rather remote handling of a maremma with how they feel dogs – even working dogs – should be treated. But treating a maremma like a pet is frowned upon by those that know and value the breed. The Maremma Sheepdog Club of America actively discourages people from acquiring maremmas as pets. Their drive to work is innate and powerful and failure to provide a job to keep them occupied will inevitably lead to trouble.

Then there's the not-insignificant fact that maremmas don't consider themselves pets. They are mistresses of their own destiny – just ask Lexie and Fly.

'A lot of the old-school people say, "You should make them fend for themselves." On the big sheep stations, maremmas will run over ten thousand acres or more and they don't get fed,' Jen says. 'They might give them food once a week to keep them coming back to the same spot, but otherwise they don't get fed at all. They have to go out and catch their food.'

Lexie and Fly are a little bit more indulged than most working maremmas, enjoying the occasional juicy bone as a treat from Jen. But she doesn't think being slightly domesticated has impacted their will to work at all. 'It's interesting that their performance hasn't been hindered. They still do whatever we want them to do. Wherever we go on the property, they'll come with us,' she says. 'I'll drive out to the back paddock and be out there planting trees and one of them will turn up and lay there while I finish my work.'

Though she grew up in the country, Jen hasn't always been a country girl. She was raised in Victor Harbor, a picturesque hamlet on South Australia's Fleurieu Peninsula, 80 kilometres south of Adelaide, but left when she was seventeen. A globetrotting career in finance and management followed before she finally settled in Sydney, where she met Ric.

'I never had any intention of living in the country ever again. I've always loved animals though and I'd wanted a horse ever since I was a kid,' she says. 'I decided the city wasn't a good environment for a horse, and when I married Ric I realised that if I was going to stay in Sydney I wanted a bit more space, so we bought a country property.'

With the purchase of the country spread came the animals. As well as the livestock, breeding horses and donkeys, the family also has fifteen free-roaming chickens and geese, two beagles – Coco and Peanut Butter – and two pet horses, Jim and Rusty, with whom Ethan competes in dressage competitions.

The plan was always for the farm to be a 'weekender', but Jen soon realised she still had the soul of a country girl, hence the permanent move to Joadja in 2011. 'I really like Sydney, but I can be out here for the whole week and I don't miss having people around,' Jen says.

When Ethan reached school age, however, Jen and Ric realised that, with school a 90-minute round trip away, three hours a day in the car was too much. Their own businesses – Jen is a management consultant and Ric has a commercial furniture and joinery business – were also flourishing, requiring frequent trips back to the city. They made the difficult decision to mostly live in Sydney during the week, with just a night or two at Eagle Rock, plus weekends and school holidays.

The maremmas stay on the property when the family are in the city and Jen says knowing they're there, guarding their flock, is a great weight off her shoulders.

'They give me total peace of mind. I always sleep well knowing they're on patrol. No one gets into this property without them telling me,' she says. 'They do bark a bit and if they bark at night you know there's something going on. They are extremely valuable to us.'

She never worries about Lexie and Fly wandering off. They're well known to people on neighbouring properties. 'We often get calls from our neighbours saying, "Your dogs are here," or, "Oh, we've had Lexie here all weekend," ' Jen laughs. 'They just cruise around everywhere, but they always come home. They can even go across the Wingecarribee River and get back home. I often think, *What do you get up to?*'

Nor does she worry about the dogs themselves posing a threat to the stock or other animals on the farm in her absence. They are unfailingly gentle with all creatures great and small. Well, almost all creatures. Lexie and her beagle friend, Coco, have taken to chasing kangaroos and both maremmas have been known to run after Jen when she's on horseback. 'I guess they're just thinking, *Something's running – this is what we do.*'

'We had a sick piglet one time and some farmhands staying here wanted to try and rear it,' she recalls. 'We named it George and Fly really bonded with that little pig. We'd see her lying out in the sun, curled up, and the piglet would be lying on her.'

Her initial concerns about having two big dogs around Ethan have proved unfounded. Maremmas are known to adore babies and small children, and at Eagle Rock Farm the feeling is mutual. 'I was worried about having a little child with a big dog, but Ethan and the dogs have become the best of friends,' Jen says.

Nevertheless, she always cautions people who tell her they'd like a maremma of their own to thoroughly research the breed. They may be independent, but these are not set-and-forget dogs. They have a purpose and they need a certain degree of autonomy in order to fulfil it, but they also need strong owners to rein them in when necessary.

'I did a lot of research and what they tell you is exactly what you get,' says Jen. 'I do tell people, "You've got to be a little bit careful because they can be *very* protective." They've got to grow up with the animals you want them to guard.'

The funny thing is that, although they're clearly a highly effective team, Lexie and Fly rarely work together.

They seem to have an unspoken agreement that while one performs her sentry duties, the other sticks close to Jen.

'Often one will stay at the house and one will come with me. Rarely will they both come with me,' she says. 'They're very different but I think they're very bonded to each other.'

And bonded to the farmer who gave them the two things they need the most: a job to do and the freedom to do it.

DAISY
DOG GUIDE DOG

It's often the worst of times that bring out the best in people. When the going gets tough, as the expression tells us, the tough get going. They do whatever it takes to cope with life's trials and tribulations. They dig deep, summon all their inner strength, and get to work. They know that being 'tough' really means being resilient. Most importantly, they know that it means never giving up hope.

The same can be said for dogs. It's often when the chips are down that a canine really proves her mettle. Sometimes she has to be at her most vulnerable, and face very dark days indeed, for her courage to shine at its brightest. Give a dog a difficult job and watch her rise to the challenge.

The collie breeds are arguably the most intelligent dogs on the planet. Not only are they extraordinarily perceptive and proactive, they also have excellent memories and are famously tireless workers. Daisy the collie mix is all of these things – and when she met River the Jack Russell terrier, Daisy's smarts told her they should stick together; that there would be safety in numbers.

Daisy and River were rescued from a cruelty situation in rural Pennsylvania in June 2016. Humane law enforcement officers from the Pennsylvania Society for the Prevention of Cruelty to Animals (PSPCA) seized the six-year-old dogs from an owner who, among other allegations, had failed to provide veterinary care.

The pair weren't in a good way when they were delivered to the PSPCA's Philadelphia shelter, 8 kilometres outside the city centre. Daisy had a large wound on her rear end; it was badly infected and had likely never been treated. She was sad, scared and in constant pain.

Pint-sized River was in an even worse state. Both of her eyes were milky white and she had trouble navigating her surroundings. She seemed to have the barest bit of vision, but was effectively blind. While PSPCA vets couldn't say for certain what caused River to lose her sight, it's possible it was a result of long-term untreated eye infections.

PSPCA staff are unfortunately accustomed to seeing abused and neglected dogs come into the shelter, but what really struck the team about Daisy and River was their devotion to each other. They clung to each other like lifeboats on a stormy sea.

Even the most seasoned employees were moved by the best friends' deep bond. 'They were superstars here. Everyone loved them,' says Gillian Kocher, PSPCA's director of public relations and marketing. 'They were always together. They clearly loved each other and needed each other.'

Just how much they needed each other – and how much River, in particular, relies on her canine companion – became clear soon after the dogs arrived at the shelter. Kennel staff quickly got used to the fact that Daisy and River were never more than a couple of feet apart, but it took a little longer for them to realise that something far more complex – and beautiful – was going on.

River stuck close to Daisy so that she never lost her companion's scent. By following it, the partially sighted terrier was able to 'map' her environment. And sometimes Daisy would use her nose to give River a little nudge, steering her in the right direction and letting her pal know she was still there if River seemed lost or disoriented.

Daisy and River are BFFs, but they're also so much more than that. Daisy is River's guide dog.

Nobody can quite agree whether or not dogs form true friendships with each other, but there's a wealth of anecdotal evidence that suggests our four-legged friends are every bit as devoted to *their* four-legged friends as we are to our human pals.

On Christmas Day in 2016, a heroic dog was filmed protecting his friend as she lay injured on snow-covered railway tracks in Uzhgorod, Ukraine. The injured dog had reportedly been hit by a train and her uninjured companion stayed by her side in sub-zero temperatures for two days, shielding her as trains roared over them. (Both dogs were eventually rescued and later adopted by a local family, who named them Lucy and Panda.)

In 2015, Irish setter mix Tillie maintained a week-long vigil by a cistern deep in a remote ravine after her curious playmate, Phoebe the basset hound, fell in. Phoebe was safely rescued. The dogs were well known by residents of Vashon Island, near Seattle, for running off and getting up to mischief together, just like any adventurous young buddies.

Tillie and Phoebe's owner, B.J. Duft, had adopted the impish basset as a friend for Tillie. And just like B.J., many dog owners instinctively seem to understand that their pets enjoy the companionship of their own kind. Multiple-dog households often become so after a second furry friend is acquired as company for the first.

There are also countless heart-wrenching stories of dogs refusing to leave canine friends that have died. Stanley Coren, an author, psychology professor and renowned dog behaviour expert, tells the story of labrador Mickey and his Chihuahua pal, Percy. When Percy was hit by a car and died, a visibly distraught Mickey could not be persuaded to move from his graveside. Several hours later, his owner, William Harrison, discovered that Mickey had opened the grave. William was horrified – until he realised that Percy was in fact still alive. Percy's life was saved because Mickey would not give up on his friend.

New puppy parents, meanwhile, are encouraged to 'socialise' their dog with others, because the ability to get along with their own species is seen as an essential skill.

We praise and reward our dogs when they play nicely with other dogs and often chastise them when they don't. We know that dogs are descended from wolves, and that wolves live in packs, and so we assume that dogs are always happy to spend time with each other.

But are they? Some scientists believe that dogs are more 'frenemies' than friends. In a 2003 study published in the *Canadian Journal of Zoology*, Washington State University researchers Traci Cipponeri and Paul Verrell charted the social structure of a pack of captive wolves and concluded that their relationships were best described as 'uneasy alliances'. They didn't play or voluntarily spend time together unless they were related. In other words, they got along when they had shared goals, but each individual was primarily motivated by his own agenda.

So wolves won't be exchanging friendship bracelets any time soon, but today's domesticated dogs bear virtually no resemblance to their wolf ancestors. They're more likely to live with a pack of humans than other dogs. They don't have to compete for food. They don't have to compete for a mate either, because most are divested of the necessary reproductive equipment at an early age. Some dogs may go days or weeks at a time without ever encountering another of their kind. So why wouldn't they not only enjoy the company of other dogs, but crave it – and form deep, enduring bonds with their canine kin when they have the opportunity?

At the PSPCA shelter, Daisy and River quickly made it clear they had eyes only for each other. Neither dog was particularly interested in her sheltermates and when they were temperament tested to assess their suitability for adoption to a home with dogs already in residence, both Daisy and River communicated in no uncertain terms that they would not like that at all, thank you very much.

'They didn't really interact with the other dogs in the shelter. They were both tested to see if they would be good with other dogs in a home and they were not,' says Gillian. 'They really are all about each other. Who knows – it might have been a protection thing in their former home. We don't know.'

Daisy's wound proved to be stubbornly resistant to antibiotics and she had to have surgery to repair it. When they were separated after the operation, both dogs became depressed.

'We tried to keep them in separate cages in order for Daisy to rest and heal, but they both stopped eating,' Gillian says. 'The solution was simply putting them back together. Once they were together in the same hospital cage they were back to their happy selves.'

Their sadness at being parted may not have been simply because they missed each other. Collies have been bred to work for hundreds of years; their desire to have a job to do is by now an innate *need*. Recuperating in her cage, unable to act as River's 'eyes', Daisy likely felt lost.

'Daisy always watches over River to make sure that she is not in harm's way. Unfortunately there is no way to tell how they communicate with each other exactly, but we are pretty sure that they know each other better than anyone.'

Daisy and River's relationship is not a one-way street, however. While Daisy serves as River's guide dog, River has assumed the role of 'therapy dog' for her faithful friend. Perhaps we could all learn from their collaborative approach to life.

'I don't think that either Daisy or River is "the boss" of the relationship. Instead, they are partners,' says Gillian. 'Daisy does at times nudge River and check in on her and River comforted Daisy as she recovered from her issues. River literally lays on top of Daisy to sleep and that is how they are most comfortable.'

River will always need Daisy to be her 'seeing eye dog'. According to PSPCA vets, the condition of her eyes can make her more prone to certain types of cancer. Eventually, it is likely they will have to be removed. But Gillian is confident River will cope well with this next challenge – especially with doting Daisy by her side.

'Dogs often operate with their other senses, like smell, and I am certain that River follows Daisy's scent to go in the right direction and follow where she leads,' she says.

Their health restored as much as possible, the next step for the inseparable pair was adoption to a loving home. Unfortunately, statistics were not on Daisy and River's side. According to US data analysis website Priceonomics, which sifted through the adoption results of more than 80 000 animals seeking new homes on Petfinder.com, large adult dogs are among the least likely to be adopted – not great news for Daisy. But, sadly, bonded pairs and dogs with special needs are the toughest sell of all, with shelters and animal rescue

groups worldwide frequently running 'choose a less adopt-
able dog' campaigns in a bid to match these forgotten pets
with the forever homes they deserve.

It can be frustrating to see dogs like River and Daisy
being overlooked by potential adopters, but the PSPCA is
nothing if not patient. 'We actually see bonded pairs of animals a lot. It does take a while for them to be adopted, but
we are always confident that we will find the right, loving
homes,' Gillian says.

Happily for Daisy and River, they are almost as fond of
human company as they are of each other. That's sometimes
not the case with bonded pairs, which can be indifferent to
anyone outside their close-knit unit.

'River and Daisy are both very sweet and super friendly
to people. They made it apparent that they love each other,
but they love people too,' she says. 'When people came to
meet them they always got up and went to the front of their
kennel and they greeted people outside when they were on
their walks.'

The shelter was adamant they would not be adopted
separately under any circumstances and that they needed to
be the only dogs in their new home, but aside from that,
their only real stipulation for their new family was that their
unique relationship be respected and Daisy be allowed to
get on with the job of guiding River through life.

'They couldn't go into a home with young children, but
respectful older children were possible,' says Gillian. 'Other
than that, they simply needed to be loved. Adopting a dog is
always a responsibility, but as long as you know what you

are getting into ahead of time, you can easily look past their additional needs. These two may have had additional medical needs, but they were also pretty cool customers.'

The great news is that Daisy and River *did* find a home together. They were adopted by a Philadelphia couple in September 2016 and have been lavished with love ever since. They even had starring roles on their dogparents' 2016 Christmas card.

But even if they had never found a home, that would have been okay – the PSPCA is a no-kill organisation and never euthanises animals for reasons of time or space. Besides, Daisy and River were not exactly lacking in love at the shelter. 'The ideal outcome for Daisy and River was always going to be finding a home together,' Gillian says. 'While we knew we would all be sad to see them go, we also couldn't wait for that moment.'

The girls' dedication to each other captured imaginations around the globe. River and Daisy's friendship was chronicled by countless media outlets, including *Huffington Post* and The Dodo. Gillian says the international attention took everyone by surprise, but it's not hard to see why the dogs' story has touched people's hearts.

'I think it is simply that they are so unique and clearly love each other and need each other,' she says. 'Sometimes when dogs – or people – come from tough circumstances, they need each other to become whole again. That is most certainly the case with Daisy and River.'

Daisy and River are made of tough stuff. They came from a terrible situation, and they certainly have the war wounds to show for it, but they have not only survived, they have thrived. Daisy knows she's doing important work. She finds solace in helping her companion 'see' the world, while River's greatest comfort is just being close to her best friend.

And they will continue to tackle anything life can throw at them head on – just as long as they're together.

CHLOE, JACKSON & SWAYZE

FILM STARS

The film and television-viewing public has always had a voracious appetite for animal stories, from *Mr Ed*'s talking horse to the titular brown bear in *Gentle Ben* and Australia's own *Skippy the Bush Kangaroo*. But the animal that has enjoyed the most screen time – and captured the most hearts – is undoubtedly man's best friend.

Dog tales, it seems, are screen gold. German shepherd Rin Tin Tin was a bona fide matinee idol. Fiercely intelligent Lassie remains the ultimate indefatigable canine hero. *The Littlest Hobo* was an after-school rite of passage for children of the 1980s, while *Old Yeller* is still breaking hearts sixty years after its release. And in 2011 and 2012, Uggie the Jack Russell terrier won almost as many awards for his role in the Oscar-winning *The Artist* as the film itself.

But even as we've devoured heartwarming tales of dogs saving human lives or travelling vast distances to make it home to their families, a rumour has been circulating. A nasty rumour implying that four-legged performers are high maintenance and unruly. A shocking suggestion that perhaps dogs don't make for ideal co-stars.

The American actor and comedian W.C. Fields famously quipped, 'Never work with children or animals.' It would be easy to dismiss the hard-drinking, acerbic Fields as an ornery old curmudgeon – if so many others in showbusiness hadn't secretly (and not-so-secretly) endorsed his opinion over the years. (Indeed, screenwriter Leo Rosten later said of Fields that 'any man who hates dogs and babies can't be all bad.')

So just how did canine screen stars earn such a bad reputation? Could it be they're divas behind the scenes? Maybe they're not suitably reverent towards A-list stars and directors. They might be too expensive or too difficult to control. Perhaps they're prone to napping at inopportune moments or mistaking prop trees and fire hydrants for the real thing.

The more likely possibility is that dogs are just, well, *dogs*. They like to sniff stuff and pilfer treats and lick certain body parts that really should not be licked in polite company. They don't always follow instructions. Dogs do things their own way and in their own time.

That's a big part of the reason why Loretta Rabbitt loves dogs so much – and poodles in particular. Loretta doesn't subscribe to the notion that dogs are hard to work with. After all, she is the owner and trainer of three of the most in-demand dog actors in Australia – and her troupe of performers are always consummate professionals. According to Loretta, the rules of a film set may mean nothing to a canine actor, but his bond with his trainer means *everything*.

'I work very hard on that bond because if it isn't there you won't get them to work. It's the same with children – people want them to be so well behaved, but they're *kids*. If you put your thumb on them the whole time they'll lose their personality and it's the same with dogs,' she says.

Loretta has always had a soft spot for animals. Growing up in Sydney's eastern suburbs, she was rarely without a pet. 'I had ducks and turtles and all sorts of things. I always had dogs as a young child. I didn't do any training with them, just had the dog that lived out in the yard and came in every so often,' she says.

When she married in 1976 and later built her dream home in Sutherland Shire, dogs were Loretta's constant companions. She dabbled in basic obedience training and found she enjoyed it, but it wasn't until she welcomed Louis, her first poodle, twenty years ago that Loretta was well and truly hooked.

'Louis was an apricot colour and he was such a well-behaved little dog. He was such a lovely dog that I realised the poodle was the breed I wanted to live with,' she says.

When Louis passed away in 2000 at the incredible age of twenty-two, Loretta got a chocolate brown poodle called Peppi. Next came Harry, a red poodle who proved to be a natural in competitive agility. Then, in 2005, Chloe arrived. Having won several agility titles with Harry, Loretta was looking for a new challenge. She found it when she discovered the sport of doggy dancing or, to use its official name, Dances with Dogs (internationally the sport is known as canine musical freestyle).

'I used to be a dancer many years ago and when I saw this new sport I thought, *I love this!* I got really involved in it and really got into competitions with Chloe,' she says.

Doggy dancing became a titled sport and Chloe became the first dog in Australia to win a dance championship. Loretta also qualified as a judge and began running workshops in canine choreography.

The pretty white poodle and her energetic owner soon became well known for their dance performances – and for the deep bond and dedicated training that produced them. In 2012, Loretta and Chloe even performed together on the TV talent show *Australia's Got Talent*. Their reputation as a symbiotic team reached beyond the canine dancing world and others started to take notice.

'When Chloe was a couple of years old I got a call from an agent. They wanted a toy poodle that was trained and somebody had said, "Loretta has a poodle and she's amazing,"' she says.

Chloe was cast in a television car commercial. The ad featured enormous animatronic crocodiles, but Chloe wasn't the least bit fazed by her reptilian co-stars. 'She had to pick up a stick and walk backwards and all this stuff she could easily do,' says Loretta.

The ad's producers were impressed and Loretta soon started fielding more casting calls for her camera-loving canine. 'I started getting more and more calls to do ad work.

If someone wants a poodle that's trained, they'll always give me a call.'

In 2009, when Chloe was four, another white poodle called Jackson joined the family. He was named after the 'King of Pop', Michael Jackson, who sadly died soon after. Like his namesake, Jackson also earned plaudits for his dance moves, following in Chloe's footsteps to appear on *Australia's Got Talent*.

Jackson very nearly upstaged celebrity chef Manu Feildel when he was cast alongside him in a series of Campbell's soup TV commercials in 2013 and 2014. 'The Campbell's ads with Manu were fun because there was a lot going on and he had to do more training,' she says. 'He worked really hard on that because he had a lot of takes to do.'

Chloe also got a taste of celebrity when she appeared in a music video with singer Dami Im, who won the fifth season of *The X Factor* and later represented Australia in the Eurovision song contest. Chloe was also cast in a production for the popular short film festival Tropfest and impressed everyone with her professionalism.

'Because of budget constraints it had to be filmed in a single day. She was there, ready to start work, at 7 a.m. and she really had to work her little bottom off that day,' says Loretta. 'If they were changing the scene she would just lay her head down and have a little sleep.'

Loretta always takes a crate with her to shoots so that the dogs have somewhere to retreat and rest when the frenetic pace of the film set gets a bit much. There's also lots of downtime on shoots – it's not all glitz and glamour.

'You might see something on TV that lasts a split second but the dog might have done that seventy times. They like going in the crate because it gives them a little bit of peace,' she says. 'There's a lot of sitting around in television. A shoot may go until 7 or 8 p.m. and you have to sit for hours, so they've learned that you catch a nap whenever you can. They know exactly how to chill out.'

But Loretta says she never has any trouble getting her dogs 'into character' when it's their time to shine. 'When they're not working I put them in the crate or they go in my lap and lay down, but as soon as I put that dog down on the ground it will be "on". It's high as a kite, ready to go. They just love to work.'

Poodles are like lollies: it's impossible to stop at just one – or even at two. Chloe and Jackson were joined in 2009 by Swayze, an exuberant white poodle that Loretta describes as 'the wild boy' of the pack. His name was inspired by *Dirty Dancing* star Patrick Swayze who, like the dogs, had started his career as a dancer before moving into acting. (Like Jackson's namesake, Patrick Swayze also passed away soon after Loretta named her dog in his honour. 'Unfortunately, every time I name a dog that person dies!' she says.)

'I just love poodles. They're such lovely dogs and they love their owners. They want to be on you all the time, but they're so tiny you can have a few of them lying all over your lap,' Loretta laughs. 'I didn't want dogs that would want to be outside all the time. They always put me in a good mood.'

Though Swayze is a much-loved pet, he was also an experiment of sorts for Loretta. With Chloe and Jackson's acting careers taking off, and with everything she had learned about training in the years since she began working with them, she was curious to see whether she could have similar success with another dog.

'It takes about three years to train a dog up to a really good level. Chloe is eleven now, so she's getting on a bit, and I thought it was a good idea to start bringing another dog up through the ranks,' she says. 'After training Chloe and Jackson I felt I was a better trainer so I thought it would be interesting to see whether I could do it again.'

It turns out she could – Swayze has taken to his training with just as much enthusiasm as his canine siblings. But it's precisely that ebullience that can make him a handful at times. 'Swayze is like an adolescent and he runs all over the place like a lunatic. It's been trouble to contain his personality,' Loretta laughs. 'He's a great working dog, but when he's not working he'll be running through the house with a toilet roll in his mouth, pulling it apart. He's always jumping up in the air.'

All three dogs have vastly different personalities. Jackson is as mellow and cuddly as Swayze is excitable. When they're not acting or dancing, the dogs are regular visitors to the Sydney Children's Hospital as part of the Delta Society's therapy dogs program – and it's Jackson who connects most deeply with the kids. 'Jackson is usually such a "go, go" dog, but with the palliative care kids he just goes and lays down and will spend forty minutes sitting there with his head on their arm, just looking at them,' she says. 'I haven't got to ask him to stay, he'll just walk in and do it. He understands he's got to be really quiet. It isn't an easy thing for a dog to do, but he just seems to love it. Swayze always has a "party" look on his face, but Jackson has a very sweet look on his.'

And while each member of the trio is staggeringly clever, Jackson is also the most biddable of the three when it comes to learning and perfecting new skills. 'Jackson is about the easiest dog you could ever get with training. He always just wants to please.'

Chloe, meanwhile, is Queen Bee – and she doesn't care who knows it. 'They're all so different that you can't have a favourite, but I suppose Chloe got me into everything so she's put up on a pedestal. She gets a lot of privileges,' Loretta admits. 'Chloe is well known to be a diva – she's like that because she's allowed to be now! She was always a very cheeky little dog. She's the princess of the house. She's a very smart dog and she takes it to the nth degree. She's not just a dog, she goes out there like she's the Queen of the World.'

And like any starlet, Chloe can be quite particular about how and with whom she works. She is decidedly *not* fond of sharing the limelight. She was not best pleased, for example, when the makers of a TV ad for celebrity fitness guru Michelle Bridges couldn't decide which dog to use. They asked Loretta to bring all three so they could decide on the day, much to Chloe's chagrin. (Chloe was chosen to appear in the ad, but so was Jackson, and she still hasn't let him live it down.)

'Chloe is always trying to get the other two out of the way. If there's a prop or something she will just get on it so they can't,' she laughs. 'She's a very pushy little girl – she likes things her own way! If we're doing dancing she likes her own numbers and she will not work with the others. Jackson and Swayze will happily work with each other, but nobody else works with Chloe.'

Being a canine screen star is a serious, time-consuming business. Loretta ensures Chloe, Jackson and Swayze get daily exercise – she even has a walking machine for them if inclement weather precludes an outdoor stroll. They eat a fresh, raw food diet that is delivered by a specialist pet nutrition company.

She drills all three dogs on their obedience fundamentals every morning before she goes to her own full-time job as an accountant and will spend more time training them to do specific tasks or tricks in the lead-up to a job. When training, she offers the dogs healthy food rewards such as raw mince or boiled chicken – no commercial, additive-packed treats. 'If the dog is really tired at the end of a long day I'll pull out something really special like a piece of cheese or one of their lovely biscuits,' she says.

Loretta is registered with three different talent agents, each of whom casts different types of projects, though the dogs' reputation as reliable (and adorable) performers is so well established that production companies and producers often contact her directly. Each dog also has his or her own professional portfolio and Loretta will sometimes shoot 'audition videos' for them.

'Agents and directors like to see the front and side view, they want to see the whole look of a dog. Often they will want to know if the dog can do something specific, so I'll film them on my phone and send it off,' she says. 'Because they do a lot of training, they can learn a new trick very quickly. I'll say, "No, they don't do that – but when I go home this afternoon they will!" Just because a dog can do something at home it doesn't mean they can do it on a set or when they're tired, but if I say my dogs can do something, they can do it.'

When she's on set with the dogs, their welfare and comfort is Loretta's chief priority. She isn't afraid to advocate for her pets or turn down work all together if she doesn't feel comfortable. Sometimes she will also bring in additional resources to help the dogs do their job to the best of their ability.

'Jackson had to ride in a motorbike side car in the Campbell's ad. I wanted to make sure he was capable of doing that so I did some lessons with him on a bike because he'd never been on one before,' she explains. 'There was one shot they would have liked of him going down the street by himself with Manu, but I said no because he wouldn't have been able to see me. If he can see me he knows he's safe. There's no pushing. In that instance they used the fake dog that I'd brought along. I go out prepared and that's why we get a lot of callbacks.'

As much as the dogs enjoy their jobs, the bottom line for Loretta is that the work must be fun. 'It's a big day and they should be enjoying the whole lot. If I get phoned for a job that I don't think is a nice job then I won't do it. Jackson doesn't like yelling, for example, so I don't put him in that position,' she says. 'If I had a dog that I didn't think had the temperament to do it, I wouldn't do it. That's why it's good to have a few dogs.'

Chloe is getting older and works a little less these days, though she does still appear in television commercials. She has also retired from her visits to Sydney Children's Hospital. But Jackson and Swayze are still very popular poodles indeed.

'The jobs we want to do more of are the tough ones where they've got to do a lot of tricks because they get to use all their skills. It's always fun to go out and do something where you're a bit of a star,' says Loretta.

People have suggested that Chloe, Jackson and Swayze only work as well as they do because there's a steady stream of tasty incentives. But Loretta knows it's their devotion to her, and the bond they share, that keeps her dogs in high demand.

'People say, "Oh, they do it for the food, Loretta." I'll get a big piece of mince out of the fridge and hand it to my husband and he'll call them, but they still come to me even if I've got nothing,' she says.

She believes any dog can achieve screen stardom if his owner is willing to put the time and effort into his training. 'Some people say, "My dog's dumb." Dogs are not dumb, but most haven't been taught to use their brains,' she says.

When the time is right for Chloe, Jackson and Swayze to retire from acting, Loretta will have no hesitation in letting them put their paws up – a stage mum she's not. 'I do see people that keep pushing their dogs along and I think, *Maybe that dog deserves a quiet life*. There comes a time when they can have a few extra sleeps up on the lounge,' she says. 'Mine do a lot of work, but they're all my pets and that's the reason I have them. I do love having them around.'

Never work with children or animals? W.C. Fields obviously never met dogs like Chloe, Jackson or Swayze.

EMMA
FOX DETECTOR DOG

Stefan Hattingh has always loved dogs. Born and raised in Johannesburg, South Africa, he owned Weimaraners and was a successful trainer of German Shorthaired Pointers (GSP) for use as gun dogs – hunting dogs used to find and retrieve game. He even trained the offspring of a South African champion.

When he moved to Australia in 2014, he wanted a pet dog whose love of our famously active, outdoorsy lifestyle would match his own. As the operations manager for Brisbane's Bulimba Creek Catchment Coordinating Committee (B4C) – a not-for-profit organisation that coordinates dozens of green groups working to protect a network of suburban creeks and tributaries – Stefan spends as much time as he can in the great outdoors. There was no doubt in his mind as to which breed would share his enthusiasm for the environment: it had to be a GSP.

Pointing breeds can be traced back to Europe and England around the 1650s and are thought to descend from the Old Spanish Pointer. The GSP was developed in Germany in the mid-nineteenth century as a hunting dog. The 'pointer' part of the name comes from the dogs' habit of freezing, lifting a paw and aiming their muzzle towards the hunter's quarry.

'Pointers love being active – they are not docile dogs. They've got to be stimulated all the time or they'll give themselves a job and start herding geckos and all sorts of things,' he laughs. 'I love canoeing, swimming, running and walking in Brisbane's parks and I wanted a dog that would do all that with me. People look at my dog and look at me and say, "You're the same."'

In 2015, Stefan found Emma, a GSP puppy whose mother had been a champion working dog in South Australia. Highly intelligent, unfailingly enthusiastic and in possession of a keen sense of smell, Emma was the perfect dog for Stefan. Their bond was immediate. 'She watches every move I make. She's so eager to learn all the time. She's almost obsessed with pleasing me.'

With Emma by his side, Stefan quickly discovered why the GSP is often ranked in the top 10 breeds for scenting ability. 'The first year I had her, I rescued so many lorikeets and a frogmouth – because Emma's nose is so sensitive, she would constantly find injured ones,' he says. 'She's a hunting dog, but now she only does rescue.'

From day one, without any training, the beautiful liver-and-white GSP also displayed her breed's instinctive pointing behaviour. 'I especially love taking her for a walk in the park after a storm because she points at everything.'

A firm believer that dogs should have the opportunity to do what they were traditionally bred to do, Stefan began to wonder whether Emma's innate need to search and find in the great outdoors could be utilised for environmental work.

'There's a massive movement towards using dogs for all sorts of things: drug detection, conservation, sniffing out certain weed species and even certain fish species,' he says. 'Dogs can even find platypuses. They are such a handy tool.'

Through his work with B4C, Stefan knew some other green groups and councils that were already using dogs in a range of ecology-focused roles. 'Brisbane, Moreton Bay and Redlands City Councils use cane toad detection dogs on Moreton Island in Moreton Bay,' he says. 'They run up and down the islands to make sure there are no cane toads.' If a wily toad does manage to find his way onto an island, the dogs will quickly track it down. 'Even if the cane toad buries himself, the dog can find him.'

Another Queensland group, OWAD Environment, uses two trained English springer spaniels, Taz and Nutmeg, to find koala and quoll habitats. Incredibly, the dogs will likely never see a koala or any of the three quoll species they're trained to sniff out. They work exclusively with the animals' droppings.

'The dog doesn't even know what a koala looks like because they only find scat, but they can find koala scat that's up to two years old,' Stefan explains. 'The argument is, "If I can't see a koala in the habitat then it's not koala habitat and doesn't need protection," but koalas move a lot and may only visit once a year. If scat is found, then by default it becomes protected koala habitat, even if there's currently no koalas in the whole park.'

Perhaps, Stefan mused, giving Emma a job could help him to be more effective in his own role. His first thought was to train his clever dog to detect fire ants, which have been found in several Brisbane suburbs. One of the world's most invasive species, these ants eat or damage seeds, causing major damage to ecosystems over time. They also attack insects and animals that pollinate native plants, and their painful sting poses a safety risk to people using public spaces.

A dog trained to detect fire ant nests can cover a hectare of land in a matter of minutes and smell a single ant from more than 30 metres away, even if the ant is 20 centimetres underground.

Ultimately, however, it was an even more virulent pest that captured Stefan's attention: *Vulpes vulpes*, better known as the European red fox.

For those outside of Brisbane, the upmarket suburb of Bulimba is perhaps best known as the home of erstwhile Prime Minister Kevin Rudd. It is also home to Bulimba Creek and lends its name to the Bulimba Creek Catchment, which spans 122 square kilometres and comprises twenty of Brisbane's eastern and south-eastern suburbs.

The catchment is ringed by significant remnant forest and contains sixteen bushland remnants, seven freshwater swamplands and ten significant riparian wetlands. Bushland vegetation and wetlands make up about 10 per cent of the catchment, which in turn makes up about 10 per cent of Brisbane's area. In environmental terms, it's kind of a big deal.

Protecting, restoring and maintaining the catchment is a massive undertaking. The once-pristine land within it is today used for a mix of residential, rural-residential, commercial, industrial, recreational and open-space purposes. As well as damaging land uses, the catchment's biggest problems include urban development, tree clearing, weeds – and foxes.

There is perhaps no more ruthless or efficient killer in the animal kingdom than the European red fox. Australian history has its fair share of dark days, but arguably none darker in an ecological sense than the day in 1855 that foxes were introduced for recreational hunting. In less than two decades, fox populations were established in the wild. Within 100 years the auburn assassins had spread across three quarters of the continent. They cost the economy an estimated $227.5 million per year in sheep production losses, environmental impact, research, eradication and management.

Today there are thought to be almost as many foxes in Australia as people. In most regions there are between one and four foxes per square kilometre, but in some places – such as swamps and semi-urban areas – there can be more than ten per square kilometre. The tropical north and a handful of offshore islands are the only regions that have managed to keep them at bay. Tasmania was fox free until the late 1990s, but illegal introductions quickly led to a low-density fox population across much of the island and eradication programs have been underway since 2002.

Savage though they may be, a fox's adaptability, resourcefulness and cunning also demand a sort of begrudging respect. Foxes are not only able to exist, but flourish, virtually anywhere. In Australia, they thrive on the coast, in the arid red centre of the continent, in alpine regions blanketed by snow in winter, and increasingly in urban areas. They're prolific reproducers, too: every year, up to 97 per cent of vixens give birth to between three and five cubs each. And though not quite an apex predator, there are few other animals that pose any real threat to a fox (though dingoes do seem to have a taste for fox cubs). While undoubtedly a vicious menace, they are about as tenacious and resilient as invasive species get.

They're also an unmitigated environmental disaster. Foxes are opportunistic omnivores – they eat almost anything, scavenging and preying on whatever is available, mainly small animals, insects and fruit. They are also accomplished hunters with adventurous appetites – virtually no animal weighing less than 6 kilograms is safe. A single fox eats less than half a kilo of food a night – around 150 kilograms per year – but they take a smorgasbord approach to their meals, killing several animals each night and eating only a small amount of each. Unlike most other predators, which kill only for survival, the fox seems to take perverse pleasure in wholesale slaughter.

In the Bulimba Creek Catchment, foxes are everywhere. 'The impact is far, far greater than people realise. Look at blue tongue lizards or bearded dragons – their numbers are going down. They're such slow things and they've never evolved to deal with these predators,' says Stefan. 'Water mice are native to Australia and live in salt marsh areas, but every single nest gets taken out by the foxes. They come all the way into the salt marshes. Those small animals are such soft targets. On the Sunshine Coast the turtle nests suffer huge losses. One fox can destroy several nests in a single night.'

This 'surplus killing' is thought to be largely responsible for the rapid mainland extinction or reduction of a huge number of native animals. According to Agriculture Victoria, foxes have had a major role in the extinction of many ground-dwelling native species in the last 130 years. They are considered a threat to fourteen species of birds, forty-eight mammals, twelve reptiles and two amphibians. Thanks to the humble fox, the orange-bellied parrot, spotted quail-thrush, herald petrel, Gilbert's potoroo and western swamp tortoise are now critically endangered. Meanwhile, efforts to save threatened species including the malleefowl, bridled nail-tail wallaby and night parrot are continually undermined by foxes. The cunning creatures also prey on newborn lambs, kid goats and poultry.

Long story short, foxes are seriously bad news. They're the animal equivalent of a movie supervillain: cold, clever and mysterious, moving unseen through the night like bloodthirsty shadows.

'When you find a fox den, within a radius of fifty metres there's not even insects. They eat literally everything that moves and then they move the den,' Stefan says. 'They're super adaptive. They can walk around without being observed. They don't cross roads – they'd rather run a couple of kilometres up the road and use a drain or culvert. They're too streetwise.'

So it's no surprise that putting an end to – or at least limiting – their collective reign of terror is a high priority for federal and state governments, local councils and conservation agencies like B4C. The strategies most commonly used to keep the dreaded butchers at bay include poison baiting, shooting, trapping, electric fencing, den fumigation and habitat manipulation.

The problem is that no single method is successful on its own and, even when a combination of measures is used, reinvasion or immigration from other areas usually happens within two to six weeks. 'The tail is almost wagging the dog at the moment because councils only deal with complaints – they go and catch foxes and feral cats when people complain about them,' Stefan says. 'But suburbia is sprawling all over and natural areas are getting fragmented more and more. You don't see foxes. You only know they're there when your chooks start disappearing, and for the ecological impact that's too little too late. It's in the natural areas that foxes are a major problem.'

That means the agencies tasked with getting rid of foxes are constantly on the lookout for new weapons to add to their collective arsenal. In recent years, for example, a growing number of organisations, as well as individual farmers, have turned to guard animals such as llamas, alpacas, donkeys and dogs in a bid to protect calves, lambs, goat kids, poultry and even fairy penguins from foxes (see Lexie and Fly's story on page 180).

Controlling fox numbers is a big part of B4C's catchment protection strategy and, like virtually everyone else working in ecology, Stefan was frustrated by their indomitable persistence. It was time to try something different, to shift the focus from safeguarding the marauders' preferred prey or waiting for foxes to wander into traps or swallow baits. It was time to take the fight right to them – with help from Emma and her amazing nose.

Stefan had been training Emma to respond to basic obedience commands since she was about nine months old. He knew she was a fast learner and an eager student. Training her to find fox dens should be as simple as introducing her to the pungent smell of fox urine. But, where animals are concerned, nothing is simple.

'Not every dog is suitable for fox detection. Some dogs get obsessed with being praised. Some will do anything for a treat. You can't use food as a reward because within two weeks the dog will figure out that I can't smell what he can smell, and he'll start faking it,' Stefan explains.

The majority of professional detection dogs are rewarded with a few minutes of play with a high-value toy. Knowing Emma had a definite soft spot for her tennis ball, Stefan decided to start there.

'With fox detection, you need to imprint the dog with the scent. I started by having Emma play with a tennis ball that I'd put fox scat and urine on, so that when she goes into the field she'll think she's looking for a tennis ball,' he says. 'In her whole life, Emma will probably never see a fox. She'll just think she needs a tennis ball that smells like a fox.'

The fact that a dog can find an underground fox den hidden in dense bushland using just her nose is impressive enough, but Emma's ability to tell the difference between fox scat and, say, possum poo is really astonishing. So just *how* does she do it? Finding and tracking the odour in the first place is made possible by the hundreds of millions of scent receptors inside the dog's nose. Their olfactory bulb – the part of the brain devoted to analysing smells – is also about forty times bigger than a human's. But scientists now believe canines can differentiate between dozens of similar smells because they have a dedicated 'smell zone' within their airways.

A team of bioengineers at Pennsylvania State University found that dogs have a fold of tissue inside their nose that splits inhaled air into two separate 'flow paths'. One goes to the lungs, for respiration, while the other detours to a nook at the back of the nose where a network of tiny bones called turbinates filters out scent molecules for the brain to interpret. Dogs can even move their nostrils independently, funnelling odours directly into the turbinates for analysis.

Training with the urine-soaked tennis ball enabled Stefan to be certain Emma would follow her nose straight to a fox den.

'I can't see what she's smelling, so I've got to test her. The tennis ball works well because I know where it goes when I throw it, but she can't see it, so she's got to use her scenting ability to find it,' he says.

After 12 months of training with Stefan and a six-week professional certification course, Emma started work as B4C's official fox sniffer dog in the winter months of 2017. Together, she and Stefan scan a sweep of land. They conduct their searches during the day, when the foxes are sleeping, rather than at night when they're on the move. When Emma locates a fox den, she's rewarded with a few precious minutes of play with her tennis ball and Stefan sends the GPS coordinates to a private contractor or, if the den is on public land, Brisbane City Council, who dispatch animal control staff to humanely exterminate the foxes.

'They have to be obsessed with catching a ball. If you watch those border patrol programs filmed at the airport, the dogs think they're finding a toy. They stare when they find that smell and then they get their toy,' says Stefan. 'It's all a game.'

Emma is extra effective because she is permitted to work on property the council doesn't have access to – B4C also works with the Queensland government's Department of Transport and Main Roads, the Port of Brisbane, electricity provider Powerlink, water retailer Queensland Urban Utilities and toll roads management corporation Transurban.

She may have more than a hundred years of hunting heritage in her DNA, but Emma never chases or kills the animals herself. 'She's not an aggressive dog, which is what makes her a suitable dog for this. A fox would turn on her and she would run away, which is what you want,' says Stefan.

Of course, Emma's training wasn't only focused on finding fox hideouts. Stefan also had to teach her how to avoid dangers she might encounter while doing her job.

'They put these fox baits out, so she's not allowed to eat anything she finds out in the field. Without even finding foxes, these are the things she's got to look for,' he says. 'When they're young they eat everything, so as part of our training I put little pieces of meat and things out and she can't eat anything until I give it to her. She's very good with that.'

Snakes are another professional hazard involved in working outside, even in the suburbs of Brisbane. 'I had to get her used to snakes so that if she smells a snake out in the field she'll back off completely,' says Stefan. 'At our depot we get quite a few carpet pythons and they shed their skin, so I just used snakeskin and droppings to start with. When I say no to her she knows she's in trouble, so I'd just get her close to the smell of a snake and give her that negative experience.'

North of Brisbane at Mon Repos, the Queensland Parks and Wildlife Service also uses dogs to detect dens during turtle mating season. An established loggerhead turtle breeding colony in the national park was all but decimated by foxes, which would sniff out the turtles' nests and eat the eggs. After losing close to 100 nests each season, the dogs were introduced. Their work means the Mon Repos area will once again become a sustainable habitat for the turtles.

For Stefan, seeing dogs successfully tackling the fox problem beyond the Bulimba Creek Catchment is heartening – not just because fragile habitats and native animals now have a fighting chance against a voracious killer, but because the dogs have the opportunity to use their considerable smarts in a role they were quite literally born to do.

So many working breeds find themselves homeless or surrendered to shelters because of so-called 'destructive behaviour', when in many cases they're only doing what their genetic makeup drives them to do.

'These dogs were bred for specific things and you've got to use those traits that they were bred for,' says Stefan. 'What's nice about this is that one dog, depending on their ability, can be trained to detect a couple of different odours. I can move the tennis ball over to another scent. It just can't be crossed with a fox scent.'

But while Emma has become a valued member of the B4C team, she remains Stefan's pet first and foremost. 'Some dogs are proper working dogs. They never go in the house and there's no interaction with their handler beyond the job,' he says. 'That's not why I got Emma and that's not what I want to do. Emma just loves people and loves attention. She always wants to run up and say hello to people. We do everything together.'

Whether at work or at play, a man and his dog can be a formidable team.

MONTGOMARY

BLOOD DONOR

Montgomary the golden retriever didn't set out to be a lifesaver. He never aspired to one of the most important jobs a dog can have. It wasn't in his plans to give an incredible gift to a total stranger. Monty was perfectly content living a quiet life in his family's Sydney apartment, enjoying multiple daily walks and cuddles on tap.

But life had another path in mind for him – because some dogs are born great, while others have greatness thrust upon them.*

Monty joined student veterinarian Kate Chambers and her family as a lively puppy in January 2012, six months after their much-loved West Highland white terrier, Angus, passed away at the age of eleven. Angus had been the perfect size for the Chambers clan during the four years they

---

* This isn't true. All dogs are, in fact, born great and that is science.

Would you work seven days a week for nothing more than treats and cuddles? Frankie the labrador does – she's a therapy dog at Sydney's Bear Cottage, a hospice for children with life-limiting illnesses. It's Frankie's job to put a smile on the faces of sick children and their families, and she always gives it 100 per cent. *(Bear Cottage)*

Coop's quiet reassurance makes it easier for young victims of violence and trauma to tell their stories. She's on track to become one of the first comfort dogs to accompany witnesses into Victorian courtrooms. *(Tessa Stow)*

Jen and Ric Dalitz were at their wits' end when foxes and wild dogs killed every lamb on their Southern Highlands property in NSW – so they turned to the maremma, an ancient herding and protecting breed. Since Lexie and Fly arrived, not a single animal has been lost. *(Jen Dalitz)*

Whoever said 'never work with children or animals' had clearly never met Loretta Rabbitt's consummate professionals, Chloe, Jackson and Swayze. The pretty poodles are among Australia's most in-demand canine actors. *(Joy Towell/Always Joy Photography)*

She's not only a much-loved pet, Emma the German shorthaired pointer is also an essential weapon in the fight against foxes. Working in Brisbane's Bulimba Creek catchment, Emma's powerful nose sniffs out fox dens, protecting native wildlife. *(Stefan Hattingh)*

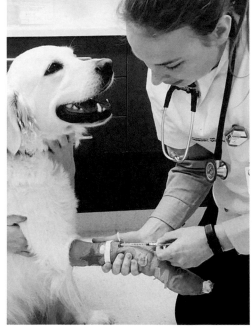

Around Australia, veterinary clinics rely on donated blood to save the lives of critically ill dogs – but few dog owners realise their pets can volunteer as blood donors. What's the official job title for dogs like Montgomary that donate blood? 'Good boy', of course. *(University Veterinary Teaching Hospital Sydney at the University of Sydney)*

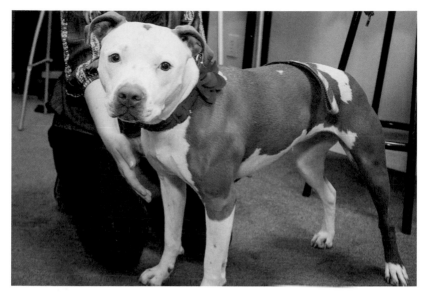

Rescued pit bull Brynneth Pawltrow – Brynn for short – isn't just the mayor of Rabbit Hash, Kentucky, she's also a tail-wagging ambassador for arguably the most misunderstood dog breed. *(Jordie Bamforth)*

When River and Daisy were rescued together from a cruelty situation in Pennsylvania, shelter staff were astonished to discover the dogs aren't just best friends – Daisy also acts as partially sighted River's guide dog. *(Pennsylvania SPCA)*

One of just a handful of accelerant detection dogs working in Australasia, Viking uses his powerful nose to zero in on the causes of suspicious fires. His reward for combing hazardous fire scenes? A few minutes of play with a rolled-up towel! *(Gianluca Bertoldi)*

Bindi and Rex are two of the dozens of working dogs helping at-risk young people through the Backtrack programs in northern NSW. They're owned by youth worker Nathan Bliss, whose own life changed for the better as a teenager after meeting Backtrack founder Bernie Shakeshaft and a dog named Girl. *(Nathan Bliss)*

He may be small, but TruMan – aka 'the dirt doxie' – is a force to be reckoned with in the world of ultramarathon running. With his colourful owner, Catra Corbett, TruMan has completed dozens of competitive races and is showing no sign of slowing down.
(Catra Corbett)

With wildlife an ever-present hazard at Michigan's Cherry Capital Airport, operations supervisor Brian Edwards was looking for a creative solution – and he found it in his indefatigable dog, Piper, whose job is to chase animals away from aircraft and runways.
(Brian Edwards)

Afghanistan veteran Scott Jackman was at rock bottom, developing PTSD after injuries ended his military career. He credits his assistance dog, Whiskey, not only with saving his life, but inspiring Scott to help other returned servicemen and women through his charity Whiskey's Wish. *(Amanda Hughes and Garth Kirkwood)*

lived in teeming Hong Kong, where Kate's father worked in taxation for an Asia Pacific company. (Angus was an exceptionally worldly dog, having also lived in France and the UK.) But after the family returned to Sydney in 2005 and Angus died, they decided they wanted a bigger, more active dog. Her parents had previously owned labradors and German shepherds and wanted a friendly and sociable dog that they could take to the park.

There was an added incentive for Kate, who was about to embark on her first year of a veterinary science degree at the University of Sydney. 'My mum thought it was important for me before starting vet school to actually see a puppy being raised and to go to puppy school and all of that,' says Kate.

Though she has loved animals all her life and juggles her studies with part-time work as a vet nurse, Kate spent more time with farm animals growing up than with the domestic pets that would likely be her bread and butter as a city vet.

'I've loved animals since I was young. I used to want to be a human doctor, but decided I didn't want to go down that track. Meeting the vets that I did through my own animals, plus my granddad has a beef cattle property and meeting the vets on the property, it just seemed like something I'd be interested in,' she says.

So Monty joined the family and soon settled in. After a rocky start, he even won over the resident cat, Casper the Birman. 'Casper is ten years old and he's got a lot of personality. He's boss of the world,' Kate laughs. 'He walks up to the dog and the dog gets out of the way. The dog will get off his bed so the cat can sleep on it. Casper beat Monty up as a puppy, but they like each other now. When I get up in the morning they'll be sharing a bed. They each get distressed if the other one's away.'

While debate rages around whether large-breed dogs are suited to living in high-density housing, Monty took to apartment living with aplomb. Rules vary from state to state, but many apartment complexes will permit residents to have a maximum of two dogs, each weighing under 10 kilograms. Monty weighs 30 kilos, but because the Chambers' apartment is in a development with a large number of Australian Defence Force members in residence – many of whom have large dogs – the rules were changed in Monty's favour.

'It took him a while to get used to going in the lift, but a couple of bags of chicken treats later he's fine with it,' she says. 'My mum is retired now and my brother is also home a lot of the time when he's not at university, so Monty goes on probably six walks a day now. He chases his ball around. He's really happy in the apartment.'

And so Monty's life may have simply trundled pleasantly on, with his walks and ball games and good-natured spats with the cat filling his days. That was until Kate discovered that canine blood stocks are dangerously low and blood donors are in incredibly short supply.

Monty was about to be put to work.

Anyone who has ever seen a Red Cross appeal for blood donations knows how important donors are. One in three people will need a blood transfusion at some point – somewhere in Australia, someone needs blood every twenty-four seconds. A single blood donation can be used in up to twenty-two different medical procedures, from cancer and blood disease treatments to surgeries and trauma cases, such as road accidents.

It's a similar story for dogs. With Australians owning millions of pet dogs, the demand for blood donations is high – and timing is critical. When a beloved family dog is rushed to the vet having been hit by a car, for example, or with internal bleeding caused by eating something toxic, having blood readily available can literally mean the difference between life and death.

But even lifelong animal lover Kate didn't appreciate the desperate shortage of doggy donors until she started studying to become a vet and working part-time as a nurse across Sydney's three Vet Med clinics in Randwick, Lindfield, and Northbridge.

'I'd heard about the canine blood donation program at Sydney's Small Animal Specialist Hospital (SASH) and at the University of Sydney. While I was at Sydney Uni's Veterinary Teaching Hospital on a three-month placement, the woman who organised the program was telling us they didn't have enough blood and that if anybody had a healthy dog she'd love for them to come in and donate,' she says.

Kate knew immediately that Monty would be an ideal candidate for donation. 'I thought it was a great opportunity for Monty to give something back, because he gets a lot! And Monty loves attention, so coming to a clinic where everyone's going to pat him is not so bad.'

Canine blood donors must usually weigh 20 kilograms or more and be aged between one and eight years. They must also be fully vaccinated, regularly wormed, have a known history of good health, a known travel history and have never received a blood transfusion themselves.

'The weight range requirement is mainly to do with the volume of blood a dog can donate. If you have a ten kilo dog, they can't give as much,' she explains. 'The bigger dogs tend to be the gutsy breeds as well, who will be willing to eat a big bowl of food after their donation.'

Potential donors receive a full veterinary examination at no cost, as well as blood screening tests to confirm their blood type. The process of donation for dogs is very similar to that of humans (though people generally don't have to have their neck shaved before giving blood). The actual donation takes just ten to fifteen minutes via a catheter inserted into the jugular vein in the neck. The jugular is used because it's a large vein, so blood can be collected quickly and causes minimal damage to the vein.

It helps if the doggy donor has a calm temperament and is able to lie still for the duration, though some clinics prefer to administer light sedation to help the donor remain relaxed.

'Once the blood is collected, the dog is kept warm and they have their vital signs (temperature, blood pressure, heart rate and breathing rate) checked every five minutes for the first half hour,' Kate says. 'After that it's every ten minutes for the next hour. Once they are fully awake they are given some water and a big bowl of food.'

Donors usually stay in hospital for a full day so vets can keep a watchful eye on them. 'They're kept in for observation and to keep them calm and quiet, rather than letting them go home where they'll maybe run around in the backyard. The vets are very careful that the dogs are constantly monitored after sedation because there can always be an unexpected reaction to a drug,' she says. 'It's also to check they're maintaining their temperature and their body is coping with the blood loss. We can always give it back to them if we need to.'

One blood donation from a dog may be used to help treat up to three others. For health reasons, a single dog should only donate blood up to four times a year, but that potentially saves the lives of twelve of his canine counterparts.

Blood transfusions aren't particularly common in general veterinary practice, but in specialist and critical care hospitals they are a daily occurrence. Kate has seen lives saved thanks to a few precious drops of blood.

'I saw a tiny little Chihuahua that had been hit by a car and received a blood transfusion. Another condition that occurs is blood in the abdominal cavity, and one of the most common causes of that is a tumour in the spleen,' she says. 'I think there was a point where the Sydney Uni program had only one bag of blood left. That's not a situation they want to be in because a large dog may need multiple bags of blood in a surgery.'

Unlike human blood donations, which are stored at blood banks around the country, there isn't a nationwide network of storage facilities for donated dog blood, though the Veterinary Teaching Hospital does have a substantial stock of donations collected on site. Instead, vet clinics and hospitals must all maintain their own blood stocks. In small practices, that often means the vet's own dog is brought in to donate blood whenever stocks need topping up. For larger clinics, having a store of blood can make a huge difference, which is why regular donors like Monty are always needed.

The great thing about canine blood is that most dogs can safely receive a first transfusion of any blood type with little or no risk of a life-threatening reaction. There are more than a dozen canine blood groups, known as Dog Erythrocyte Antigens (DEAs), with eight recognised as international standards. Around 98 per cent of dogs are DEA 1.1, which means they can serve as blood donors for the majority of the canine population.

Monty went to work and gave his first blood donation at the Sydney University Veterinary Teaching Hospital in September 2016. 'He's quite used to the vet clinic scenario because he's been to work with me a lot. At uni, we had prac classes and sometimes we'd bring our own dogs in to do physical exams on,' says Kate. 'I was a bit worried about how he would handle the situation, because we can't explain to a dog what's happening or why we're doing the things we're doing. It's only a tiny bit of pain, but having a catheter put in and having your blood taken is mildly uncomfortable.'

But as is typical of his generally laid-back approach to life, the sweet golden retriever took it all in his stride.

'Monty seemed to take it really well. I was there all day and a lot of my friends that he knows quite well were on that day as well, so if I wasn't sitting with him then someone else that he knows was. He got the gold star treatment.'

As with human donors, some dogs can feel tired and grumpy after giving blood. Monty was certainly worn out – 'He had his dinner and went straight to sleep,' says Kate – but by the next morning 'he was back to his old self'.

Dogs are able to donate two blood products: packed red blood cells (pRBC), which are used to treat trauma, cancer and autoimmune disorders; and plasma, which contains antibodies that can tackle infectious diseases such as parvo-virus. Donated pRBC can be stored for up to four weeks and plasma for up to a year, so a single donation can go a very long way indeed.

Monty's blood was used within two weeks of his dona-tion; it went to a dog who'd had surgery to remove his spleen due to a tumour causing bleeding. One of the advantages of being a student of the university whose veterinary hospital Monty gave his donation to was that Kate was able to meet the dog whose life was saved by his gift. 'It was good to know that it was being used. You see the family that owns the dog and it's nice to know you're doing a little bit extra to help them,' she says.

All being well, it won't be long before five-year-old Monty makes his next blood donation – and Kate hopes all dog owners whose pets are eligible will consider signing them up as donors, too.

'Blood donation is a great thing and it does benefit the owners as well – a free vet check and blood tests is always useful,' she says. 'It's also just nice to know that, if Monty ever needed blood in the future, he's done his part.'

Good job, Monty. Good job.

BRYNNETH PAWLTROW

MAYOR OF RABBIT HASH, KENTUCKY

The tiny town of Rabbit Hash, Kentucky, is little more than a speck on the map. But what it lacks in size, this diminutive hamlet more than makes up for in heart – and sense of humour.

Comprising seven buildings on just three-and-a-half acres of land in Boone County, the town's fortunes once rose and fell with the waters of the Ohio River, on whose banks it sits. Devastating floods frequently washed buildings clean away, while in winter the river froze so solid that cars and trucks could drive across it and ferryboats would be crushed and buried by the ice.

These days, however, Rabbit Hash's prospects are a little more stable – and that's due in large part to its four-legged residents and the headline-grabbing political spectacle that unfolds there every four years.

But we'll get to that. We're on Rabbit Hash time now. There's no rush.

Rabbit Hash was 'born' around 1813, though back then it was called Carlton, most likely after an early settler family. Carlton was little more than a ferry landing, from where people, livestock and farm products would be shunted across the river to Rising Sun, the town on the opposite bank in the state of Indiana.

With the advent of steamboat transport, the area's population grew, and more and more goods needed to be shuttled back and forth between the two towns. A group of farmers got together and built a storehouse on the Carlton side so that these wares could be kept somewhere safe and dry until the next steamer arrived. Opening in 1831, the general store was originally run by seventeen-year-old James A. Wilson and has been trading ever since; 186 years later, it's still the centre of the Rabbit Hash universe.

As Christmas approached in 1847, the town was in the grip of yet another calamitous flood. A group of townsfolk watched helplessly as trees, haystacks, livestock and even buildings were swept downstream in the roiling waters of the Ohio. Talk turned to what they would serve for Christmas dinner. A resident called Frank, who was by all accounts something of a comedian, observed all the ground-dwelling wildlife fleeing to higher ground and remarked that there would surely be no shortage of rabbit hash (rabbit cooked with potatoes, onions and spices).

'Rabbit Hash' immediately became Frank's nickname and, soon after, the colloquial name for the thriving little town itself. So when the United States Postal Service asked the good people of Carlton to pick a new name for their post office – because their steamboat-delivered mail kept getting mixed up with the larger town of Carrolton, 62 kilometres down the river – the decision to officially become Rabbit Hash was an easy one.

By the northern winter of 1978–79, however, the future looked bleak for Rabbit Hash. Cars were by then ubiquitous and had rendered the riverboat trade all but obsolete. Local businesses shut up shop as the monolithic shopping complexes popping up across the US leeched their trade. The town's historic buildings, now abandoned, slipped deeper into decay. Just five or six people actually lived within the three acres. The once vibrant village was withering and its demise seemed inevitable.

But local resident Lowell Scott – known to all as Louie – had other ideas. Born and raised in Rabbit Hash, he was determined to preserve the town he loved. He had already bought the Ryle Brothers Feed and Seed Store from an uncle and in 1979 he bought the general store. He slept on a fold-out bed next to the stove as he worked to stabilise the building, which had been significantly flood-damaged in 1937 and still had river mud in the attic. (Only an ingenious hook-and-anchor system devised by a local blacksmith in the 1880s kept the building from being swept away.)

Over the next two decades, Louie Scott continued to buy the buildings of Rabbit Hash until he owned the entire town. When asked why he had poured his life savings into protecting the dilapidated hamlet, Louie reportedly said, 'It just needed saving.'

His enthusiasm for his home town proved infectious. In 1984, a group of like-minded Boone County residents formed the not-for-profit Rabbit Hash Historical Society (RHHS), dedicated to preserving and promoting the town and its history. Thanks to a generous bequest from a late resident, Edna Flowers, the volunteer-run RHHS was able to buy Rabbit Hash outright from Louie Scott in 2002 and is now solely responsible for its upkeep. The entire town was added to the National Register of Historic Places in 2003.

Though the population of the greater Rabbit Hash area was 315 in the most recent census, nobody actually lives within the original three acres anymore. But locals say the town's population is 'one half', because while he may spend most of the year in Florida, Louie Scott returns whenever he can to the hamlet he fought so hard to save.

And this may well have been where the Rabbit Hash story ended. The pretty little town might have gone quietly on for another 200-odd years, unknown to all but those passionate about her.

But then the church needed renovating and a dog named Goofy changed everything.

Fast forward to 1998. Boone County turned 150 and the Kentucky government asked all of the county's towns and villages to plan events to mark the occasion. The RHHS was in the throes of restoring Rabbit Hash's 200-year-old church at the time and was rapidly running out of money to do it.

They decided to hold an event that would both celebrate the county and raise money for the church.

'The people we call old-timers gathered together and decided they would hold an election for an honorary mayor of Rabbit Hash,' says RHHS secretary Bobbi Kayser. 'Our town is unincorporated so we don't really *need* a mayor, but everybody knows that in an election whoever has the most money is going to win. We decided to be upfront about it and charged people a dollar to vote. We also encouraged drinking at the polls because we know people are a little bit looser with their wallets when they've had a drink.'

Open to anyone, initially all the mayoral candidates were humans. But about a month into the campaign, local couple Jane and Randy Cochran entered their black labrador retriever, Herb, into the race. Not wanting to be outdone, Ed Borneman and his son, Mike Calhoun, entered their thirteen-year-old mutt, Goofy.

Goofy was well known the to residents of Rabbit Hash. Adopted by the Bornemans in 1985, he was a familiar sight on the journey between his home in Lower River Road and the Rabbit Hash General Store, where he would greet neighbours and purloin any scraps he could find (including town chickens on one occasion, to his eternal disgrace).

Ed's campaign strategy for Goofy was simple: everyone in town knew and liked his dog and he deserved their votes. He was right – Goofy won by a mile, beating local wood-carver 'Crazy Clifford' Pottorf as well as his four-legged rival, Herb. The election not only made headlines, it also made more than $9000 for the restoration of the church.

'The dogs just ran away with the election and we ended up with Mayor Goofy. He'd been arrested a couple of times as a stray because he wasn't wearing a collar. We got him out pretty quickly, but it was a scandal,' laughs Bobbi.

Sadly, Goofy wasn't able to see out his full term. In 2001, at the very impressive age of sixteen, he was diagnosed with cancer and had to be put to sleep. 'We honestly thought we were going to start a worldwide epidemic of euthanising public officials,' Bobbi says. 'We still can't figure out why that didn't happen.'

Many people expected the novelty of a dog mayor to die with Goofy, but further repairs to Rabbit Hash buildings were needed in 2001 and so another fundraising election was called. This time there was only one human candidate – two-year-old Ruby Markesbery, whose mother, Terrie, is the proprietor of the Rabbit Hash General Store. 'It was otherwise old dogs and a mini jackass,' laughs Bobbi.

Perhaps still smarting from their 1998 defeat, the Cochrans – whose previous candidate, Herb, had since joined Goofy in the great City Hall in the sky – entered their black labrador, Junior, and he was duly elected. 'He was our first black mayor,' Bobbi says.

Junior was a popular leader from day one. 'I always felt he was like (late President) Kennedy. He had a lot of charisma, only with black hair and a wet nose,' one Rabbit Hashian said of the new mayor.

With Junior's election came the decision that the mayoral term would be for life, and so the lovable lab was in office until he passed away in 2008. In his seven years in office he did much to raise the profile of Rabbit Hash, starring in a documentary, *Rabbit Hash: Center of the Universe*, and also an Animal Planet TV special, *Mayor Dog*. Junior also completed a nationwide tour in the Cochrans' RV and became 'spokespet' for a local women's crisis centre.

New rules were introduced for the 2008 election: candidates had to be able to chase a duck from wherever they resided into the centre of Rabbit Hash in under an hour. Ducks and geese were not eligible. Because that would just be silly.

Bobbi, who had moved to Rabbit Hash in 2001, decided to enter her eighteen-month-old red and white border collie, Lucy Lou, in the mayoral race. She campaigned under the slogan 'the bitch you can count on' and shattered the glass ceiling when she was elected in a landslide as the town's first female mayor. With the fee-per-vote still a very reasonable $1, the election raised more than $21 000 for Rabbit Hash's ongoing maintenance, including $8000 raised by Lucy Lou's own campaign.

'My husband and I are roofers and right before the election we'd been contracted to do an extensive amount of repair work on all the buildings in Rabbit Hash,' Bobbi explains. 'We offered to do all the labour for free, but as a non-profit they had to pay us, so we just took all the profit and put it in as votes. We bought the election fair and square!'

Lucy Lou was featured in countless magazines and TV shows and served as Grand Marshal of several pet parades. She was also named as a finalist in *Cincinnati Magazine*'s annual list of best elected officials four years running, and one year won the top honour over incumbent Cincinnati mayor John Cranley.

At the age of ten, Lucy Lou had years of benevolent governance ahead of her, but in 2016, after just two years in office, she decided to resign. Two major crises had befallen Rabbit Hash in quick succession and the RHHS urgently needed funds for restoration work – another election was urgently needed.

In June 2015, a landslide had wiped out the back of one of the town's historic buildings, with repairs totaling $100 000. Then, on 13 February 2016, a fire sparked by an electrical fault destroyed the beloved general store. All that remained were three partial walls and the foundation. 'It was horrific,' says Bobbi, 'but in the spirit of Rabbit Hash we decided to restore it.'

It was easier said than done. Not only was the rebuild going to cost in the region of $350 000, holding onto the town's historic significance designation meant a raft of strict guidelines had to be met. 'Our little non-profit just does not have that kind of money,' she says. 'Lucy Lou decided to step down and she also imposed term limits, so we'll now have an election every four years.'

The 2016 mayoral election was held on November 8 – the same night, coincidentally, as America's Presidential election. But while the people of the United States controversially voted a snarling, snapping and arguably dangerous creature into office, electors in Rabbit Hash chose a pit bull.

*

Like many people, Jordie Bamforth once harboured a negative bias toward pit bulls. She had seen all the bad press – the stories of dog fighting rings, their allegedly vicious temperament and so-called 'locking jaws' – and believed the breed deserved its fearsome reputation.

That was until she met one.

'The first time I was introduced to a pit bull, I was terrified. He had this big old, fat, meaty head. I was like many other people that you come across. I grew up watching Animal Planet and I learned lots about dog fighting and things,' Jordie says. 'Then I ended up living with my roommate's male pit bull, Blake, and he was the sweetest dog I've ever met. He'd come from a rural animal shelter. We didn't know his past, and he had some scars on him, but he was so forgiving of people and did great with other animals.'

She began to suspect her preconceptions about the breed might have been wide of the mark. 'As I learned about the breed and how they work, something changed in me. The media just paints a terrible picture of these dogs. If there's a hurting animal, I want to be their voice.'

So when she decided to adopt a rescue dog of her own in late 2012, there was no question about which breed the then twenty-year-old Jordie would choose.

'I wanted a pit bull because they're such great dogs, and I wanted to show the world that someone my age can be a responsible dog owner to a pit bull and that it can be a kind, loving animal,' she says.

She spent more than six months combing the websites of local animal shelters and rescue groups and went to meet several dogs and puppies, but none felt like quite the right fit. 'I wanted to make an educated decision so I could be a good voice for the breed,' Jordie says.

Then she discovered a tiny private rescue in the neighbouring state of Ohio, run virtually singlehandedly by a woman who would save pregnant dogs from shelters and provide a safe, calm environment for them to give birth, later rehoming the puppies. A recent arrival had delivered nine puppies and when Jordie saw one in particular on the rescue's website, something clicked.

'There was something about her little scrawny picture; I just knew that this was my dog. There was something about her that spoke to me. I contacted the lady and said, "Please hold her until she's eight weeks old. I'll drive to wherever to come get her,"' she says.

'Wherever' turned out to be north-east Ohio, a two-hour drive 'into the middle of nowhere' from Jordie's home in Kentucky. She scarcely remembers the journey in mid-May, 2013.

'It was just a blur. I got lost in this little tiny town. I was very overwhelmed. I met her foster mum at a baseball field, signed my little contract and drove her home,' she recalls. 'Animals are very special to me. I'm an only child and my parents surrounded me with animals growing up. I just knew this dog was going to be my best friend. Me and her, we're a team.'

She had decided to name her new little sidekick Brynn. 'I picked out Brynn for no specific reason. I just wanted a one-syllable name that started with a B,' she laughs.

Within days, Brynn had well and truly settled in. Blake, her male pit bull roommate, was initially terrified of the tiny puppy, but she soon won him over, playfully chewing on his ears and joining forces with him to chase the household's cat, Yoda. (A third dog, Pomeranian mix Jack Jack, joined the family when Brynn was about eighteen months old.)

'She is one of the happiest dogs I've ever met. She loves virtually everyone. I made sure she was raised around kids and small animals and people from all walks of life,' says Jordie, now twenty-four. 'She's constantly licking and her tail is almost always wagging – unless she's in trouble!'

It didn't take long for others to notice Brynn's easygoing nature, too. Jordie is often approached by strangers drawn in by the friendly dog's wide 'Pibble' smile and unusual red and white markings. She relishes every opportunity to be an advocate for the much-maligned breed.

'People are constantly asking me in the pet store or in the park, "Oh, your dog is so nice – is she a bulldog?" It makes my heart so warm to say, "No, she's a pit bull," and to be able to show people that these dogs are not vicious,' she says. 'It was one of those things where I took it upon myself to be a teacher to the public.'

But while cheerfulness and compliance are her default settings, Brynn is not without her diva moments. 'She hates rain and if it's raining she will refuse to go out. If there's something she doesn't want to do, I have to make her do it. She's a 25-kilogram dog, so there are times when I have to pick her up and put her outside,' says Jordie. 'If it's cold in the mornings and I open the back door and the cold hits her, she will turn right around and go lie in her dog bed. She's known nothing but a life of comfort.'

It was one of these rare moments of recalcitrance that earned Brynn her extended nickname, Brynneth Pawltrow, after the famously fussy Oscar-winning actress Gwyneth Paltrow.

'"Brynneth Pawltrow" didn't really develop until she was a year old. It was a joke between me and one of my girl-friends. She has children, and you know how you say their entire name so they'll listen to you? One day Brynn wasn't listening to me so I said, "Brynneth Pawltrow, get over here!" and it stuck,' she laughs. 'Now whenever we intro-duce her my boyfriend will say, "Her full name is Brynneth Pawltrow."'

Brynn was already a popular fixture in Rabbit Hash when the 2016 election was announced – she and Jordie have long been twice-weekly visitors to the town, travelling from their home in nearby Union to catch up with friends and listen to live music at the general store, which reopened in April 2017. Jordie also has a weekend job at a wine store in town (one of three jobs she has on top of her college studies) and Brynn often goes to work with her.

'Brynn has been a regular in Rabbit Hash for a little over two years now. She loves to go and see all her favourite people. As soon as I change my clothes, she's sitting by the door waiting to go,' she says. 'My mum used to bring me to Rabbit Hash when I was about ten years old and I didn't like it very much. My, how things have changed!'

When Bobbi Kayser asked Jordie if she would consider entering Brynn in the mayoral race, she was initially hesitant.

'I'm the least competitive person in the world, so I said I'd think about it. Then I had Brynn in Rabbit Hash one afternoon and she kept lying in the middle of the road. It's a tiny one-lane main street and every time she would do it a car would come and she wouldn't come when I called her,' she says. 'I'd have to go grab her by the collar and pull her over to where I was sitting and someone made the comment, "She really is a Rabbit Hash dog – she keeps going back and lying in the middle of the road like she owns it!"'

By the time they left Rabbit Hash that afternoon, Brynn was in the running for mayor. 'In the days following, one of my friends made buttons that said *Peace and Brynn*, Bobbi made posters and before I knew it, it was a big campaign.'

The votes started trickling in and soon Brynn was in third place. Then an anonymous sponsor made a large donation to Brynn's campaign and suggested Jordie reach out to local businesses and encourage them to put their hands in their pockets, too.

'It grew and grew. She went from being in third place to first place overnight, and she stayed in first place until she won,' says Jordie.

Brynn romped home by more than 1000 votes, raising $3367 in an election that netted nearly $9000 for the RHHS. She was 'indawgurated' at a formal ball on January 20, 2017, the same day as President Donald Trump. The second and third place-getters, Bourbon and Lady, were also honoured for their, ahem, *dogged* campaigns; they were made Ambassadors to Rabbit Hash and will fill in for Brynn if she's ever unavailable. The event was attended by Cincinnati City Councilman Chris Seelbach, a vocal opponent of discriminatory breed-specific legislation, which targets pit bulls.

'I thought it was so awesome of him to want to be involved,' Jordie says. 'I've really taken this as an opportunity to be a breed advocate, to say, "Hey, she's not only a girl, but she's a pit bull. You can come to Rabbit Hash and meet her and she'll lick your face."'

Brynn's ascension to high office made international headlines, in no small part because the feel-good story of a tight-knit community raising money for their town by choosing a canine mayor was a refreshing counterpoint to that fraught and bitter *other* election happening at the same time.

'Everybody gets so stressed out with the politics and the name calling and the negativity. We're a relief, a break from all that. I loved Brynn's campaign of peace, love and understanding because we need that right now. If you're a dog lover, then you're going to fall in love with this,' Bobbi Kayser says of the mayoral elections' quirky appeal. 'If you were to come to Rabbit Hash, you'd get it immediately. There's something just so soothing about this place. I've heard people say, "My blood pressure lowers 10 per cent every time I come here."'

Jordie and Brynn have partnered with a Cincinnati-based no-kill shelter, Save the Animals Foundation, and partial proceeds from a range of Brynn merchandise will support the shelter's work, as well as the RHHS. Brynn's primary job as mayor, however, will be to greet visitors to the town and continue promoting that unique Rabbit Hash *je ne sais quoi*. She may even stand for a second term in 2020 'if she's ageing gracefully'.

'We're just taking it as it comes. As long as she doesn't seem stressed or overwhelmed by any of the situations, we'll keep going. We've had a few families bring their small children down to get a picture with the mayor and that has just made my day.'

One thing that definitely *won't* happen, says Jordie, is the newly acquired political power going to Brynn's head. It shouldn't be a problem – as an adopted Rabbit Hashian, Brynn grew used to a steady stream of pats and attention long ago, anyway. 'Nothing in Brynn's life has changed so far other than having to sit for a picture every now and then,' says Jordie. 'She's the mayor, so she has some leeway in town, but she is a dog and I want her to stay a dog. No ego – she's stubborn enough as it is!'

With a team of tireless supporters behind her, friendly Brynn will no doubt do a first-rate job as the first pit bull mayor of Rabbit Hash. And with her passionate campaign manager, Jordie, at the end of her leash, she might just make a real difference for pit bulls, too.

VIKING

ACCELERANT DETECTION DOG

The aftermath of a house fire is chaotic. What's left when the flames have been extinguished by thousands of litres of water and fire retardant foam is a smouldering mess of charred wood and twisted metal. The acrid stench of smoke is overpowering. The home's contents that haven't been reduced to ash are scorched or waterlogged. In some tragic cases, people and pets have been injured or lost their lives. But even when everyone has safely escaped the inferno, the scene is still one of utter devastation.

Imagine, then, having to walk into that setting and figure out what caused the blaze. Visualise for a moment having to pick through the detritus of somebody's life in the search for clues. Consider the challenge of trying to isolate the source of the fire with smoke filling your nostrils and stinging your eyes. Think about trying to work under the scrutiny of distraught homeowners, shocked neighbours and bustling fire crews.

Now picture doing all of this with only your nose to guide you. Impossible, right? Maybe for some – but not for a dog like Viking.

Viking, a black labrador, is a 'sniffer dog' in the truest sense of the word. His official job title is accelerant detection canine (ADC), and his powerful nose makes him an invaluable weapon in the fire cause and origin investigation arsenal.

'Everything in a fire leaves a footprint. The dogs' main purpose is to confirm or dismiss the presence of ignitable liquid,' says Station Officer Phil Etienne, who works with Fire & Rescue NSW's (FRNSW) Fire Investigation and Research Unit (FIRU) and is Viking's handler. 'Everyone thinks their role is only to find, but that's not always the case. We need to rule out deliberate actions where possible, too. If we have a fatal fire and the dog can rule out the presence of ignitable liquid, the investigation can swing in another direction.'

Dogs are, of course, well known for their incredible sense of smell. The power of the canine nose has been harnessed for all manner of purposes, from hunting to tracking, for centuries. Using a dog to sniff out the source of a fire might seem obvious, but in fact the technique is relatively new in fire investigation in Australia.

FRNSW employed its first canine officer in 1995. Sabre the German shepherd was donated by NSW Police and while his nose was undoubtedly on point – German shepherds are one of the best dog breeds for scenting ability – his training wasn't.

'He was well trained by his handler but it was police-style training, so very obedience oriented,' says Phil. He could home in on ignitable liquids with ease, but the training had failed to take into account the need for a measured response from such a large dog. As with most dogs that work in detection, Sabre's reward for a 'hit' was lavish praise and a few minutes of play. Unfortunately, he was a little too enthusiastic about the play part of proceedings. "He was working well with detection, but when he would play he would destroy the scene."

Sabre retired from accelerant detection work after a year and was redeployed as a public education dog, visiting schools with Superintendent Ian Krimmer and demonstrating the 'Get down low and go, go, go' fire safety message for children.

But while Sabre hadn't been quite the right dog for the role, he had proven that dogs are a force to be reckoned with when it comes to pinpointing the presence of ignitable liquids at fire scenes. His successes led to the official creation of FRNSW's accelerant detection dog program in 1996, when Kova the labrador joined the ranks. The program was the first of its kind for Australasian fire services and remains the only such scheme in Australasia.

Kova came from the Australian Customs Service (now called Australian Border Force), but his training again followed police procedure. He was exceptional at his job, but when Kova's handler retired there was a period of several months when he didn't work. Instead, he lived in a family home and enjoyed life as a pet. He enjoyed it so much, in fact, that when Kova started working with his new handler he had lost some of his passion and drive for detection work. He was retired in 2000 and spent the rest of his days being doted on by FIRU operations officer Inspector Bob Alexander, passing away in 2008.

The next cab off the canine rank was Ellie the golden labrador. She came to FRNSW in 2000 from the renowned Australian Border Force (ABF) breeding program in Bulla, Victoria. Phil became Ellie's handler in 2003.

'Ellie is the most tested accelerant detection dog in Australia. She's even had an honours thesis done on her by forensic science students at the University of Technology, Sydney, comparing the dog's scenting ability to chemical analysis,' he says. 'It was the first time a university had been involved. They weren't sure what the research was going to do, but it became a valuable tool for when we'd present in court. It was no longer hearsay: "I think this is a wonderful dog." Instead it became, "I *know* she's good."'

Thanks to scientific quantification of Ellie's abilities, evidence uncovered by accelerant detection dogs at fire scenes can now be used in FRNSW, NSW Police and State Coroner investigations. Ellie retired from active duty in 2008.

Sheba and Winna, both labradors, followed in Ellie's pawsteps. Like their predecessor, they were also bred by ABF. When a new dog arrives, Phil can have him or her operational within three months. 'All our dogs now come from ABF. I believe their breeding program is fantastic. If it's not broken, why fix it?' he says.

Sheba and Winna both retired in 2015 and Viking started work in May of the same year. Also on the FIRU accelerant detection dog team is a golden labrador, Earl, whose handler is Qualified Firefighter Tim Garrett, and a black lab called Opal, who works with Senior Firefighter Joel Walton.

The dogs are used in investigations of suspicious and fatal fires across NSW, regardless of where or what type of fire it is. They will sometimes also attend fire scenes in Queensland and Victoria. 'We attend structure fires, bush fires and mobile property fires, such as vehicles,' says Phil. The dog team also assists police in warrant searches and lineups. If a dog doesn't locate accelerant at the scene of a suspicious fire, he'll often find it in a suspect's home or on their clothing instead.

Accelerant detection is an incredibly demanding job for both the dog and the handler. 'Since 1996 there's only been seven accelerant detection dog handlers in the whole of FRNSW, including myself. We are on call twenty-four hours a day, seven days a week. That really affects your life.'

Matching dogs with handlers is a serious business. Perhaps surprisingly, Phil says people who are real dog lovers often don't make great detector dog handlers because they get too attached to their canine colleague.

'You can love the dog but you have to know where to draw the line. You can see the difference between people who can draw that line and those who can't,' he says. 'This job is dynamic and changes all the time. You do have to adapt to the dog and you'll find that the dog will adapt to you.'

Funnily enough, the dogs that best suit the accelerant detection program are those that, for various reasons, didn't make the grade in the ABF's own detection training programs. That can be because ABF detector dogs need to nail both passive and active alerts (an active response to a detection might mean pawing or digging at the scent, while a passive alert will usually be a sit, drop or stare), but accelerant detection dogs need only the passive response.

'Ours will sit and stare at the odour. We then tell them to "show me" and they'll put their nose as close as they can,' Phil explains. 'We want the dog as close as it can get to the scent, because we can't see a scent. They have to push into those little gaps to show us.'

They're trained to not give active reactions primarily for security reasons: the more low-key the dog's response, the less likely the investigation scene will be damaged or contaminated. But safety is also a factor, says Phil.

'We remove any active interaction because it reduces the risk of them hurting their paws,' he says. 'We teach the dogs search patterns and how to search, but there's no reliance on the handler to say where next. With some of the other agencies, their dogs are very handler focused. We couldn't do that in a fire scene because it's just a mess.'

But just what are dogs like Viking looking for? It's one thing to say they're searching for a smell, but the reality is infintely more complex.

Accelerant detection dogs are trained to sniff out the five most common ignitable liquids used to start fires: petrol, kerosene, mineral turpentine, paint thinners and methylated spirits. Viking's predecessors were trained on a whopping twelve scents, but Phil has removed some that are frequently found at fire scenes for legitimate reasons, such as diesel fuel.

It's amazing enough that a humble canine can differentiate between five different-yet-similar smells. What's really remarkable, however, is that they can they can sniff them out in incredibly tiny amounts *and* amid the pungent smell of smoke and chemicals.

'Petrol is a very strong smell, so if the dog hits it very quickly, you've got an idea it's petrol. If it takes longer, it's either down to kerosene and thinners or it's very evaporated,' Phil says.

The extent to which an odour has evaporated is an ADC's biggest challenge. A blaze may be started with a jerry can's worth of petrol, for example, but what the fire itself doesn't consume will be largely washed away by the firefighters' hoses. Time is always an enemy in fire investigation, too.

'Once an accelerant hits the ground, it evaporates and changes. When it's set on fire, it evaporates and changes. We put water on it; it evaporates and changes. In the time it takes for us to arrive to investigate, it evaporates and changes,' he says. 'The dogs are trained to detect the five substances at five levels of evaporation: neat, as in a cup of fresh petrol, 75 per cent evaporated, 50 per cent, 25 per cent and 90 per cent evaporated.'

Scent changes, he says, in a similar fashion to the way fruit decays. 'If I buy a fresh mandarin from the shop, you can smell it. When it starts to wither and shrink, it's got a totally different smell but it's still a mandarin. If I leave it for a week, it's a rotten mess with flies all over it – but it's still a mandarin.'

To a highly trained accelerant detection dog like Viking, the smell of an ignitable liquid is always the proverbial mandarin, regardless of what has happened to change it.

If an accelerant is present, it rarely takes Viking very long to zero in on it. Dogs can detect some odours in parts per trillion. According to Alexandra Horowitz, a dog cognition researcher at New York's Barnard College, if a human being would notice a teaspoon of sugar in a cup of coffee, a dog could detect a teaspoon of sugar in a million gallons of water. That's two Olympic swimming pools.

'The dogs have twenty-five little 'scent pockets' in their head. They can detect 0.5 of a microlitre. That's a pinhead-size drop,' says Phil. 'If I put a drop of accelerant on someone's foot, it might take Viking a while but he'll find it.'

When Viking locates an accelerant, it's always a big moment. All the accelerant detection dogs are rewarded with the same thing: playtime with a rolled-up towel and plenty of loud, enthusiastic praise.

'It's fantastic when you see them with the towel. When Earl gets the towel, he wants to run around and show everyone like, *I found this – how good am I?*' Phil laughs. 'Opal wants to run her towel back to the car. Viking wants to play tug-o-war with me and wrestle.'

It may not seem like much of a treat to a human, but Phil says the dogs' desire for 'towel time' is a powerful motivator. 'For Viking, this job is his time to play. I don't play with him or wrestle until he's found an odour he's trained to detect,' he says. 'There's no "good boy" for anything else. If he wants to play, he goes and finds an odour. I want the "want" for the towel.'

There are times when he feels awkward about going through Viking's praise routine. At the scene of a fatal blaze, with heartbroken family members and friends of the victims present, having to jump around, whooping and cheering with his dog, feels terribly inappropriate – but failing to do so is confusing for the dog and can affect his working ability. In those situations, Phil tries to be as discreet as possible, and reminds himself that Viking doing his job well can bring a sense of peace and resolution to the bereaved family.

'The biggest thing for the dog is the handler. If I'm feeling uncomfortable, Viking will pick up on it. Fatalities are the hardest because I still have to carry on and scream and shout and tell him he's the best dog in the world. Everything is about energy. If my energy's high, the dog's energy is high,' he says. 'If we've been to a fatality and I'm different, the next watch Viking will be quieter because I was different last time. Without even realising, I'm transferring that to the dog. I try not to change, but if I have the dog picks up on it.'

As well as teaching the dogs to hunt for odours, a large part of their training focuses on coping with conditions at a fire scene. They are always unpleasant and often dangerous, such as when a building is unstable or there is asbestos present. The dog's ability to follow his nose quickly through a burnt building means it's safer for firefighters – if the dog can rapidly detect the location of an accelerant, it reduces the amount of time investigators have to spend excavating the scene.

'Most dogs don't want to go into a fire scene. It's disgusting. It's hot, it's smelly, you have the noisy generators going,' Phil says. 'A lot of our initial work is condition training. We put them through different agility courses, put them in dark boxes. We might then have to train at night because people forget that part – most house fires happen at night or in the early hours of the morning. We might have to drive six hours to a fire scene and then work in the dark. Dogs that come through training without any fear of that are what suits us.'

That's another reason why there's very little obedience training in the ADC curriculum: handlers need the dogs to be savvy enough to avoid hazards. 'Everyone expects the dogs to know sit, stay, drop and wait, but the only time we make our dogs wait is for food, to try to teach them not to eat the things they find at a fire scene,' he says. 'Although Viking did eat a glass bottle once.'

When they're searching a fire scene, Viking's safety is Phil's number one concern. Viking is never off leash during an investigation because the terrain in a razed building or scorched area of bush is just too unpredictable. 'It's purely to make it safe, so if Viking falls I can grab him,' he says.

'We don't send the dogs anywhere that we wouldn't go ourselves. If a scene is not safe for you or me, it's not safe for the dog.'

Of course, the dog's own clumsiness can't be helped – Viking was once so engrossed in following a scent trail that he walked straight through a wall. Each handler gives his dog a basic health check after every investigation, paying particular attention to the paws as the dogs don't wear booties and fire scenes are overflowing with debris. 'The handler knows the dog's demeanour and if there's something that's not right they'll get straight to the vet.'

All of the accelerant detection dogs live with their handlers, but they're not house pets. Viking has a purpose-built kennel and runs and doesn't get cuddles, treats or food from anyone but Phil. It may sound tough, but that slightly hands-off relationship is essential to his success as a working dog.

Viking is three years old and will keep working with Phil until he's eight or nine. When he retires, Viking will be adopted by a FRNSW member and Phil will train a new dog. He's learned the hard way that a dog needs to be fully retired and ensconced with a new family before his replacement comes on board.

'Twice now I've had my current detection dog at home while I'm training a new one and it's the worst thing. You spend time training the new dog and it's getting better and better but the old dog is going, *I'm missing out*, and his skills start declining,' he says. 'You think you have two great dogs, but you actually have two 50-per-cent dogs.'

That's the bottom line for Phil – and for all the FRNSW accelerant detection dog handlers. He loves Viking, but more than that, he respects his skills and knows how important it is that he remembers Viking has a job to do – everything he does with Viking must enable him to do that job to the best of his ability.

THE BACKTRACK GANG
HIGH JUMPERS/FARM DOGS/ LIFE CHANGERS

Nathan Bliss was sliding down a slippery slope. As a teenager growing up in Armidale, in the Northern Tablelands region of New South Wales, his chief priorities in life were sports, girls and parties – in that order. He fell in with the wrong crowd, dabbled in drugs and was generally getting up to no good. His father wasn't in the picture and, while his mum did her best with Nathan and his siblings, his unruly behaviour didn't help to make his home life any more harmonious.

School wasn't even on his radar – Nathan was constantly at odds with teachers and by the time he was fifteen he was rarely at school at all. 'School was never for me. I liked learning with my hands and doing things differently. I couldn't be in the classroom,' he says.

Then, in 2005, Nathan met a girl. Well, to be precise, he met *the* Girl – a border collie puppy named Girl who was every bit as wild as he was.

He was enrolled in a job-readiness course at Armidale TAFE for Year 10 boys who had drifted away or been excluded from mainstream schooling. The program included welding and metalwork skills and basic computer training. Trouble was, it wasn't working – it seemed nothing could get through to these rowdy young lads.

'We were really struggling with these kids. We tried everything – from computers to art to rock climbing – and we couldn't get the right thing to chill them out,' says social worker Bernie Shakeshaft, who taught the course.

But Bernie had an idea. A lifelong dog lover and working-dog enthusiast, he had a litter of border collie puppies at home that were all but feral. They couldn't be handled and he was at a loss as to how he would ever get them to work. Maybe, he thought, his teenage rebels could do something with them.

'Bernie always had dogs on the back of his ute and these dogs were a bit wild so I think he thought, *Might as well put the wild boys with the wild pups*,' Nathan recalls.

Bernie went to his higher-ups at TAFE and pitched the concept of having the boys train the dogs as part of his course. 'These kids were in need of the same thing as the dogs,' he says. 'I spoke to the TAFE about pairing them up and it was a point blank no. I couldn't believe it. I was like, "You're worried about puppies hurting these kids?"'

He wasn't about to take no for an answer. Bernie had worked with a lot of troubled kids and a *whole* lot of tough dogs in his time and something told him they could help each other. So he went ahead and threw them together.

'I just tipped the pups out on the lawn at TAFE one day and while I was inside getting a dressing down from the TAFE manager, I had one eye watching over his shoulder. It was the first time, with these little black and white border collie pups, that these kids had any chill on them,' Bernie says. 'I had about twenty wild kids and a bunch of wild dogs. It was a great mix. What do they say – never work with kids or animals? I was doing both.'

The boys spent several months training the puppies in basic obedience. For Nathan, working with Girl was a turning point in his life. He loved the training – not just the work itself, but the sense of accomplishment. He could see the little dog making progress and the fact that he was able to say, 'I did that' was huge; it wasn't something he was used to.

But more than the satisfaction of tangible achievement, Nathan loved the bond he shared with Girl. There had always been dogs in his life, but they weren't *his* – not the way Girl was. 'She was calm, chilled. I'm kind of like that and I think she recognised that in me,' he says.

Even as a sixteen-year-old rebel, he began to understand what a difference a dog can make. 'We trained the dogs, but we also talked to them. At the start it was just that friendship, that bond you get with your dogs. You can tell them anything,' he says. 'You can have the hardest time of your life and tell your dog about it and know they're not going to run and blurt it out to the next friend. They're going to keep it in. They're always going to be there for you.'

Bernie was also astonished by the transformation in his motley crew of kids and dogs. Even after the TAFE course finished and the boys returned to mainstream schooling or moved into employment, he couldn't shake the idea that there was untapped potential in dogs' innate ability to get through to wayward teens. He had seen it time and time again not only in his career, but in his personal life too.

Bernie struggled at school himself. He's dyslexic and couldn't keep up with the workload, so truancy and play-ground punch-ups seemed like better options. Thanks to a sympathetic school chaplain, he spent time in India working at Kalighat, Mother Teresa's hospice for the destitute, when he was sixteen. The experience certainly fired his social conscience.

Through it all, there were dogs. 'I've always been around dogs. By the time I was a young teenager, working dogs were an everyday part of my life,' he says. 'My career started in farms, working as a station hand and stockman.'

In his early twenties, Bernie moved to the Northern Territory to work as a tracker with the National Parks and Wildlife Service. He was part of the NT's first catch-and-release program, trapping dingoes, fitting them with radio collars and sending them back into the bush. He stayed in the Top End for more than a decade and it was there that he started working with recalcitrant teenagers, often taking local Indigenous kids with him on his tracking expeditions. When they had the opportunity to spend time with his working dogs, the teens would invariably thrive.

Back in Armidale, his experience with the TAFE boys only confirmed it: give a kid a dog and, while it may not change the world, the whole world can change for that kid.

With that in mind, in 2006 Bernie founded BackTrack, his own network of programs for at-risk youth in Armidale and the surrounding areas. The organisation's mission is simple: to help as many young people having a hard time as possible.

In the years since, BackTrack has worked with nearly 1000 Northern Tablelands teenagers. Most are boys and around three quarters are Indigenous – 'the Indigenous kids get the animal thing so much faster,' says Bernie.

BackTrack is 'the last stop' for the majority of the kids he works with. 'Your standard kid that comes to us has kind of hit the end of the rope. They've been through every other service and they're out of options. They'll probably be out of the education system – thirteen or fourteen years old and either completely kicked out of school or on that spiral of long-term suspension after long-term suspension,' he says. 'There's lots of drug and alcohol issues. All of them have got some kind of contact with the legal system and some have already been inside. We worked with 180 kids just last year across all our programs. We've always got between twenty and forty kids that are at the really tough end of the business.'

BackTrack started with a welding workshop in an old council works depot on the outskirts of town. Bernie had seven boys in that program – the Magnificent Seven, as they're now known – and they learned to make everything from dog kennels to sculptures.

Nathan Bliss was one of the seven. He remembers well the day it all began.

'About twelve months after I finished the TAFE course I caught up with Bernie again. He was having a meeting and I butted in as usual. He mentioned he was thinking about starting this program and said, "Do you want to participate?" I said, "Yeah, no worries,"' he says. 'He gave me a date and said, "I'll pick you up at this time." It was a Sunday. I went in to have a look and start cleaning up the welding shed.'

From day one, there were always working dogs hanging around the shed. They've proved to be useful in more ways than one. 'If a couple of boys are about to go the biffo, we give them a dog each and send them around the block in different directions,' says Bernie. 'By the time they meet in the middle, they have some chill on them.'

Nathan moved on from BackTrack when he landed a painting apprenticeship, but a year later Bernie came to him with a proposition. 'He was looking for mentors because he had a new bunch of kids. I put my hand up and said, "Yeah, I'll have a go at it,"' he says.

Undoubtedly thanks to his own experiences, Nathan was a natural when it came to connecting with young blokes who were exactly where he had been just a couple of years previously. He was so good at it, in fact, that Bernie offered him a traineeship, which allowed him to complete a Certificate III in Community Services at the same TAFE college where he first encountered Bernie and his feral puppies. The next year Nathan – or 'Blissy', as he's known to pretty much everyone – did a Certificate IV in Youth Work and for the past four years has been on staff as a full-time youth worker.

Dogs became an even more integral part of BackTrack's work in March 2007. Bernie was at a barbeque when a mate called him from the Armidale Show, which was on in town that weekend. There was a dog high-jump competition on, his mate said, and he reckoned Bernie should get down there with some dogs to have a crack at it. He duly rounded up a few dogs and headed into town.

'He won it – came first and second – and thought, *I could do this with the boys*,' Nathan laughs. 'So we built a dog high jump in the welding shed.'

That first jump evolved into Paws Up, a phenomenally successful high-jumping team that travels to country shows and invitational events throughout NSW and interstate. In the past decade, the Paws Up team has competed in around 700 events, missing out on first place just a handful of times. One of the competition dogs, Zorro the border collie, set an Australian dog high-jump record at 299 centimetres (9'10").

'It just took off to the point we were doing thirty-five events a year. We'd have boys and dogs packed tight onto the truck and be running around New South Wales competing. We've never been on a dog trip to compete or do a demonstration where there's been a spare seat on the truck,' says Bernie. 'I think we ruined the sport in this state. Now we do a lot more demonstrations, since we've trashed the sport.'

BackTrack's offering soon grew to include AgLads, an agricultural contracting business that provides the boys with on-the-job training and paid work on local properties. Working dogs, not surprisingly, also play a central role,

with the AgLads boys training BackTrack's canine contin-
gent to work stock. Every time a team goes out to a job,
they'll have several dogs in tow.

'I've got a bit of the old-school farm thing that only one
man can be the handler for one dog and you don't touch
another man's dog,' Bernie says. 'But something never sat
right with me about that and I wondered what would happen if we trained the boys to work with different dogs. All
of a sudden these dogs had a dozen different handlers and a
couple of different jobs each. Our dogs do so many different
jobs. Unless you're a dog person, you don't really get how
much dogs can do.'

But while the dogs are trained to work with any handler,
the training itself is very much one-on-one. Just as he did
with his litter of crazy canines on the TAFE lawn all those
years ago, Bernie lets the dog choose his handler.

'The dog picks the kid. When a new kid comes in, we'll
just let ten or fifteen dogs off and just wander around,
pretending nobody's looking at anything. That dog will find
a kid with the same personality every single time,' he says.
'The barking dog that never shuts up will pick the kid that
never shuts up. The ADHD dog that's always bouncing
around will pick the ADHD kid. The dog that might bite
you if you don't handle him right will choose the kid that
might bite you if you don't handle him right. We use that as
a tool now to get a feel for what the kids are like. It saves us
six months of work.'

The choice is always easy for the dogs, Bernie says,
because they're not burdened by that uniquely human habit

of overthinking everything. 'Dogs don't do the thinking thing. They leave that out and it's all around energy. It's a pretty good place to start for kids that have come from such chaotic backgrounds,' he says. 'We have some dogs that will just sit quietly and be nice and gentle with the kids. We have others that are good at working with the sad kids. We just put them together and they're all part of a big pack. That dog will treat you the way you treat the dog.'

The first time he saw that natural selection in action, Nathan was blown away. 'You notice the bond straight up when you get one of the new kids coming through. You see the dogs sniffing around and if it has a connection it'll stay there but if it doesn't it'll go off to the next kid,' he says. 'I love watching that.'

Working with Bernie on Paws Up and AgLads took Nathan's love of dogs to the next level. 'Doing the cattle work is when I really started getting into it. I like the ag stuff. I'm not from a farming background, but when I started doing bits and pieces with Bernie I just found a love for it. I've taken it a couple of steps further than most people do with training,' he says.

Girl the border collie was still a part of the BackTrack gang, and Nathan worked with her as often as he could, but he wanted a dog he could take home at the end of each day. Enter Bindi, a black and white kelpie. He trained her to jump and she held the dog high-jump world record until 2016.

'I think she's the right build for it. She's nice and thin and athletic. It's a bit of the training and a bit of the nature of the dog,' says Nathan. 'It's a game to her, like chasing a tennis ball – but she's got to get over the jump to get the ball or, in her case, a pat from me.'

The success of the Paws Up and AgLads programs led Bernie to start breeding working dogs specifically for BackTrack. There are about twenty dogs working with the organisation at any given time and they live between Bernie's place and a couple of training farms, including a residential facility that houses about eight boys.

'It's dogs everywhere, all the time. There's always a dozen or so at my place. We rotate them through to keep them fresh and give them a break from the kids,' he laughs. 'We've got to keep the younger dogs coming through that are really energetic and tough for the work that they do.'

With so many dogs in the program, it's not always happy families – but even when there's a bit of argy-bargy among the canines, Bernie expects the boys to learn from it. 'They're a pack of dogs and when you've got twenty of them together, they're forever trying to work out the pecking order. We've had some incredible dog fights,' he says. 'If these dogs all ran away one day there might be one or two that wouldn't stay together because they don't really like each other, but when they're down here, doing stuff with us, they just have to respect each other's differences.'

He adds wryly: 'We're forever telling the boys stories like that. Kids really get metaphors.'

For a while, the constant demand for young, exuberant dogs created a bit of a problem: what to do with the older canines that no longer had the get-up-and-go to chase sheep and cattle all day or leap 3 metres over a vertical jump. Bernie solved that one in 2015 by introducing the Barking Books program, which uses the older dogs to help primary school students who are struggling with reading.

'A teacher will take the dog in and these kids that just won't have a go at reading will read to the dog for thirty minutes. It's pretty extraordinary,' he says. 'A dog doesn't judge. Even if the book's upside down the dog won't point it out, and I've never heard a dog stop and say, "You didn't say that right." A dog doesn't know if you've been locked up or care about the colour of your skin. He just treats you how you treat him in the moment and the kids get that.'

While BackTrack works mainly with boys, it also runs a couple of girls' and mixed gender programs. One, Imagine This, sees teenage girls taking the dogs to visit residents of local aged care facilities.

'Ordinarily a little Indigenous girl isn't going to be talking to some old cocky sitting up there in a retirement home. That stuff will bring a tear to your eye. It's extraordinary, it really is,' says Bernie. 'That and the reading program are far more suited to the older dogs that are chilled out, so we've given them retirement jobs now. Jobs for the pensioner dogs. How many jobs can one dog have? We're really testing the limits.'

Just like the dogs, there's no cut-off for kids in the BackTrack family. Some are in the programs for six months before returning to mainstream schooling or going into employment; for others that can take years. 'Our aim is keeping them alive, keeping them out of jail and getting them chasing their hopes and dreams,' says Bernie.

His ultimate ambition is to take BackTrack national. The programs have already expanded beyond Armidale into Condoblin, Dubbo and Lake Cargelligo. 'Dogs are in every town, so I think it's a good place to start,' he says.

Funding the organisation is a constant struggle, however. The AgLads program is commercially viable and provides some of the necessary funding; the rest comes from donations and sporadic government grants. 'Funding for long-term programs in Australia is siloed around education or homelessness, but we have to look at the whole business,' Bernie explains. 'We're constantly overloaded with referrals from schools, police and magistrates, and having to turn kids away. The highest number, particularly in the Armidale district, come in because other kids are already here and they know someone.'

They may come because their mates are there, but the dogs are a big part of the reason the kids stay. 'We've saved hundreds and hundreds of kids. One might like mechanics and another one might prefer working in the bush, but the dogs are the consistent factor,' he says. Aside from anything else, working with the dogs 'teaches the kids a lot of responsibility'.

'A lot of people think the kids take the dogs home, but a lot of the kids don't have homes to go to,' Bernie says. Instead, the BackTrack gang – both two-legged and four-legged members – become a home of sorts.

And just as Nathan discovered back in 2005, talking to the dogs helps in a way that can't necessarily be defined in words, but is profound nonetheless.

'We teach the kids how the dogs are good at absorbing energy. If you've had a shit day and you sit down with your dog, they somehow take that bad stuff out. If you've got something heavy going on in your life and you don't want to tell anyone, but you want to get rid of it, that really works,' says Bernie. 'We teach the kids how to speak "dog language", so they can go anywhere and have a conversation with a dog. It's real and we know it's real because of the impact on the dogs. It really sucks the energy out of them.'

As to the dogs themselves, Bernie has no doubt his ragtag bunch of bush canines understand they're doing something that matters. 'They absolutely understand that they're working and that they're doing an important job,' he says. 'They're different around the kids than when they're with me just going out to muster cattle or something. They get what they're doing.'

What the dogs – and Bernie – did for Nathan was truly transformative. Now twenty-eight, he's married with three young kids of his own and has big plans for the future.

'The three things I'm most thankful for in the last twelve years are Bernie; my dog I trained at BackTrack, Girl; and my wife, Erin. We met at school and she helped me to see that there's other paths,' he says. (Girl, by the way, is nearly twelve and 'still kicking around'.)

He also has three dogs, two of which, Bindi and Rex, are BackTrack's two best high jumpers. 'I'm always going to have dogs in my life. Taking what I've learned from Bernie and other trainers that work with BackTrack, and putting all that different training together to get one trained dog out of it is pretty fun. You never stop learning,' says Nathan. 'My wife and I are talking about saving up for our own property and running a farm, so if we do that I'll definitely need a couple more dogs.'

Dogs are known for their loyalty and ultimately that is the foundation of BackTrack's success. Dogs are loyal to their masters through thick and thin; Bernie sticks by his boys no matter what and expects the same in return. In the end, that's what binds them all together.

For troubled kids who probably haven't seen a lot of loyalty in their lives, that's an incredibly powerful thing. 'Everywhere we go, the dogs come with us. Loyalty just becomes standard. It's such a normal part of life,' Bernie says. 'It really makes a difference.'

PIPER

WILDLIFE CONTROL K-9

Think of a dangerous animal. Chances are a bird isn't the first creature that springs to mind. Lions and tigers – now *they're* dangerous. Australia's own eastern brown snake is one of the deadliest critters on the planet. Sharks pose an ever-present threat to ocean swimmers. And they've got nothing on the mosquito, which kills a staggering 725 000 people every year.

But a fluffy owl or a tiny swallow? Surely not. How much harm can a bird possibly do?

Plenty, it turns out – especially at airports.

Wildlife strikes are a serious aviation safety issue. More than 95 per cent of strikes involve birds and they're on the increase thanks to growing populations of large birds and more aircraft crowding the skies.

The first recorded bird strike to a powered aircraft happened, fittingly, to one of the first people to ever fly a powered aircraft. Orville Wright, one of the famed Wright brothers, struck and killed a bird while flying over an Ohio cornfield in 1908. Four years later, American aviation pioneer Cal Rodgers became the first person to die as a result of a bird strike when he flew into a flock of seagulls over Long Beach, California. One bird jammed his plane's rudder control, causing him to crash.

The most famous recent bird strike occurred on 15 January 2009, when US Airways flight 1549 ditched in New York's Hudson River after striking a flock of Canada geese on take-off from LaGuardia Airport. Both engines lost power, but veteran pilot Chesley 'Sully' Sullenberger saved the lives of 155 passengers and crew by making a textbook forced water landing.

Closer to home, 16 609 bird strikes were reported to the Australian Transport Safety Bureau (ATSB) between 2006 and 2015. (In the United States, the Federal Aviation Administration received 13 795 bird strike reports in 2015 alone.) Rather gruesomely, Australian aircraft collided with 766 kilograms of flying animals in that period, mostly bats/flying foxes, swallows and martins, kites, lapwings and plovers. Galahs are the bird most commonly involved in multiple-bird strikes.

Ground-based animal strikes are relatively rare, but hares and rabbits, kangaroos, wallabies and foxes fare worst in those types of collisions in Australia.

Domestic high-capacity aircraft – the Boeing 737s and Airbus 320s that shuttle daily between Australian capital cities – are the planes most commonly involved in bird strikes. They're most likely to occur during takeoff and landing between 7.30 a.m. and 10.30 a.m., though there's also a spike in bat collisions between six and eight at night. Larger planes, such as Boeing 747s and Airbus 380s, have a significantly lower strike rate. (The birds are presumably better at seeing them coming.)

It's no surprise, then, that wildlife control is a major concern for airports worldwide. The good news is that airborne collisions between aircraft and birds are rarely dangerous to humans. (Sadly, the same cannot be said for the birds.) Since 1988, animal strikes have killed 262 people around the world. But while passenger safety is always the chief priority for airports, minimising damage to multi-million-dollar aircraft and airport infrastructure is also pretty high on the list of day-to-day operational challenges. More than 247 aircraft globally have been destroyed by animal strikes in the last three decades. Between 1990 and 2012, the FAA estimates that wildlife strikes to US civil aircraft cost as much as US$957 million.

Airports employ various methods of keeping birds and wildlife away from runways and taxiways. Wildlife mitigation strategies include lights and sirens, traps and noisy pyrotechnics called 'bangers' and 'screamers'. Good planning is also essential. There's no use building an airport close to a wetland, sewage treatment plant or putrescible waste dump – they're like supermarkets for hazardous wildlife.

One of the most common techniques for keeping critters at bay is habitat deterrence – creating an area around the airport that is unattractive to potentially hazardous animals.

That's why the land surrounding most airports is featureless and uninspiring: animals aren't fond of hanging out in places where there's no food or shelter on offer.

For some airports, however, using the landscape as a weapon against bird and wildlife strike simply isn't an option. Cherry Capital Airport in Traverse City, Michigan, is one of those airports. Flanked on two sides by Mitchel Creek, the small airport has the stunning 339-acre Boardman Lake five minutes to the west and is less than 5 kilometres south of Lake Michigan, which is one half of the largest body of fresh water in the world. 'Uninspiring' is something this part of the world will never be.

It's never going to be possible to keep wildlife entirely at bay at Cherry Capital, not that airport management would want to. Its existence depends in large part on the tourists who flock to Traverse City throughout the year to revel in the area's natural beauty and reputation as a food and wine destination. The city is the largest producer of tart cherries in the US, and its National Cherry Festival alone attracts more than half a million visitors each July.

No, Cherry Capital Airport is always going to have more than its fair share of feathered and furred visitors. Gulls, loons, ducks and geese are a problem throughout the summer months. In winter, it's low-flying snowy owls. Between 2010 and 2015, the airport recorded thirty-seven bird strikes and one rather pungent skunk strike. The most serious recent incident was in May 2014, when an aircraft struck a loon 15 kilometres from the airport and the bird crashed through the windscreen into the cockpit.

Fortunately the pilot, who was flying at an altitude of just 1000 metres as he descended toward the runway, was able to safely land his plane, but it was badly damaged.

The constant presence of wildlife means that Brian Edwards, one of six airport operations supervisors tasked with keeping wildlife away from planes, has his work cut out. Bangers and screamers were once the main weapon in the airport's arsenal, but they were becoming less and less effective. The trouble with the airport's existing wildlife mitigation strategies, he felt, was that the wildlife inevitably became desensitised to them – they stopped seeing them as dangerous.

'They make a hard, cold, startling noise. It would deafen somebody if it blew up next to them. The problem is, if you use it too much, the birds become aware that there's no threat,' says Brian. 'They come back again half an hour later or move down the runway so we have to chase them off again. Eventually, over the course of time, if you're not threatening the birds they will be able to get closer and closer to the aircraft.'

Brian knew he'd have to get creative and find something the birds would never get comfortable with. Something that was so fast and unpredictable, they would never feel braver than it. Something a little bit scary.

Something like Piper.

Brian is an outdoorsy guy. He runs most days and has competed in obstacle races and ultramarathons. In Michigan's notoriously frigid winters, he likes to hike in the snow. So when Brian decided to get a dog, he knew he wanted a companion with similar *joie de vivre*. In early 2013, he found his perfect match.

Piper the border collie was five years old when Brian learned the handsome black and white dog was looking for a new home. He didn't hesitate to offer his.

'Piper is just really cool. He's always been very well mannered. He's extremely loving, extremely loyal. Border collies are loyal in the first place, but he does not let me out of his sight,' he says. 'This guy goes everywhere with me and wants to go everywhere with me. I couldn't ask for a better companion.'

Brian was always going to keep Piper as a pet first and foremost, but he also had a benevolent ulterior motive. In his never-ending quest to find a way to keep Cherry Capital's runways clear of wildlife, he had read about other airports that used dogs to do the job. It was far from a common strategy, but from what he was reading, it seemed to work.

In 1999, Southwest Florida International Airport at Fort Myers was the first commercial airport in America to employ a wildlife control dog, Jet the border collie. Its current dog, Aero, is the fourth to hold the position; her training cost more than $12 000. Several US military bases also have bird-chasing dogs on patrol. 'I had read about the border collies at Fort Myers long before I met Piper. It costs a lot of money if you were to actually purchase a dog for wildlife mitigation,' says Brian. 'Because we are a smaller airport, we don't have a lot of money and the airport could never afford it.'

But the more he got to know Piper, the more Brian began to wonder if his faithful pet might be up to the task. 'My plan was, if I could get Piper to a point where I thought he was good enough, then I'd present the idea to my boss,' he says. 'There was no timetable because I didn't even know if we were going to be able to do it.'

He used the internet as a starting point, reading as much as possible about advanced, task-specific training for dogs. He also reached out to a handful of professional dog trainers, but none was overly keen to share a career's worth of hard-won knowledge. 'A lot of the time I'd talk to somebody that does this for a living and they wouldn't want to give up their knowledge. I don't blame anybody for that – I feel a little bit that way myself now!'

His training methods may have been somewhat ad hoc, but it wasn't long before Brian could see they were sinking in. He was essentially encouraging Piper's natural herding instinct and focusing it on the particular animals that liked to frequent the airport. As well as the birds, ground-dwelling animals like foxes, moles and voles are also an issue.

'Border collies are working dogs, so he is doing what he's bred to do. A lot of people know that a border collie needs a job, needs to go out and run, but most people forget the mental stimulation,' he says. 'We're constantly training and learning new things, because the mental activity is as important to them as the physical.'

Brian was also working on building Piper's fitness and stamina, since chasing wildlife away from runways would certainly involve a whole lot of running.

'I have a second job on top of working at the airport, and we did all this in my free time. There were times when we couldn't do any training for a week because I was so busy with the two jobs plus racing,' he says. 'I was running a lot of obstacle races and ultras, so Piper was my training partner for that stuff. Outside of just going out every day and running a lot of miles, I added in the obedience training. I'm not a trainer, so I didn't have eight hours a day to devote to training. What we did is just what I felt was right.'

When he felt his eager-to-please dog was ready, Brian prepared to broach the idea of 'employing' Piper with his boss, the airport director. 'It ended up taking a year or a year and a half to get him to a point where I thought he was responsive enough. Once I got to a point where I thought, *I can't take this any further*, I was going to bring it to my boss.'

But before he could raise the issue, Brian was scheduled to attend an airports conference. Having never left Piper in a boarding kennel, he was reluctant to go – but when Piper was given permission to tag along, he figured it was an opportunity to show his boss just how smart and dedicated his canine companion is.

'They found me a dog-friendly room at the hotel and there was a dinner one night where delegates brought their kids out. I said, 'Well, Piper is my kid, so I'm bringing him," he laughs. 'He was playing with kids all night and it was perfect. The next week I went back to my boss, we talked about it for a little bit and decided to give it a go.'

Piper was on the airport's payroll (except not really, since he's paid in praise and treats). He started work on a trial basis in August 2014. The trial was necessary to see how he would cope with aircraft noise. The racket made by a commercial jet on takeoff can exceed 120 decibels – a rock concert, by comparison, is around 105 decibels. For all his committed training, Brian doesn't have helicopters and planes in his backyard. 'We could have paid somebody $100 000 to train a dog to chase geese away, but if they can't work in that environment there's no point.'

Fortunately, easygoing Piper had no trouble with the noise and was given the go-ahead to officially start work in January 2015. He is the only wildlife control K-9 on staff at a Michigan airport, and one of just a handful working at commercial airports across the US.

Piper now works alongside Brian at the airport four days a week. Together, the pair complete regular patrols of the entire facility, with Piper digging up the burrows of moles, voles and foxes and sending them on their way. They are also on call to respond to immediate threats such as a flock of geese on a runway.

'I carry around a phone that people will call if they have issues. If somebody reports that there's a flock of geese on the runway, that is an immediate threat. We will go out and respond to that within five to ten minutes,' Brian says. 'If there's days when I don't have much desk work then we can spend a lot more time being proactive and going out patrolling.'

When they do head out on patrol, there is no doubt Piper is raring to get to work. This is a dog that takes his job very seriously indeed.

'If he's in the truck and he happens to see something outside, I can tell because he snaps to attention and starts whining. He's trying to push the door open and he wants out,' says Brian. 'It can be very, very loud and can be very high pitched. He just gets really worked up. I always wonder what people think if they hear that and can't see him – it sounds like I'm beating him!'

Unlike other airports that use dogs for wildlife control, Cherry Capital Airport doesn't own Piper – he's still Brian's pet and they only ever work together.

'Most of the time, a dog working at an airport is an airport-owned asset like any other vehicle. It's kenneled at the airport and any trained employee would be able to use the dog at any time,' he explains. 'There's a lot of red tape that would make that difficult to do here, because Piper is my dog. I'm his everything. My bringing my own dog isn't costing the airport anything, but they're getting the benefit – but I get the benefit of working with my dog every day, so it's a fair trade if you ask me.'

To a casual bystander watching Piper at work, it may not look like he's doing anything particularly specialised. Brian will simply drive his maroon airport SUV onto the airfield, let Piper out of the vehicle and watch the sleek canine take off in pursuit of whatever critter is causing trouble – but his work is far more strategic and considered than it appears. Piper seems to understand that his job is to move the animals on rather than catch them. In any case, his quarry is generally much faster than he is.

'He can run fast; not as fast as a fox, but for much longer. A fox can run at 65 kilometres per hour – they're like sprinters and Piper is more like a marathoner,' Brian says. 'Most of the stuff that he could catch up to, I don't mind him catching. We're trying to be non-lethal, but we do hunt moles and things because they attract larger things like coyotes, hawks and foxes. When we're out at night looking for a fox, he knows that's what we're looking for and that it's different from the daytime. I didn't teach him that.'

Perhaps surprisingly, Piper's job doesn't take him onto runways or close to aircraft as much as other parts of the airfield. Brian regularly runs 'termination drills' where he will call off a chase, in case he ever needs to steer Piper away from a hazard. Again, that's a strategy with a precise goal behind it.

'We don't want him scaring up birds into an aircraft. A lot of times it's actually better not to chase anything and hope it doesn't fly up into the aircraft,' says Brian. 'Our number one goal is to improve safety, not cause a safety incident. We spend most of our time on the taxiways and surrounding areas. We're only on the runway if there's something that needs to be chased off.'

Winter is Piper's favourite season. His thick double coat insulates him against the icy Traverse City climate, where winter temperatures can plummet to –9 °C and up to a metre of snow is common. Brian tried him in protective booties, but ditched them after Piper jumped awkwardly out of the vehicle and broke his toe. Now, they just keep their outdoor patrols shorter in cold weather.

'He loves the snow. He loves bounding around, chasing the snowy owls. Border collies are bred on the borders of England and Scotland. They are meant to be outside and they're very capable of dealing with stuff,' he says.

Brian doesn't see Piper as his employee – to him, they are a team whose success depends on how well they work together. 'I don't want to set the dog up for failure. I'm always between the runway and wherever he is so I can block him with the truck or send him in a different direction if I need to,' he says. 'My responsibility as a handler is not to put him in a situation where he may fail, because that's my fault, not his.'

But failure doesn't seem to be an option for tenacious Piper. He has been so successful in his role as wildlife control K-9 that the other wildlife mitigation techniques employed by the airport have also become more useful.

'Nobody but me is using Piper so we still have to use the other tools of management, but now that we have him we use the loud noises less, which makes them more effective,' Brian explains. 'The reason Piper is effective is that there's always a perceived threat. To the wildlife, Piper is a predator. A goose isn't going to get desensitised to Piper chasing it. The fight-or-flight instinct always kicks in.'

It's testament to his border collie smarts that Piper never tries to chase or harm wildlife when he's off the clock.

In fact, when he's not working he can most likely be found napping or playing with his ball.

'I'm lucky with Piper because he's got a great off switch. He thinks his ball is his main job in life. If he's got his ball, everything is hunky-dory,' Brian laughs. 'Most listings rank border collies as the smartest breed of dog and I would agree with that. It's like working with a five-year-old kid.'

Piper has also become something of a celebrity. Images of the handsome hound wearing his flight goggles went viral after being shared on Reddit. His Instagram posts racked up more than 675 000 likes in 2016 and he has nearly 20 000 Facebook fans. He visits local schools and is recognised on the streets of Traverse City. Visitors to the airport frequently ask to meet the indefatigable bird-chasing dog and Brian never refuses.

'We have an open door policy, so anybody who wants to meet him can come say hi. He's definitely a part of the culture of the airport, but also the community,' he says. 'He's become a kind of mascot for the area. That's what I really set out to do from the beginning. I didn't want him to be some cool guy behind a fence that nobody had access to.'

Piper is nine now and Brian knows retirement may be imminent. He doesn't have a particular cut-off date in mind; rather, he's relying on Piper to let him know when he's had enough. 'We do a lot of stuff outside work to keep him in shape and moving, but if tomorrow I decide that Piper isn't capable of chasing stuff anymore then he won't do it.'

He might have a job on his hands getting Piper to quit *his* job, however. There's no doubt Piper loves what he does – even if he doesn't understand that he is actually working.

'I don't think he understands that he's helping people be safer by doing what's in his blood. To him, it's all play. Everything is a game,' says Brian. 'He's never on a leash. He gets to chase stuff, dig stuff up. When he goes and chases a flock of geese, he makes these big, sweeping turns like he's really proud of himself. It's a dream job.'

It's a pretty sweet gig for Brian, too. 'Nothing in my life is more fulfilling than going out and watching him do that work and seeing him do it on his own,' he says. 'I don't have to tell him because we've put so much blood, sweat and tears into it. He's just an awesome dog.'

And when your boss thinks that highly of you, why would you want to work anywhere else?

WHISKEY

PTSD SUPPORT DOG AND CHARITY MASCOT

The dog was in a terrible state. He might have been a handsome, muscular working dog once upon a time, but now the blue heeler was little more than skin and bone. The heavy-duty chain fastened with a D-shackle around his neck was too tight and the flesh had grown over it. He was vomiting and had diarrhoea, too. All evidence suggested the poor dog was not long for this world.

When she got the call to collect a dog that had been cruelly abandoned outside the a petfood manufacturing facility in Bathurst, New South Wales, local animal rescuer Louise Kelly expected to find an elderly canine. But this dog was young, only about eight months old; it was his physical condition and defeated demeanour that made him seem like a little old man. Wandering around by the factory's security boom gate like an offering, the dog's spirit was broken and Louise knew she had to do everything in her power to repair it.

The security guard at the factory had called Louise because he knew she was involved with a newly established dog-training program at the local jail. He wondered if this dog might be suitable for that program. Louise wondered, too.

Blue heelers are bred to work. If they're not given a job to do they'll often invent one for themselves, and when they're domestic pets that can be a cause of consternation for their owners. All too often, working breeds find themselves surrendered to pounds and animal welfare groups or – like Louise's forlorn factory foundling – simply dumped by owners unable or unwilling to meet their need for mental and physical stimulation.

This dog was a mess, cowering and shying away from any human interaction. All evidence suggested he was a lost cause, but Louise felt that, beyond his pitiful appearance, this puppy had the soul of a fighter. She believed having a job, a purpose, would accelerate his recovery, so she named him Whiskey and took him to Bathurst Correctional Complex.

In 2012, in partnership with Corrective Services NSW, a veterans' welfare organisation launched an Australian-first program that paired minimum-security inmates at the prison with sick, neglected or abused rescue dogs. The inmates rehabilitated the dogs and spent six months training them to work as support dogs for veterans with physical or psychological injuries such as post-traumatic stress disorder (PTSD).

Louise had provided rescued dogs to the program and thought her sad young charge would be a perfect fit – and she was right. Once he had been nursed back to health at the prison, Whiskey took to his training with aplomb.

It wasn't all smooth sailing, though. The first inmate Whiskey had been paired with didn't have the patience for the still ailing little dog's messy health problems. So Whiskey was matched with another prisoner, one who had previously been expelled from the training program and sent back to maximum security. He wasn't really a fan of cattle dogs, but he was desperate to redeem himself and get back into the program, so he took Whiskey on. Eager to show he was worthy of his second chance, the inmate worked tirelessly to give Whiskey a second chance of his own.

Slowly, Whiskey regained his health. He grew bigger and stronger and surprised everyone not only with his intelligence, but his empathy. Whiskey was a sensitive dog, always able to 'read the temperature' of a room, and was extremely protective of those who needed a friend. At one stage his trainer became ill and it took three prison guards to safely remove Whiskey from his side – he had sensed the man was unwell and was determined to protect him.

Finally, Whiskey's training was complete and he was matched with a veteran suffering from PTSD and major depression. Nobody could have imagined that their time together would be so heartbreakingly brief, nor that Whiskey's dedication to his job would inspire a crusade that would save dozens of lives.

*

Unlike many career soldiers, Scott Jackman came to the Army relatively late in life. He grew up on a Victorian dairy farm and, after leaving school, completed a fitting and machining apprenticeship. In 1994, at the age of twenty-three, though he had a full-time job in a gas cylinder factory in the border town of Echuca, Scott surprised everyone – including himself – by joining the 1st Armoured Regiment in the Australian Army Reserve.

'My youngest brother, Dean, didn't have a job and my mother wanted me to take him somewhere and get him motivated, so I took him to an open day at Puckapunyal [the Australian Army training facility in central Victoria],' he says. 'We saw the tanks do live fire demonstrations and stuff and Dean said, "Bugger that, I don't want to join," but I loved it and signed up on the spot.'

The following year, the regiment relocated to the newly built Robertson Barracks in Darwin. Scott went up there a couple of times, but ultimately the distance and clashes with work commitments proved too challenging. He was discharged from the Army Reserve in 2004.

Outside of his work as a reservist, Scott had tired of factory work by 2001 and went back to dairy farming, working as a farmhand. He later worked as an industrial irrigation installer and self-employed welder before taking a job at a local abattoir. In 2007, the drought tightened its grip and farming became increasingly difficult. Work at the abattoir dwindled and Scott made the decision to join the infantry. He repeated his basic training at Wagga Wagga, NSW, and was assigned to the newly re-raised

8th/9th Battalion, Royal Australian Regiment (8/9 RAR), as a rifleman. His was the first new platoon in the resurrected battalion, but even with the influx of new members there were just sixty-seven people in the division. He was thirty-six.

'In all my other jobs I'd been a leading hand or a foreman. I wanted a job where I could just be one of the guys,' Scott says. He wasn't part of the rank-and-file for long though, being promoted to the rank of Lance Corporal in 2009.

In 2010, he was deployed to East Timor as a detachment commander in the battalion's signals platoon under Operation Astute, an Australian-led military campaign to return stability to the country in the wake of military-led unrest, violence and a coup attempt. While in East Timor, Scott learned that 8/9 RAR were raising another rifle company and would soon start pre-deployment training for Afghanistan's Uruzgan Province. He was determined to be among the soldiers who made the trip to the Middle East.

'I knew they were raising Charlie Company to go to Afghanistan and I just kept begging the Major, who was pegged to command the new company. He said he wanted good NCOs (non-commissioned officers),' he says.

Scott had moved to Brisbane with wife Liz and their three sons in 2008, and in January 2012 he was one of 730 Brisbane-based soldiers deployed with 8/9 RAR to Afghanistan as part of Mentoring Task Force 4 (MTF-4). Their job was to train and mentor the Afghan National Army's 4th Brigade and they were also trained in bomb detection so they could assist the unit's engineers in searching for improvised explosive devices (IEDs). 'We did a lot of jobs. We'd travel to different bases for a week or two weeks.'

But almost immediately, his time in Afghanistan was troubled. Soon after arriving, Scott developed severe pneumonia and was ordered to rest and perform only light duties for two weeks. He didn't much like the sound of that. 'As soon as the doctor wasn't looking I took off for the first patrol,' he says. 'I could hardly walk properly. It was the middle of winter, it was snowing and the cold air was burning my lungs.'

The situation in Afghanistan was confronting, to say the least. Horrific events were virtually a daily occurrence. 'I had experiences overseas. We had casualties come into our patrol base from Afghan police checkpoints. Two Afghan police were in the makeshift hospital – a shipping container – when I came on picquet. One bloke had been shot in the face; the other had gut wounds from a rocket-propelled grenade. On another occasion we had an eleven-year-old child who'd had three fingers blown off because his dad had been showing him how to make bombs,' says Scott. 'We found body parts everywhere. We saw burned babies and all sorts of things.'

It felt like death was never far away. Scott says he and his fellow troops were almost resigned to it. He had completed some of his heavy weapons training alongside Private Nathan Bewes, who was killed by an IED in Afghanistan in 2010. Few of Scott's ancestors had made it home from the great wars, and it seemed inevitable that he wouldn't make it home either. 'We just expected it. You get in a room and they say, "Some of you aren't going to make it back," and you just think, *Well, it's probably going to be me*,' he says.

On one occasion, when the task force's engineers were occupied searching the proposed site of the new Patrol Base Zafar in the Chaka Juy area, Scott was sent to search a large swath of nearby land for IEDs so that recovery vehicles could get safely through to salvage a Bushmaster armoured vehicle that was on the verge of rolling after sliding down an embankment. Scott had been travelling in the vehicle when it slid; he and his fellow soldiers managed to scramble to safety as the vehicle teetered on the edge of the precipice.

Further ahead of him, at the location where Zafar would be built, engineers had discovered two IEDs and were preparing to 'BIP' them – blow them up *in situ*. Scott had no idea an explosion was imminent – he had relinquished his radio so as not to trigger any IEDs that might lay in his search area. At the precise moment his metal detector picked up a weak indication of a metal hit in his own area, the bomb further away was BIP-ed.

'It was only 130 metres away as the crow flies, but you can't have a radio on you so I didn't know what was going on at the top,' he says. 'When they blew up the first one, the shock wave just went through me and for a split second I thought I was dead.'

He looked up and saw a group of infantry soldiers 30 metres away who were behind cover and had been protected from the shock wave. They were laughing at him – unlike Scott, they had heard radio warnings of the impending explosion.

Recovering his composure, Scott took another step – exactly as the second IED was detonated. 'That caused exactly the same reaction from me and the group of infantry soldiers. I nearly had to change my ballistic undies that day.'

Another near miss came at the end of Scott's deployment. On his last patrol from Patrol Base Wali, the lead vehicle in Scott's convoy inadvertently detonated a roadside bomb. The plan had been to drop the convoy, half of whose members were trained to find the deadly IEDs, 5 kilometres further along a ridge, from where they would search their way back and put a roadblock in place.

'They couldn't drop us there anymore as the vehicles were damaged. As it happened, an American unmanned aerial vehicle (UAV) was in the area and checked out the drop-off point. It picked up two more IEDs using heat sensors,' Scott says. 'We'll never know whether we would have found those IEDs or not. We might have found them the wrong way.'

The irony was that Scott wasn't even meant to be on that patrol. He was a last-minute replacement for a soldier who had been injured. 'One of their blokes rolled his ankle, so I took his spot. We were trained for all core searches – I had done a course on how to find bombs, so I was put on that patrol for that reason,' he says.

Despite these narrow escapes, every member of MTF-4 returned safely to Australia in July 2012. But though he was happy to be reunited with Liz and their sons, Tim, Matt and Sam, Scott was struggling. He wasn't sure where he now fit in civilian life and began to feel depressed.

'Ours was the only troop where everybody came back. There's a lot of survivor guilt that goes with that,' he says. 'It was a like a movie with a happy ending, but I was almost sad that we survived. They teach you how to go away, but they don't really teach you how to come back.'

Compounding Scott's disquiet was the fact that he was in terrible pain. He had fallen backwards down a mountain on a night patrol just six weeks before he returned to Australia, but had hidden his injuries because he didn't want to be sent home early. Now, 'it felt like a knitting needle being pushed under my collarbone'. He was scheduled to start a training course that would enable his promotion from Lance Corporal to Corporal status and didn't want to miss out, so he asked his GP to prescribe painkillers. Instead, he was sent for scans – and the news was not good.

'They found out I had two discs that were ruptured or bulged. It was compounded by a degenerative bone condition from carrying all the weight that infantry soldiers carry all the time,' Scott says. 'One disc was pushing out to the left and impinging on the nerve that goes down my arm, so if I try to work on the computer or hang out the clothes my arm goes numb. The other was pushing out the other way and pinching my spinal cord.'

Surgery was not – and still isn't – possible because the problem is too close to Scott's spinal cord. He was put on heavy-duty pain relief, but was still hopeful of remaining in the Army. 'My plan if I couldn't continue in the infantry was to join another corps and just do whatever,' he says.

Scott was admitted to the Army's Soldier Recovery Centre at Enoggera Barracks in Brisbane for rehabilitation from the debilitating injury. His dreams of promotion looked set to remain just that. 'Then I heard I might be able to stay in another way, but the day I found out they wanted to keep me there I got my medical discharge papers, so that was another kick in the gut.'

The involuntary end of his military career was, Scott says, the straw that broke the camel's back. The depression and PTSD that had been lurking since his return from Afghanistan suddenly overwhelmed him. He sank into alcoholism and gambling addiction and abused his prescription medication. It wasn't unusual for him to down five bottles of scotch over a four-day bender. He was hypervigilant, sometimes staying awake for two days without sleep. He felt powerless to control his feelings of anger and aggression.

For more than a year, Scott felt trapped in a vicious cycle of despair and desperation. He contemplated suicide. Then he met another veteran who also struggled with PTSD – but he had a dog to help him with it. 'I was hanging shit on him and saying, "How did *you* get a dog?" The bloke said, "Why, do you want one?"'

Scott's initial reaction was to scoff. What difference could a dog possibly make to the war raging inside his head? But he knew he had to do something. He owed it to his family – and himself. 'I thought about it and said, "Yes, I do want one," he says.

Luckily, the perfect dog was waiting.

When Scott met Whiskey at a meet-and-greet in Bathurst in July 2013, it was as if they immediately recognised something in each other. Whiskey was two by then and the frail little puppy was long gone. In his place was a big, stocky blue heeler who'd been through a lot and was ready to move on – much like his new owner.

Scott went back to Bathurst to collect Whiskey in September. 'He'd been beaten around a bit and was a really good judge of character. Most of the blokes I knew that turned out to be real pricks, he picked that up before I did,' he says.

Psychiatric support dogs are trained to detect and diffuse the signs of mounting anxiety, but it went deeper than that with Whiskey. 'He always had a really protective streak. If someone was really suffering or had really bad mental problems, he'd go up to them and put his head on their lap.'

Whiskey became Scott's constant companion and, just as his soldier owner had been in the Afghanistan desert, was always on the lookout for signs that something wasn't right. 'Dogs like Whiskey are always looking around. They're doing the hard yards and searching for things that might trigger you because they know you very well. They're very focused,' he says. 'When you get home and you take the [assistance dog] jacket off and you take the leash off, they're just a puppy and they're knackered. They're exhausted because they're working so hard.'

In September 2014, Scott and Liz went to Canada on holiday. When they returned, Scott was concerned to see that Whiskey had lost a large amount of weight. But he was in good spirits and as dedicated to his job as ever, so Scott tried not to worry too much. Then, on a routine weekend shopping trip a few weeks later, he discovered the lymph nodes in his faithful dog's neck were enlarged.

'I leaned down to pat him and felt that his glands were really big and sore. I freaked out and rang the vet and she said, "He's probably got a tooth infection. Bring him in on Monday and we'll figure out which tooth is rotten and do an operation to take it out,"' he recalls. 'I went in and the vet felt his glands and looked like she was about to cry. She said, "I think he's got cancer and I think it's the bad one." I just broke down.'

With treatment, the vet thought she could ensure Whiskey continued to enjoy a good quality of life for about three months. But there would be no cure; Whiskey would eventually succumb to the cancer.

'We really spoiled him,' says Scott of his last days with Whiskey. 'We fed him Cornettos, took him to the beach, did all the things we shouldn't have done.'

In the end, Whiskey had three more love-filled weeks. He passed away on 7 October 2014, after just a year by Scott's side. He was only three years old.

The day before Whiskey's death, a professional photographer friend of Scott's had photographed the Jackman family with their loyal dog. Scott printed one of those pictures on canvas and gave it to Louise Kelly. Across the top he wrote, 'Thanks for saving my life so that I could save a soldier's.'

Whiskey's loss was a crushing blow to Scott, who once again found himself feeling suicidal. He also felt that the ex-serviceman's group that had trained Whiskey for him had little empathy for his profound grief.

'I got a call and they said something like, "Mate, we'll get you a new pup, don't worry." It was the last thing I wanted to hear,' he says. 'I was devastated and angry.'

Two days after Whiskey's death, Liz and the couple's friend Marilyn Kench came to Scott with an idea. Liz had befriended Marilyn through her work in the special needs community (one of the couple's adult sons has Asperger's syndrome). Marilyn, who was holidaying with the Jackman family at the time of Whiskey's death, had served with the Army for twenty years and her partner, Paul, was an Australian SAS member who was tragically killed on a training exercise in 1992.

'It was lucky that Marilyn was there because she had a friend who was an SAS chaplain that I could talk to,' Scott says. 'I was feeling heartbroken and a bit lost and Marilyn suggested to Liz and myself that we should do something in Whiskey's honour. She said, "Let's do our own program and call it Whiskey's Wish."'

At first, Scott rejected the idea – 'I said, "No, I can't replace Whiskey" – but it niggled at him. For all the training he had received to equip him to work with Whiskey, Scott felt there was nothing in place to help him cope with the unexpected death of the dog that had quite literally been his saviour. He didn't want other veterans to have to go through what he had.

With the encouragement of Liz, Marilyn and another veteran friend, Scott decided to set up an initiative that would provide veterans with psychiatric support dogs and, crucially, stick with them for life – not just the life of the dog. And, of course, he would name it after the plucky blue heeler who had pulled him back from the brink more than once.

Whiskey's Wish was launched in November 2014. Scott serves as president and training coordinator, while Liz is secretary and treasurer and Marilyn is vice president. Scott's mother, Cassandra Friswell, is also involved on the committee – she stayed with the family for twelve months to help ensure Scott didn't harm himself at the height of his PTSD. She also fosters puppies in Tongala, Victoria, along with Scott's brother, Dean, and his children Jesse, James and Jett.

Whiskey's Wish procures and trains rescue dogs to work as psychiatric support and mobility assistance dogs for veterans and first responders.

'When we started off we were only supplying Army guys. The first three dogs were from shelters and then we started to get a few from reputable breeders – I was thinking about longevity because with Whiskey we didn't know what his background was – but we've gone back to rescues now,' Scott says.

'I like the working breeds – kelpies, cattle dogs. When they get out there, they're mentally challenged all the time. We've got a really good relationship with Brisbane-based Best Friends Rescue. I can ring them up and say, "I've got three blokes that need kelpie crosses" and they'll find them for us.'

Training a PTSD dog costs around $12 000 and takes between twelve and eighteen months. The first six months is spent with a foster carer who drills the puppies on basic obedience commands such as sit, drop, stay, walk-to-heel and toileting on cue. At six months, the dog dons his L-plates – the red 'in training' jacket that affords public access – and moves in with his designated veteran. This is reportedly the prime age for developing a strong dog–human bond. The pair trains as a team until the dog is fourteen months old, when the canine half of the operation takes his Public Access Test (PAT). Passing it earns him the blue jacket of a fully qualified assistance dog and means he can go almost everywhere his owner can.

In the three years since its inception, Whiskey's Wish has placed more than a dozen psychiatric support dogs with veterans and first responders and three have already passed their PAT. There are more than forty dogs currently in the program, including some veterans who are training dogs they already owned. 'We're really proud of that because we're writing all our own procedures and doing things a bit differently,' says Scott.

All dogs provide companionship and comfort to their owners, but a psychiatric service dog's skills go further.

These dogs can be trained to confirm the safety of a room by patrolling its perimeter, for example, so the veteran feels it's safe to enter. They can remind the veteran to take medication and can prevent a veteran from being startled by nudging him when someone is approaching or by blocking a person who is coming too close. 'Veterans with PTSD don't tend to like people rushing up behind them,' Scott says. 'Little things like that make you a bit jumpy.'

While there is still surprisingly little scientific data supporting the efficacy of psychiatric support dogs, anecdotal evidence reveals what an enormous difference dogs like Whiskey make to the lives of returned servicemen and women. Veterans report their quality of life improves once they begin to manage their PTSD symptoms after being paired with a service dog. They also tend to re-engage in many life tasks that their symptoms previously prevented them from participating in, including employment, study, and socialising with family and friends. Veterans with dogs also say they depend less on medications that have side effects, such as drowsiness, to cope with symptoms.

Whiskey's Wish is helping to add to the research canon. Scott and Liz are working with the Gallipoli Medical Research Foundation's (GMRF) PTSD Initiative to help design the structure and scientifically evaluate the benefit of canine therapy programs for veterans.

Of course, none of this is news to Scott – he sees the incredible benefits of canine therapy every day via the dogs Whiskey's Wish has trained. 'We have a lady in Alice Springs who has a really bad back, so she's trained her dog to pick up water bottles and stuff and bring them to her,' he says. 'We've got a guy in Canberra who's quite disabled on one side so we're teaching his dog how to turn on lights and things.'

Another dog, the colourfully named Sergeant Kester, lives in NSW's Blue Mountains with his owner, Luke Simon. On their first night together, 'Sarge' woke Luke from a nightmare by licking the back of his neck. Sarge is named after a close friend of Scott's, Sergeant Michael Kester, a former US Marine, a veteran of Desert Storm and several other US deployments and an Australian Army soldier, who suffered from PTSD and passed away in 2015.

One of the few downsides of having a psychiatric support dog, says Scott, is that people often want to talk to their handlers – which can be the last thing a veteran wants. Whiskey's Wish has developed what Scott calls 'get lost cards' to combat this.

'Having one of these dogs means you've got someone to be with you who doesn't judge you that you can pat and cuddle, but it's also a draw card for other people to want to approach you,' he explains. 'We hand these cards out in schools with the dog's name that say, "I'm in training, so before you come and have a chat, have a look at this card. Don't make noises that might distract me. Speak to my handler before approaching. Don't ask personal questions about my handler's disability. Don't be upset if we don't stop and chat."'

Amid the whirlwind of setting up the charity, in 2014 Scott also welcomed a new support dog of his own. Roxy the blue heeler was born on Scott's discharge date and, just like Whiskey before her, she's fiercely protective of her human best friend. 'She's a funny little thing. She doesn't like being crowded. Everyone calls her "a little nip of Whiskey" because she's a bit of a nipper,' he says. 'She can be aggressive because she's so protective of me. That's probably because I've been so focused on everyone else's dogs I've neglected training my own. I love her to death.'

Roxy, now two years old, has a big personality and is prone to holding grudges. 'She'll crack it with me if I go out and leave her behind. Then she'll ignore me for half the day, but talk to Liz – she'll walk up and give Liz her ball, but she won't give me the ball just to rub it in.'

But she's perceptive – 'There's certain people she doesn't like and she's usually spot on' – and doesn't miss a beat when it comes to staying on top of Scott's PTSD.

'One thing Roxy does is, if I start to get aggressive or angry, she'll grab my hand or jump up and push me away. You can't train that. It's instinctive,' he says. 'If I go to the ATM, Roxy will sit in front of me and look behind so I know she's watching my back, and that makes me feel safe.'

Whiskey's Wish dogs are part of a big family, and it's a family that's there for life. When a dog approaches retirement age – usually at around ten years old – the organisation starts training a younger dog to succeed him. But veterans have the option of keeping their PTSD dogs as pets after their retirement. If staying with their handler isn't an option, a dog will spend the rest of their days with Scott or another Whiskey's Wish volunteer.

Scott's own wish for the charity is that the GMRF study will deliver empirical evidence that the program works, so that it can become a candidate for government funding. At the moment, Whiskey's Wish is funded entirely by donations and from the three founders' own pockets.

But ultimately, growth isn't what it's about for Scott. 'It doesn't matter if we never get any bigger and we only ever have forty dogs in the program,' he says. 'We want to provide a program that works. I've been told ten or fifteen times that I've saved somebody's life. I'm not a therapist or a social worker; I just listen to their stories and try to be as understanding as I can. They'll talk until they can't talk anymore and then they feel better. All you've got to do is listen.

'We want veterans to feel safe, happy and have good lives. If we can only save one life a year, we'll do it properly and we'll save that life.'

For the most part, Scott feels safe and happy these days, too. He still has PTSD and depression, he's still hypervigilant and sometimes he struggles to sleep, but now he has a family of more than forty veterans to look after and a four-legged friend to look after him. He's on a mission to save as many lives as possible and that's in large part due to a tenacious dog called Whiskey. He couldn't stay long, but he did an incredible job while he was here and now Scott is determined to do an incredible job in his honour.

MORE INFORMATION

FIGO
guidedog.org

MOLLY POLLY
facebook.com/MollyPollyAssistanceDog
minddog.org.au
diabeticalertdoguniversity.com

AKAROA DOLPHIN DOGS
akaroadolphins.co.nz

TUNA
tunameltsmyheart.com
Instagram: @tunameltsmyheart & @thetravelingtuna

HOLLY
storydogs.org.au

TRUMAN
facebook.com/dirtdiva333
Instagram: @dirtdiva333

BAILEY

anmm.gov.au

ROWDY

whiteeyedrowdy.com
facebook.com/rowdyumbenhower
Instagram: @white_eyed_rowdy

INDI

border.gov.au/australian-border-force-abf/protecting/
detector-dog-program

MIA, COOPER & HOPPY

smilingsamoyed.com.au

CHARLIE

asdog.org.au
scia.org.au

TIFFANY

thepinkteam.com.au
Facebook: Tiffany the Pink Property Pooch

FRANKIE

www.bearcottage.chw.edu.au
assistancedogs.org.au

COOP

k9support.com.au

LEXIE & FLY

eaglerockfarm.com.au

DAISY
pspca.org

CHLOE, JACKSON & SWAYZE
lorettasdancingpoodles.com

EMMA
bulimbacreek.org.au

MONTGOMARY
uvths.com.au/canine-blood-bank/

BRYNNETH PAWLTROW
rabbithashhistsoc.org

VIKING
facebook.com/frnsw

THE BACKTRACK GANG
backtrack.org.au

PIPER
tvcairport.com/airportk9
facebook.com/airportk9

WHISKEY
whiskeyswish.org.au

ACKNOWLEDGEMENTS

Like anyone who's really great at their job, none of these remarkable dogs works alone. My heartfelt thanks to the human co-workers whose assistance in telling the stories of these indefatigable canines was truly invaluable.

FIGO: Audrey Stone; Doug Wiggin, Bill Krol and Andrew Rubenstein at Guide Dog Foundation.

MOLLY POLLY: Adrienne Cottell, Martin Weber and Hannah and Olivia Weber.

AKAROA DOLPHIN DOGS: Hugh Waghorn; Julia Waghorn.

TUNA: Courtney Dasher.

HOLLY: Petra Westphal; Janine Sigley at Story Dogs.

TRUMAN: Catra Corbett.

BAILEY: Adrian Snelling; Shirani Aththas at Australian National Maritime Museum.

ROWDY: Niki Umbenhower and the whole Umbenhower family.

INDI: Mick; Justine Bonner at ABF Detector Dog Program; Daniella Jukic at Immigration and Border Protection.

MIA, COOPER & HOPPY: Kate Henning and Simon Dunstone.

CHARLIE: Dan Holt; Elle Reid at Brand New Solutions.

TIFFANY: Tracey Ashley.

FRANKIE: Annie Denison and Bronwen Simmons at Bear Cottage.

COOP: Tessa Stow.

LEXIE & FLY: Jen, Ric and Ethan Dalitz.

RIVER & DAISY: Gillian Kocher at Pennsylvania SPCA.

CHLOE, JACKSON & SWAYZE: Loretta Rabbitt.

EMMA: Stefan Hattingh; Genevieve Robey at B4C.

MONTGOMARY: Kate Chambers; Dr Christine Griebsch and Jennie Bohns at University Veterinary Teaching Hospital Sydney; Vivienne Reiner at the University of Sydney.

BRYNNETH PAWLTROW: Jordie Bamforth; Bobbi Kayser and the Rabbit Hash Historical Society.

VIKING: Station Officer Phil Etienne; Peter Walker at Fire & Rescue NSW.

THE BACKTRACK GANG: Bernie Shakeshaft and Nathan Bliss at BackTrack.

PIPER: Brian Edwards; Susan Wilcox Olson at Cherry Capital Airport.

WHISKEY: Scott and Liz Jackman at Whiskey's Wish.

Thanks also to the many wonderful friends and family members who alerted me to stories of hard-working dogs all over the globe.

At Penguin Random House I am so very fortunate to be able to work with Kim Atkins, Johannes Jakob and Andrea Davison. Thank you all for your support and editorial insight, and for never making me feel too weird about loving dogs as much as I do. Thanks also to Louisa Maggio for creating such beautiful covers.

To my erstwhile editor at PRH, Sarah Fairhall: you may have gone globetrotting, but you'll always have my gratitude for starting me on this doggy journey.

As with my last book, I'm really hoping my dogs' vet, Kay Gerry from Sydney Road Veterinary Clinic, will accept my sincerest thanks for answering all my canine and veterinary research questions in lieu of actual money.

I can't really thank them, because they're often more of a hindrance than a help when I'm trying to write, but I do want to say that my dogs, Tex and Delilah, are the cutest and most wonderful dogs that have ever lived and that is a science fact.

And most of all, love and thanks to Mark and Pickle for all the support and cups of tea, and for merely nodding resignedly when I talk about the sanctuary for old, sick dogs that we will definitely start someday. You know it's happening.